LONDON
UNDERGROUND
GUIDE 2017

Written by Jason Cross
Edited by Nick Meskell
Designed by Jason Prescott

Published by Train Crazy Publishing
© 2017 Train Crazy Publishing

on Underground Guide 2017

Contents

Introduction

Welcome to the fourth edition of the London Underground Guide Book. Fully updated and revised to the end of January 2017, it includes historical and operational information about every line, the trains that operate on the system (including a full fleet list) and an A-Z of all 270 stations with opening dates, station renaming and items of interest to look out for.

The book has been written by an enthusiast for enthusiasts, tourists and anybody else who is interested in this wonderful railway system. With a book of this size, it is not possible to provide a full in depth look at all aspects of the Underground's operation. Timetables, opening hours and the full range of ticketing options are not included. This information is subject to change at short notice and can be found on the TfL website at www.tfl.gov.uk. Web links to pages with specific details are included where appropriate. For details of which stations have step-free access, please refer to the official London Underground map contained within this Guide Book.

The information contained within this book has come from official sources and our own observations and research. All of the photographs were taken by the author. Some were taken from areas not accessible to the public, including several views from the driving cabs of trains, all of which were taken with full official permission. The author would like to thank the many members of staff who have been most helpful with assistance and information that has contributed to this book. The author would also like to thank Brian Hardy for his expert advice, assistance and proof reading skills, a much valued contribution that helps to ensure that this book is accurate.

I hope that all readers enjoy this book as much as your author has enjoyed writing and illustrating it. I hope it helps make your experience of the London Underground a pleasurable one.

Jason Cross

Jason Cross – Leicester, February 2017

Content - The information provided in this book has been obtained from official sources as well as our observations, updated to 21 February 2017 (stock list is up to date to 31 January 2017).

Maps - Excluding the official underground map on the inside back cover (fold out), the individual line maps used in this publication are our own versions. These are to be used only as a rough guide. Connections to railway stations and other lines are not shown. Not all of the stations are open all of the day or at weekends and some do not have step-free access. Please use the official TfL map provided or check with TfL before travelling.

Front cover: *Arriving at Arsenal on the Piccadilly Line is a train of 1973 Tube Stock led by unit 103-503-303 with a Cockfosters to Heathrow Terminal 4 service on 20 August 2016. The whole train is covered in a vinyl wrap advertising the Night Tube service which began operating during 2016.*

Rear cover: *The north end of East Finchley station with a train of 1995 Tube Stock heading north with 51597 at the rear while working train 015, the 0805 East Finchley to High Barnet service on 19 June 2016. It is crossing over onto the northbound line shortly after departing from platform 2 at East Finchley, having started empty from Highgate Sidings. Note the abandoned former Great Northern Railway signal box towards the centre of the train (for a closer picture, see page 117).*

Changes Since The 2016 Edition

London Underground launched its Night Tube 24 hour train service on the night of 19/20 August 2016. Initially, this was confined to just a part of the Central Line (Ealing Broadway to Hainault via Newbury Park and to Loughton via Woodford) and the whole of the Victoria Line. It was later augmented by the Jubilee Line on 7/8 October 2016, part of the Northern Line (High Barnet and Edgware to Morden via Charing Cross) on 18/19 November and part of the Piccadilly Line (Cockfosters to Heathrow Terminal 5) on 16/17 December. Night Tube operates every Friday night into Saturday and every Saturday night into Sunday. More details can be found on page 6.

There was much fanfare on 10 November 2016 when London Underground's Ruislip Depot welcomed the 192nd and final S Stock train to be built. This was indeed a milestone, as it was technically the last S Stock train to be built by Bombardier in Derby. The order for 192 trains was not completed at this point in time as there were still two trains (21467-21468 and 21547-21548) which were yet to be delivered. As this book went to press, these two trains were based at the Old Dalby test track where they were undergoing trials associated with the new Automatic Train Operation (ATO) that is to be rolled out across the sub-surface network. The entire fleet of S Stock trains will have to be retro-fitted with ATO equipment, for which they are being returned to Bombardier in Derby. This has meant a stay of execution for the remaining D Stock trains. At the time of writing, eight D Stock trains remained in traffic, with an expectation that they are likely to remain in traffic until about May 2017. It has to be said that when the 2016 Guide Book was written, your author was not expecting to be including D Stock in the 2017 Guide Book!

Meanwhile, some of the withdrawn D Stock is living on elsewhere. The first of two 5-car D Stock Rail Adhesion Trains was released from Acton Works for testing in November 2016, and is expected to take over from the A Stock Rail Adhesion Train for the autumn 2017 season. Many D Stock vehicles have been sold on to a company called Vivarail which has an innovative scheme to convert them into diesel trains for use on Network Rail. The prototype train, numbered 230001, made its first mainline test runs between Tyseley and Leamington Spa on 28 November 2016. However, on 30 December 2016 it suffered a fire in one of its diesel engine modules, which is expected to delay its introduction into passenger service. More details of the class 230 can be found on page 95.

GENERAL INFORMATION

Night Tube

London Underground has introduced a new service known as 'Night Tube', which involves continuous operation of selected lines from the start of traffic on Friday morning until the close of traffic on Sunday night. The service was introduced in stages during 2016, with the whole of the Victoria Line and part of the Central Line the first to operate from 19/20 August. This was followed by the entire Jubilee Line on 7/8 October, part of the Northern Line from 18/19 November and part of the Piccadilly Line from 16 December. Night Tube only operates through Friday night into Saturday morning, and through Saturday night into Sunday morning. On all other nights, the Underground shuts down completely in order to allow maintenance to be undertaken.

A photograph taken on 18 November 2016, the night on which the Northern Line Night Tube service started. One of the roundels on the northbound platform at Leicester Square is seen decorated in Night Tube colours to promote the launch. A train of 1995 Tube Stock is departing.

Details of the routes used and train frequencies are as follows:

Central Line:

The Central Line remains open through the night between Ealing Broadway at the west end and Hainault and Loughton in the east. The service is every 20 minutes between Ealing Broadway and Hainault (via Newbury Park) and between White City and Loughton in the eastbound direction. In the westbound direction, trains run between Hainault and White City (via Newbury Park) and between Loughton and Ealing Broadway (via Woodford), providing a ten minute frequency between White City and Leytonstone. The West Ruislip branch, Loughton to Epping and Woodford to Hainault (via Chigwell) are not served by Night Tube.

Victoria Line:

The Victoria Line's Night Tube consists of a 10 minute interval service over the entire length of the line between Walthamstow Central and Brixton with no booked short workings.

Jubilee Line:

The Night Tube service on the Jubilee Line consists of a 10 minute interval service over the entire length of the line between Stanmore and Stratford with no booked short workings.

Northern Line:

The Northern Line's Night Tube service offers the highest frequency of service through Central London of all the Night Tube routes. Trains operate a 15 minute interval service between High Barnet and Morden, and a 15 minute interval service between Edgware and Morden. This gives a 7 ½ minute interval service south of Camden Town. All trains are routed via Charing Cross, and there are no Night Tube services on the Bank branch or the Mill Hill East branch.

Piccadilly Line:

The Piccadilly Line has a 10 minute interval service between Cockfosters and Heathrow Terminal 5 during Night Tube. The loop to Heathrow Terminal 4 and the Uxbridge branch are not served by Night Tube. All Piccadilly Line services are booked to call at Turnham Green during Night Tube.

Please see the section about ticketing on page 11 for more information on how the use of One Day Travelcards applies on Night Tube.

A train of Piccadilly Line 1973 Tube Stock had carried a vinyl wrap promoting the Night Tube since 2015, however the service didn't launch on the Piccadilly Line until 16 December 2016. Here the special liveried train formed 252-652-452+303-503-103 is seen passing Chiswick Park on 2 April 2016 with an Uxbridge to Cockfosters service. It is expected to have its vinyl wrap removed during the early part of 2017.

USEFUL INFORMATION, FACTS AND TIPS

Train sizes, signalling, ticketing, and some interesting facts that will help readers as they go through the book.

Train Sizes – Tube or Surface

The London Underground has two different sizes of train known as Tube Stock and Surface Stock. Although Transport for London often refers to the London Underground on their website, in their literature and on the official map as 'The Tube', this is a technically incorrect term, as not all of the system is built to tube size. To confuse matters further, signage at stations displays the word 'Underground' rather than 'tube'. For reasons of clarity, this book will only use the word 'tube' when describing matters relating to any of the seven lines that are built to tube gauge. When referring to the system as a whole, the term 'Underground' will be used.

There are four sub-surface lines, and seven tube lines. The earliest underground railways in London were built by the 'cut and cover' method, which involved digging a large trench in the ground (usually down the centre of a road). Side walls were built and railway tracks laid in the bottom of the trench, before a roof was fabricated over the top and the road on the surface restored. This was a very disruptive method which severely affected life on the surface while construction was taking place. These railways were built to generous dimensions however, and the trains which could operate on them could be the same height as those which operate today on Network Rail. These are known as sub-surface lines; the Metropolitan, Hammersmith & City, Circle and District lines are all built to this size.

Later lines were built at a much deeper level using 'Greathead Shields' (the 19th century equivalent of today's tunnel boring machines), and these are what we know today as the tube lines. These could be built without disturbing life on the surface, but the size of the trains was dictated by the overall diameter of the tube tunnel, which was much smaller than those built by the 'cut and cover' method. The tube lines are made up of the Bakerloo, Central, Jubilee, Northern, Piccadilly, Victoria and Waterloo & City lines.

This view clearly shows the difference in height between Tube Stock and Surface Stock. The picture was taken at Chiswick Park and shows two eastbound trains. On the left is a Piccadilly Line train of 1973 Tube Stock, while on the right is a District Line train of Surface Stock of the S Stock type.

Preventing Surface Stock from Entering Tube Tunnels

There are a number of locations where full sized Surface Stock operates alongside the smaller Tube Stock. Where this occurs, there has to be a safeguard to prevent a train of Surface Stock from being wrongly routed into tube tunnel. Between Hammersmith and Barons Court (eastbound Piccadilly), and between Hounslow Central and Hounslow West (westbound Piccadilly) there are gantries from which three glass hoops are suspended above the track. The hoops are of a length that allows a train of Tube Stock to pass beneath without making contact, but a taller train of Surface Stock would

strike the tubes and smash them if one was to try and pass beneath. Inside the glass hoops is a conductive paint which makes a circuit. Breaking the hoop would break the circuit and throw the signals to danger, which in turn would raise the associated train stop and the Surface Stock train would be stopped before it reached the tube tunnel. There used to be a similar gantry at Finchley Road on the Jubilee Line, but since the connection here between the Metropolitan Line and the Jubilee Line was removed, there is no longer any need for the glass hoops here and they have been removed, although the actual gantry is still in place. Any Surface Stock wrongly routed onto the Jubilee Line would now be tripped by fixed train stops at Neasden, which is the last physical connection between the two lines before tube tunnel can be reached. As the Jubilee Line trains operate automatically on the TBTC signalling system, they do not have tripcocks, and so are not affected by the fixed train stops at Neasden. Until 1973, there were also glass hoops at East Finchley on the Northern Line, which were to prevent steam hauled freight trains from reaching the tube tunnels.

Signals and Train Stops

There are a number of different signalling systems in use across London Underground. The Jubilee, Northern, Victoria and Central lines all have signalling systems associated with automatic operation, which is explained in more detail later in this chapter. At the moment, the Piccadilly, Bakerloo, Circle, Hammersmith & City, District, Metropolitan and Waterloo & City lines are signalled manually with colour light signals fitted with train stops. A train stop is a 'T' shaped piece of metal which is raised whenever a signal shows a red aspect. If a train passes a signal at red, a device on the train known as a tripcock will come into contact with the raised train stop which will release the air in the train braking system, thus instigating a full emergency brake application. In the case of the new S Stock trains, the air is released from a valve, which triggers the emergency brake application electronically. There are also several speed related train stops around the system (on the approach to terminus platforms for example), which have to be reached below a pre-set speed in order for them to lower. Advancing towards them too fast will cause them to remain raised and the train will be 'tripped'.

It is also possible for a full height train from the Watford DC Line to be routed into the Bakerloo's tube tunnel at Queen's Park, but the train stop will only lower here if current is being drawn from the central (negative) conductor rail, and the London Overground class 378 units only collect power from the outer (positive) conductor rail, so if one were to be wrongly routed, it would be 'tripped' (the London Overground class 378s also being fitted with tripcocks).

The above views show a signal on the outer rail Circle Line / westbound District Line at Cannon Street. The left view depicts the signal showing a red aspect with the train stop raised. The right hand view was taken after the signal had cleared to a yellow aspect and shows the train stop in its lowered position. This particular signal is a draw-up automatic signal.

Automatic Train Operation

There are several lines where passenger trains are controlled automatically with Train Operators (the LU term for a train driver) opening and closing the doors and pressing buttons to start the train automatically. Across all lines, Train Operators still need to have the skills and knowledge required to drive a train manually and to be able to deal with a whole range of other potential incidents which could arise, regardless of whether they are working on an automatic line or a manually operated line.

On automatically operated lines, the train will receive commands which allow or forbid it to proceed and set target speeds depending on the status of the track ahead. The signalling systems are either 'fixed block' or 'moving block'; the best way to describe the difference between the two is to imagine a train departing from a station. With a 'fixed block' system, the line is divided up into sections (or 'blocks'). When a train is given a start command from a station, it looks at the block ahead, and if it is clear, the train can proceed. With a 'moving block' system, the line is not divided up into sections. Instead, each train has a safe zone around it, so when it receives a start command, it can proceed provided it is not infringing on another train's safe zone. The safe zone around each train varies in size according to that train's speed, which means that as its speed decreases, the size of its safe zone also decreases, allowing trains to get as close to each other as is safely possible. This allows more trains on the line and therefore an increase in the frequency of service. With 'moving block', it is possible, at busy times, to sometimes see a train enter a platform as soon as the previous train has departed from it.

Both the Northern Line and the Jubilee Line operate using a 'moving block' system, specifically the Thales 'Seltrac' Transmission Based Train Control (TBTC), which sends commands to the train via a wire loop between the running rails. Unlike the Central and Victoria lines, the Northern and Jubilee lines do not generally require trackside signals.

The Central Line is fitted with a fixed block ATO/ATP system, with the Automatic Train Operation (ATO) driving the train and the Automatic Train Protection (ATP) picking up target speeds through codes transmitted through the track. There are colour light signals at the start of each block section, which mostly display either a green, white or red aspect. Green is go and is applicable to all trains; red is stop and is applicable to all trains; white is go for a train in automatic mode, but stop for a train being driven manually.

The Victoria Line is fitted with the fixed block Invensys (formerly Westinghouse) Distance-to-Go – Radio (DTG-R) system. ATO and ATP commands are transmitted via a radio link to the trains. Being radio based, it was possible to 'overlay' the DTG-R system on top of the original Westinghouse Automatic Train Control (ATC) system which was installed when the Victoria Line was opened. This allowed the new trains of 2009 Tube Stock to operate alongside the old 1967 Tube Stock during the period of transition. Once the 1967 Tube Stock had been withdrawn, the old system was completely replaced by DTG-R, which allowed train frequencies to be increased. Should the ATP fail, trains can be moved manually in conjunction with trackside signals at a top speed of 15km/h. Should the ATO fail, the train can be driven manually at full line speed in accordance with the target speeds set by the ATP.

None of the automatically operated lines require the use of train stops, so trains operating over them do not require tripcocks. There are occasions when engineering trains have to use these automatic lines; to do so, they either have to be fitted with the relevant equipment to interface with the signalling. Alternately they can operate under an 'incompatible train movement plan', which allows a train to move under its own power under strictly controlled conditions on a line for which it does not have the required signalling equipment on board.

At the time of releasing the 2017 Guide Book the sub-surface lines of the Metropolitan, Circle, Hammersmith & City and District are still manually operated by trackside signals and are to be fitted out for automatic operation using the Thales 'moving block' TBTC system. Unlike the cable based ('wiggly wire') system employed on the Jubilee and Northern lines, the sub-surface lines are to receive a radio based version of TBTC. The S Stock fleet is currently in the process of being returned to Derby to be fitted with ATO equipment (along with other engineering modifications). Two trains were, at the time of writing, based on the Old Dalby test track for ATO tests (21467-468 and 21547-548). The first section of the sub-surface lines expected to go over to ATO should be the Hammersmith branch of the Circle and Hammersmith & City lines. There will be complexities where the sub-surface railway shares tracks with other railways, namely the District Line with the Piccadilly Line west of Barons Court, the District Line with Network Rail on the Wimbledon and Richmond branches, the Metropolitan Line with the Piccadilly Line between Rayners Lane and Uxbridge, and the Metropolitan Line with Chiltern Railways trains north of Harrow-on-the-Hill. Exactly how trains will be signalled in these areas remains to be seen, but these sections could well retain conventional signalling and manual operation.

Traction Current

The entire London Underground system is electrified using a standard four rail DC system (two running rails and two electrified rails). One conductor rail, energised at -210V, is located centrally between the two running rails, while the second conductor rail is outside of the running rails and is energised at +420V, which gives a potential difference of 630V. The outer conductor rail can swap sides but is always on the opposite side to the platform edge in stations, except when a track has a platform on both sides. Where running is shared between the Underground and Network Rail, such as East Putney to Wimbledon, Gunnersbury to Richmond and Queen's Park (and Kilburn High Road) to Harrow & Wealdstone, the centre rail is bonded to the running rails. Work is underway to upgrade parts of the system to 750V supply.

Ticketing

The Underground and other transport modes within London are split up into zones; 1 is Central London, with 6 being the outer zone. There are also zones 7 to 9 which cover the Metropolitan Line north of Moor Park. The specific zones used and the number of which are passed through determine the price, with zone 1 being the most expensive.

The Underground and other transport modes within London are split up into zones; 1 is Central London, with 6 being the outer zone. There are also zones 7 to 9 which cover the Metropolitan Line north of Moor Park. The specific zones used and the number which are passed through determine the price, with zone 1 being the most expensive.

The bulk of journeys on London Underground are made using an Oyster Card; this is a plastic card onto which users can pre-load season tickets and add credit with which travel can be paid for on a pay-as-you-go basis. An Oyster Card can be topped up with credit at ticket machines in Underground stations, online via the Oyster website, in local shops, or it can be set to automatically top up direct from your bank account as soon as the amount of credit drops below £10. A contactless debit card can also be used as in the same way as a pay-as-you-go card, with the advantage that you do not have to top up as the system deducts the amount payable straight from the card owner's bank account. Both Oyster and contactless cards work by the user 'touching in' on the yellow Oyster pads on the gate line at the start of their journey and then 'touching out' at the end of their journey. It may also be necessary to touch at an interchange point, and where this is the case, the readers are identifiable as they are pink in colour. The system will then charge the card with the cheapest possible fare. If multiple journeys are made during a day, the system will cap the cost at a value determined by the number of zones used. The Oyster and contactless system is time based, and it expects journeys to be made within a certain timescale. If the user goes over these time periods, the system will apply a maximum fare, which is added onto the daily price cap. If used to make normal journeys, the system works well, but if you wish to pause to watch trains, you need to be aware of the time limits and make sure you touch out before exceeding them. Time limits vary depending on the time of day and the number of zones you have passed through. Details can be found at:

https://tfl.gov.uk/fares-and-payments/oyster/using-oyster/maximum-journey-times

If you wish to spend some time travelling on the Underground, and wish to linger to watch trains without worrying about Oyster time limits, it is recommended that a paper One Day Travelcard is purchased from a ticket machine at an Underground (or Network Rail) station. A zone 1 to 6 card will cover the entire Underground except for the Metropolitan line north of Moor Park. It costs just £12.30 off peak (Mon-Fri after 0930, and all day Saturdays, Sundays and Bank Holidays) or £17.50 anytime (Mon-Fri for use before 0930). If you intend to travel north of Moor Park, then a zone 1 to 9 card is available at £13.10 off peak or £22.10 anytime.

The use of paper single tickets purchased from cash machines is not recommended, as a journey within zone 1 will cost £4.90 as a cash single, but just £2.40 with a card.

Oyster Cards, contactless and paper tickets are all valid on local Network Rail services, London Buses and Tramlink as well as the Underground.

If using Night Tube services with a contactless debit card or an Oyster card, there is little difference to using those cards during the day. However, if using a paper One Day Travelcard (ODTC), then there are time restraints that you will need to be aware of. An ODTC purchased at any time between the start of traffic on Friday morning and 2359 that day will be valid until 0430 on Saturday morning. An ODTC purchased between 0230 and 2359 on a Saturday will be valid until 0430 on Sunday morning, and an ODTC purchased between 0230 and 2359 on a Sunday will be valid until 0430 on Monday morning. Due to the way the ticketing system is set up, it is not possible to purchase an ODTC between 0000 and 0229.

Car Parking

A lot of Underground stations outside the centre of London have car parks. Visitors from outside London who are travelling by car are recommended to park outside London. Parking at Underground stations is very well priced, especially at weekends. Most car parks cost £5 on weekdays, £2 on Saturdays and £1.50 on Sundays (please note these prices are subject to change). Upgrading of car parks with number plate recognition (ANPR) technology is ongoing. Where this has yet to be fitted, payment is on the 'pay and display' principle. At car parks with the new ANPR technology fitted, the system logs your vehicle as it enters and leaves. You have the option of paying instantly at the machine, via a mobile phone app, by text, or over the internet. There is no requirement to display a ticket in your car, and if you are in a rush, you do not have to pay immediately; you can pay later using one of the methods listed above. It is also possible to register online, so that each time the system sees your car entering and leaving a car park, it charges your account automatically. More details can be found at:

https://ukparking.dashcardservices.com/dashtube/client/tube2home.aspx

Taking Photographs on London Underground

For any tourists or enthusiasts wishing to take photographs on London Underground, your attention is drawn to section 4.5 of the TfL Conditions of Carriage, which clearly states that the use of tripods and other camera supporting equipment is forbidden, and that camera flash must NOT be used. Drivers spend a lot of time driving in dark tunnels, to which their eyes will have adjusted. To suddenly have a flash go off in their direction as they enter a station can actually cause short term vision impairment and is therefore very dangerous. Some modern cameras are fitted with an 'auto focus assist' light which can also be very bright with much the same effect as a flash. Before attempting any photography on the Underground, it is recommended that you disable this function.

The above text in this Guide Book regarding photography does not grant the reader the right to take photographs on London Underground and should not be quoted as such. Station staff have the right to stop people taking photographs and move them along at busy times, for operational and security reasons or if the person taking photographs is causing an obstruction to other passengers.

History of the London Underground (Timeline)

Elsewhere throughout this book, the history of each of the London Underground lines is described in order to explain how the system became what it is today. Below is an overview 'timeline' covering all lines:

10.01.1863 – Metropolitan Railway (MR) opened to the public between Paddington (Bishop's Road) and Farringdon Street.

13.06.1864 – Hammersmith & City Railway opened between Paddington and Hammersmith.

23.12.1865 – MR extended from Farringdon Street to Moorgate Street.

13.04.1868 – Metropolitan & St John's Wood Railway opened from Baker Street to Swiss Cottage.

01.10.1868 – MR opened Edgware Road to Brompton (Gloucester Road).

24.12.1868 – Metropolitan District Railway (MDR) opened South Kensington to Westminster Bridge. MR extended from Brompton (Gloucester Road) to South Kensington to connect with the MDR.

12.04.1869 – MDR extended from South Kensington to West Brompton.

07.12.1869 – East London Railway (ELR) opened New Cross (later renamed New Cross Gate) to Wapping.

30.05.1870 – MDR extended from Westminster Bridge to Blackfriars.

03.07.1871 – MDR extended from Blackfriars to Mansion House and from High Street Kensington to Earl's Court.

01.02.1872 – MDR opened Earl's Court to Addison Road (now Kensington Olympia).

10.04.1872 – ELR extended from Wapping to Shoreditch.

09.09.1874 – MDR extended from West Kensington East Junction to Hammersmith.

01.02.1875 – MR extended from Moorgate Street to Liverpool Street (Great Eastern Railway terminus).

12.07.1875 – MR opened Bishopsgate (the current Liverpool Street sub-surface station).

18.11.1876 – MR extended from Bishopsgate to Aldgate.

01.06.1877 – MDR extended west from Hammersmith to join the London South Western Railway (LSWR), allowing MDR trains to run through to Richmond.

30.06.1879 – Metropolitan & St John's Wood Railway extended from Swiss Cottage to West Hampstead.

01.07.1879 – MDR opened branch from the LSWR line at Turnham Green to Ealing Broadway.

24.11.1879 – Metropolitan & St John's Wood Railway extended from West Hampstead to Willesden Green.

01.03.1880 – MDR extended from West Brompton to Putney Bridge & Fulham.

01.04.1880 – ELR opened between Deptford Road (now Surrey Quays) and New Cross.

A Wimbledon to Edgware Road train of S Stock with 21308 at the rear crosses the Fulham Railway Bridge on 5 June 2016.

02.08.1880 – Metropolitan & St John's Wood Railway opened beyond Willesden Green to Harrow (now Harrow-on-the-Hill).

03.07.1882 – Metropolitan & St John's Wood Railway became part of the Metropolitan Railway.

25.09.1882 – MR extended from Aldgate to Tower of London.

01.05.1883 – MDR opened from Mill Hill Park (now Acton Town) to Hounslow.

21.07.1884 – MDR opened to Hounslow Barracks.

03.03.1884 – A branch off the ELR to St Mary's was opened. It would eventually form a link between the ELR and the MDR (which would also be used by the MR).

06.10.1884 – MDR extended from Mansion House to Whitechapel, joining up with the MR at Tower of London (which closed and was replaced by Mark Lane station), thus completing the Inner Circle.

25.05.1885 – MR opened from Harrow to Pinner.

31.03.1886 – MDR closed branch to Hounslow Town.

01.09.1887 – MR extended from Pinner to Rickmansworth.

03.06.1889 – With the building of the Fulham Railway Bridge over the River Thames, MDR trains began running beyond Putney Bridge & Fulham over LSWR tracks to Wimbledon.

08.07.1889 – MR opened Rickmansworth to Chesham.

18.12.1890 – The first deep level tube railway was opened by the City & South London Railway (C&SLR) between Stockwell and King William Street. This was also London's first electric railway.

01.09.1892 – MR trains began running beyond Chalfont Road (now Chalfont & Latimer) to Aylesbury South Junction.

01.01.1894 – Aylesbury South Junction to Aylesbury North Junction opened, allowing MR trains to run through to Verney Junction.

08.08.1898 – Waterloo & City Railway opened between Waterloo and City (now Bank).

01.12.1899 – MR took over the operation of the Quainton Road to Brill branch.

25.02.1900 – C&SLR opened an extension from Borough to Moorgate Street which avoided the C&SLR's original terminus at King William Street which was closed.

03.06.1900 – C&SLR opened extension from Stockwell to Clapham Common.

30.07.1900 – Central London Railway (CLR) opened between Shepherd's Bush and Bank.

17.11.1901 – C&SLR extended from Moorgate Street to Angel.

02.06.1902 – MDR extended services eastwards from Whitechapel to Barking over the tracks of the Whitechapel & Bow Railway.

01.03.1903 – MDR re-opened the Hounslow Town branch, along with a new spur towards Hounslow Barracks.

23.06.1903 – MDR opened from Hanger Lane Junction to Park Royal & Twyford Abbey.

28.06.1903 – MDR extended beyond Park Royal & Twyford Abbey to South Harrow.

14.02.1904 – Great Northern & City Railway (GN&CR) opened between Moorgate and Finsbury Park.

04.07.1904 – MR opened Harrow to Uxbridge.

13.06.1905 – MDR opened a short branch from Mill Hill Park (now Acton Town) to South Acton.

10.03.1906 – Baker Street & Waterloo Railway (BS&WR) opened between Baker Street and Kennington Road (now Lambeth North).

05.08.1906 – BS&WR extended from Kennington Road to Elephant & Castle.

15.12.1906 – Great Northern, Piccadilly & Brompton Railway (GNP&BR) opened from Finsbury Park to Hammersmith.

27.03.1907 – BS&WR extended Baker Street to Great Central (now Marylebone).

12.05.1907 – C&SLR extended from Angel to Euston.

15.06.1907 – BS&WR extended from Great Central to Edgware Road.

22.06.1907 – Charing Cross, Euston & Hampstead Railway (CCE&HR) opened from Charing Cross to Golders Green and Highgate (now Archway).

30.11.1907 – GNP&BR opened the short branch from Holborn to Strand (later Aldwych).

14.05.1908 – CLR opened Shepherd's Bush to Wood Lane.

01.05.1909 – MDR closed Hounslow Town branch (again!).

01.03.1910 – A short extension from South Harrow to Rayners Lane allowed MDR trains to run through to Uxbridge over MR tracks.

01.07.1910 – BS&WR (Bakerloo), CCE&HR (Hampstead Tube) and GNP&BR (Piccadilly) amalgamated to form the London Electric Railway.

28.07.1912 – CLR extended from Bank to Liverpool Street.

01.12.1913 – Bakerloo extended from Edgware Road to Paddington.

06.04.1914 – Hampstead Tube extended from Charing Cross (Strand) to Charing Cross (Embankment) – the station we today know as Embankment.

31.01.1915 – Bakerloo extension to Queen's Park opened as far as Kilburn Park.

11.02.1915 – Bakerloo extended beyond Kilburn Park to Queen's Park.

10.05.1915 – Bakerloo extended over London & North Western Railway (L&NWR) tracks from Queen's Park to Willesden Junction.

16.04.1917 – Bakerloo services began through running over L&NWR tracks beyond Willesden Junction to Watford Junction.

03.08.1920 – CLR services extended through to Ealing Broadway over the tracks of the Great Western Railway built Ealing & Shepherd's Bush Railway.

19.11.1923 – Hampstead Tube extended from Golders Green to Hendon.

20.04.1924 – C&SLR extended from Euston to Camden Town where it joined the Hampstead Tube.

18.08.1924 – Hampstead Tube extended from Hendon to Edgware.

02.11.1925 – MR opened branch from Watford South Junction to Watford.

13.09.1926 – Hampstead Tube extended from Charing Cross (Embankment) to Kennington to join up with the C&SLR. C&SLR extended from Clapham Common to Morden.

04.07.1932 – Piccadilly Line trains began operating over MDR (District) tracks to South Harrow.

12.09.1932 – District trains extended from Barking to Upminster over LMS tracks.

19.09.1932 – Piccadilly Line extended from Finsbury Park to Arnos Grove.

10.12.1932 – MR opened branch from Wembley Park to Stanmore.

13.03.1933 – Piccadilly Line extended at both ends, from Arnos Grove to Enfield West (now Oakwood) over newly built line, and over District Railway tracks from Acton Town to Hounslow West.

01.07.1933 – The London Transport Passenger Board acquired the City & South London Railway, the Central London Railway, London Electric Railway (made up of the Bakerloo, Hampstead and Piccadilly), the Metropolitan Railway and the District Railway.

31.07.1933 – Piccadilly Line extended from Enfield West to Cockfosters.

23.10.1933 – Piccadilly Line services began operating beyond South Harrow through to Uxbridge.

30.11.1935 – The Metropolitan's Brill branch is closed.

04.07.1936 – Metropolitan Line trains ceased to operate between Aylesbury and Verney Junction.

28.08.1937 – The lines of the former CCE&HR (Hampstead Tube) and C&SLR become known as the Northern Line.

03.07.1939 – Northern Line extended from Archway (Highgate) to East Finchley.

20.11.1939 – Bakerloo Line began operating through to Stanmore over former Metropolitan Line tracks and through new tube tunnels between Finchley Road and Baker Street.

14.04.1940 – Northern Line extended from East Finchley to High Barnet over former London & North Eastern Railway (LNER) tracks.

21.09.1940 – Piccadilly Line closed branch from Holborn to Aldwych.

18.05.1941 – Northern Line trains began operating between Finchley Central and Mill Hill East.

01.07.1946 – Piccadilly Line re-opened branch from Holborn to Aldwych.

04.12.1946 – Central Line extended from Liverpool Street to Stratford.

05.05.1947 – Central Line extended, partly over former LNER tracks and partly in new tube tunnel, from Stratford to Leytonstone.

01.07.1947 – First section of the new Central Line western extension opened between North Acton and Greenford.

14.12.1947 – Central Line extended from Leytonstone to Newbury Park (in new tube tunnel) and from Leytonstone to Woodford (over former LNER tracks).

31.05.1948 – Central Line trains began operating between Newbury Park and Hainault, replacing British Railways steam trains.

21.11.1948 – Central Line trains take over from British Railways steam trains between Hainault and Woodford and from Woodford to Loughton. The western extension opened between Greenford and West Ruislip.

25.09.1949 – Central Line extended over former British Railways tracks from Loughton to Epping. The Epping to Ongar section was also transferred on this day, but as this section was not electrified, it continued to be operated by British Railways steam trains.

18.11.1957 – Electrification of the Ongar branch of the Central Line saw British Railways steam trains replaced by Tube Stock.

28.02.1959 – The District Line's Acton Town to South Acton branch closes.

12.09.1960 – Electrification of the Metropolitan Line north of Rickmansworth to Chesham and Amersham.

09.09.1961 – Operation of the line beyond Amersham towards Aylesbury transferred to British Railways.

03.10.1964 – The former GN&CR, known at this point as the Northern City line, was cut back to Drayton Park so that the station tunnels at Finsbury Park could be adapted to accommodate the new Victoria Line.

01.09.1968 – First section of the new Victoria Line opened between Walthamstow Central and Highbury & Islington.

01.12.1968 – Services commenced on the second section of the Victoria Line to open, south of Highbury & Islington to Warren Street.

07.03.1969 – Victoria Line opened Warren Street to Victoria with a formal ceremony performed by HM Queen Elizabeth II.

06.06.1971 – Steam traction (which had been used to haul engineering trains) was used on the Underground for the final time with a commemorative run from Barbican to Neasden Depot.

23.07.1971 – Victoria Line extension opened from Victoria to Brixton.

The former Northern City Line is now part of Network Rail and is operated by the Great Northern franchise. All trains are currently operated by class 313 electric multiple units. In this view 313040 arrives at Highbury & Islington with a Welwyn Garden City to Moorgate service.

04.10.1975 – The Northern City Line between Moorgate and Drayton Park ran with London Underground stock for the final time in preparation for the line's transfer to British Rail.

30.04.1979 – The new Jubilee Line was opened by HRH Prince of Wales. This line included a new tube tunnel section between Baker Street and Charing Cross plus the Baker Street to Stanmore branch of the Bakerloo, which was transferred to the Jubilee on the same day.

24.09.1982 – Bakerloo Line services withdrawn between Stonebridge Park and Watford Junction.

04.06.1984 – Bakerloo Line services re-introduced between Stonebridge Park and Harrow & Wealdstone.

12.04.1986 – Piccadilly Line opened a new loop line to serve Heathrow Terminal 4.

01.04.1994 – Ownership of the Waterloo & City Line transferred from British Rail to London Underground.

30.09.1994 – The Central Line's Epping to Ongar branch and the Piccadilly Line's Holborn to Aldwych branch were both closed to passengers.

14.05.1999 – Jubilee Line Extension (JLE) opened between Stratford and North Greenwich.

17.09.1999 – JLE opened between North Greenwich and Bermondsey.

24.09.1999 – JLE opened between Bermondsey and Waterloo.

19.11.1999 – Jubilee Line's Charing Cross terminus closed to passengers.

20.11.1999 – JLE opened between Waterloo and Green Park thus completing the extension and allowing Jubilee Line trains to operate over the full length of the line between Stanmore and Stratford.

22.12.2007 – East London Line closed to Underground trains prior to being transferred to the London Overground network.

27.03.2008 – Piccadilly Line opened a short branch from Heathrow Terminals 1, 2, 3 to serve Heathrow Terminal 5.

FUTURE EXTENSIONS

Work is currently underway on two extensions on the London Underground network, these being the Metropolitan Line extension to Watford Junction, and the Northern Line extension to Battersea:

Metropolitan Line

The Watford branch of the Metropolitan Line is being extended to Watford Junction where there will be interchange with Network Rail services on the West Coast Main Line, and also with the London Overground route to London Euston. The new line will diverge from the existing line to the east of Croxley, cross the A412 road and the Grand Union Canal (on a new viaduct) and use the currently disused track bed of the Croxley Green branch to join the existing London Euston to Watford Junction DC lines close to Watford High Street station. Metropolitan Line trains will then share the tracks between Watford High Street and Watford Junction with London Overground services. Two new stations will open at Cassiobridge and Watford Vicarage Road, and the existing stations at Watford High Street and Watford Junction will also join the Metropolitan Line map. The current Watford Metropolitan Line terminus will close, although it is expected to be kept as a train stabling point. The current estimate for the opening of this extension is 2020, although at the time of going to press, there were some concerns emerging regarding the funding of this extension.

Northern Line

The Northern Line is being extended from Kennington to Battersea. The new route will diverge from the existing Kennington loop and will serve new stations at Nine Elms and Battersea. The two tunnel boring machines for this project were being assembled at the end of 2016 and tunnelling is expected to begin during 2017. Both machines have been named; one is called Helen (after the astronaut Helen Sharman) and the other is called Amy (after the aviator Amy Johnson). They are expected to take around six months to bore the tunnels. The expected completion date for this extension is 2020.

Tube Lines

HARROW & WEALDSTONE
KENTON
SOUTH KENTON
NORTH WEMBLEY
WEMBLEY CENTRAL

Stonebridge Park Depot

STONEBRIDGE PARK
HARLESDEN
WILLESDEN JUNCTION
KENSAL GREEN
QUEEN'S PARK

Kilburn High Road (reversing moves without passengers)

KILBURN PARK
MAIDA VALE
WARWICK AVENUE
PADDINGTON
EDGWARE ROAD

Connection with Jubilee Line (engineering trains only)

MARYLEBONE
BAKER STREET
REGENT'S PARK
OXFORD CIRCUS
PICCADILLY CIRCUS
CHARING CROSS
EMBANKMENT
WATERLOO

London Road Depot

LAMBETH NORTH
ELEPHANT & CASTLE

BAKERLOO LINE
Overview:

Route: Elephant & Castle to Harrow & Wealdstone

Night Tube: Not applicable

Route type: Tube

First section opened: Baker Street to Kennington Road (now Lambeth North) opened by the Baker Street & Waterloo Railway on 10 March 1906

Method of train operation: Manually driven

Signalling: Colour light signals protected by train stops

Direction of route: Northbound / Southbound

Route length: 14.4 miles

Number of stations: 25

Trains: 1972 MkII Tube Stock with a few cars of 1972 MkI Tube Stock incorporated into the fleet

Max number of trains required for service: 31 (morning and evening peaks)

Depot: Stonebridge Park

Stabling points: Queen's Park / London Road / Elephant & Castle

HISTORY

The Bakerloo Line began life as the Baker Street & Waterloo Railway. The first section opened between Baker Street and Kennington Road (now called Lambeth North) on 10 March 1906. The section from Kennington Road to the current southern terminus at Elephant & Castle was opened on 5 August of the same year. Extension to the northern end of the line took place in stages, to Great Central (now called Marylebone) on 27 March 1907, to Edgware Road on 15 June 1907, and with backing from the Great Western Railway, to Paddington on 1 December 1913. Beyond Paddington, the Bakerloo was extended in two stages to Queen's Park, first of all to Kilburn Park on 31 January 1915, and then to Queen's Park on 11 February 1915. At Queen's Park, the Bakerloo met the recently built tracks of the London & North Western Railway's line between London Euston and Watford Junction (often referred to as the Watford DC Lines or 'new' line). Bakerloo trains operated over LNWR tracks to Willesden Junction from 10 May 1915, and to Watford Junction from 16 April 1917.

The next expansion of the Bakerloo came as part of the '1935-1940 New Works Programme' with a new section of tube tunnel from Baker Street to Finchley Road where it joined the route of the Metropolitan Line. The opening of this new tube tunnel section took place on the 20 November 1939, and on the same day, the Bakerloo took over the Stanmore branch from the Metropolitan. The adjacent Metropolitan Railway route from Finchley Road through to Baker Street, with trains from Aylesbury (and beyond), Chesham, Watford, Uxbridge and Stanmore all feeding into this two track section, had become congested. The new tube tunnels were built to relieve that stretch of line by transferring the Stanmore branch trains to the Bakerloo and routing them through the new tube tunnels. Baker Street then had three platforms serving the Bakerloo. Platform 7 was southbound serving trains from the Stanmore branch. Platform 8 was southbound serving trains from the Watford / Queen's Park branch, and platform 9 was northbound serving both the Stanmore and Watford branches. It wasn't long before the single northbound platform became a bottleneck, and the solution came with the construction of a new platform serving the northbound Stanmore line. At the same time, a new tube tunnel route was built southwards from the Stanmore branch platforms to Charing Cross. This became the Jubilee Line, which opened on 1 May 1979 and saw the transfer of the Stanmore branch from the Bakerloo to the Jubilee. The junction between the Jubilee and the Bakerloo still exists at Baker Street, but today is only usually used by engineering trains (and occasional stock movements) which reach the Bakerloo from Ruislip Depot via the Jubilee Line.

The opening of the new Jubilee Line left the Bakerloo with just the Elephant & Castle to Watford Junction route after 1979. Bakerloo Line services were withdrawn north of Stonebridge Park in 1982, and reinstated in 1984, but only as far as Harrow & Wealdstone, which is the current northern terminus of the Bakerloo Line.

Between Harrow & Wealdstone and Wembley Central, the tracks of the Bakerloo Line (and Watford DC Line) parallel the Network Rail West Coast Main Line on its west side. In this view, a southbound Bakerloo Line train is being overtaken near South Kenton by a London Midland class 350 which is heading for London Euston. The Bakerloo Line train is headed by unit 3265-4265-4365-3365, one of several 1972 MkI units that have been incorporated into the 1972 MkII Tube Stock fleet. 25 September 2016.

THE ROUTE AND OPERATIONS

The Bakerloo is currently operated by a fleet of 1972 MkII Tube Stock (see page 46). There are a number of 1972 MkI Tube Stock cars incorporated into the fleet which are highlighted in the list on page 48. Since the withdrawal of the C Stock in 2014, the 1972 Tube Stock is the oldest passenger stock in regular service on the London Underground. The Bakerloo Line's main depot is at Stonebridge Park, but trains also stable in two sidings south of Elephant & Castle, in the platforms at Elephant & Castle, in London Road Depot (Lambeth) and at Queen's Park in either the North Carriage Shed or the South Carriage Shed.

The southern section of the line is entirely in tube tunnel from the southern terminus at Elephant & Castle for a distance of just under 6 ¾ miles to Queen's Park. Whilst in tube tunnel, the line passes beneath the River Thames between Waterloo and Embankment, serves the West End shopping area (running directly beneath Regent Street in the process) and the mainline railway termini at Waterloo, Charing Cross, Marylebone and Paddington before eventually emerging into daylight on the approach to Queen's Park station. The Bakerloo rises up between the 'up' and 'down' tracks of the Watford DC Line which is operated by London Overground class 378s. Also situated between the Watford DC tracks is Queen's Park South Carriage Shed where up to four trains can be stabled. Queen's Park station consists of four platforms (plus two on the adjacent West Coast Main Line that see little use) with the inner two platforms (2 and 3) being served by the Bakerloo Line, while 1 and 4 are served by London Overground. To the north of the platforms is Queen's Park North Carriage Shed, which has four roads numbered 21-24. All can be used for stabling trains, but during traffic hours roads 21 and 24 are the northbound and southbound Bakerloo Line tracks respectively, while roads 22 and 23 are used to reverse trains that have terminated at Queen's Park. At the north end of the North Carriage Shed, the four tracks of the Bakerloo and Watford DC lines reduce to two tracks at Queen's Park Junction. North of here the Bakerloo Line and London Overground trains

On 25 September 2016, a train of 1972 Tube Stock with 3247 on the rear can be seen entering the central reversing siding at Harrow & Wealdstone. In the background, a Virgin Trains class 390 'Pendolino' heads south on the West Coast Main Line towards London Euston.

share the same tracks all the way to Harrow & Wealdstone (with the London Overground trains continuing to Watford Junction). The signalling north of Queen's Park is controlled by Network Rail, and all signals are fitted with the Network Rail AWS and TPWS systems. However, the Bakerloo Line 1972 MkII Tube Stock is incompatible with both of these, so the signals have London Underground train stops which are compatible with the tripcocks on the 1972 Tube Stock and the class 378s (which are also fitted with tripcocks in addition to AWS and TPWS). Train stops are fitted to all signals on the Watford DC line between Harrow & Wealdstone and Kilburn High Road, which is the first station south of Queen's Park towards London Euston. At times of disruption London Underground trains can run out of service to Kilburn High Road, and the central conductor rail is in place to just beyond the south end of the station platforms for this purpose. It is rare to see a Bakerloo Line train run to Kilburn High Road in daylight, but there are night time paths which occasionally run, especially during icy weather, when they shuttle between Kilburn High Road and Harrow & Wealdstone to keep the conductor rails free of ice. These trains also occasionally operate to prevent the build up of rust on the centre conductor rail between Queen's Park and Kilburn High Road.

Under normal circumstances, all southbound trains run through to the southern terminus at Elephant & Castle. However in the northbound direction, roughly 50% terminate at Queen's Park while a further approximately 20% run through to Stonebridge Park where they terminate in the platform, and then run empty into either road 21 or road 22 at the entrance to Stonebridge Park Depot. The remaining approximately 30% of trains run through to Harrow & Wealdstone where they terminate and de-train in platform 1 before proceeding empty into a reversing siding located centrally between the 'up' and 'down' Watford DC tracks. Once the driver has changed ends, trains leave the siding and move into platform 2 from where they form a southbound service.

First trains:
0537 Elephant & Castle to Harrow & Wealdstone 0627 (Mon-Sat)
0716 Elephant & Castle to Harrow & Wealdstone 0806 (Sun)
0538 Harrow & Wealdstone to Elephant & Castle 0628 (Mon-Sat)
0723 Harrow & Wealdstone to Elephant & Castle 0812 (Sun)

Last trains:
2346 Elephant & Castle to Harrow & Wealdstone 0036 (Mon-Sat)
2337 Elephant & Castle to Harrow & Wealdstone 0026 (Sun)
2354 Harrow & Wealdstone to Elephant & Castle 0043 (Mon-Sat)
2313 Harrow & Wealdstone to Elephant & Castle 0001 (Sun)

Note: *The above trains are the first and last to travel the full length of the line. There are other shorter workings before and after those listed above.*

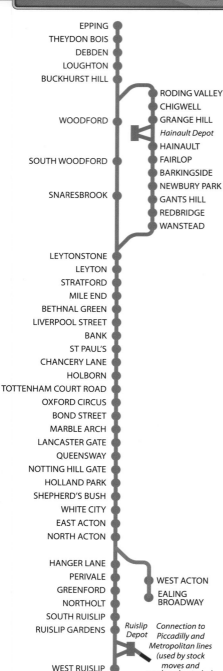

EPPING
THEYDON BOIS
DEBDEN
LOUGHTON
BUCKHURST HILL
RODING VALLEY
CHIGWELL
WOODFORD
GRANGE HILL
Hainault Depot
HAINAULT
SOUTH WOODFORD
FAIRLOP
BARKINGSIDE
NEWBURY PARK
SNARESBROOK
GANTS HILL
REDBRIDGE
WANSTEAD
LEYTONSTONE
LEYTON
STRATFORD
MILE END
BETHNAL GREEN
LIVERPOOL STREET
BANK
ST PAUL'S
CHANCERY LANE
HOLBORN
TOTTENHAM COURT ROAD
OXFORD CIRCUS
BOND STREET
MARBLE ARCH
LANCASTER GATE
QUEENSWAY
NOTTING HILL GATE
HOLLAND PARK
SHEPHERD'S BUSH
WHITE CITY
EAST ACTON
NORTH ACTON
HANGER LANE
PERIVALE
GREENFORD
NORTHOLT
SOUTH RUISLIP
RUISLIP GARDENS
WEST ACTON
EALING BROADWAY
Ruislip Depot — *Connection to Piccadilly and Metropolitan lines (used by stock moves and engineering trains)*
WEST RUISLIP

CENTRAL LINE

Overview:

Route: West Ruislip and Ealing Broadway to Hainault, Woodford and Epping

Night Tube: Ealing Broadway to Hainault and Loughton

Route Type: Tube

First section opened: Shepherd's Bush to Bank, opened (to the public) by the Central London Railway on 30 July 1900

Method of train operation: Automatic

Signalling: ATO/ATP

Direction of route: Eastbound / Westbound (plus inner rail and outer rail Leytonstone to Woodford via Newbury Park)

Route length: 46 miles

Number of stations: 49

Trains: 1992 Tube Stock

Max number of trains required for service: 78 (morning and evening peaks)

Depots: Hainault and Ruislip

Stabling points: White City / Loughton / Woodford

HISTORY

The first part of the Central London Railway was opened by the Prince of Wales on 27 June 1900 between Shepherd's Bush and Bank, with opening to the public following on 30 July of the same year. To begin with, the line was operated by electric locomotives, but these machines caused too much vibration, plus there was the added complication of reversing at each terminus, so by 1903 they were replaced by motor carriages. The first extension was to Wood Lane which was situated on a balloon shaped loop to the west of the original terminus at Shepherd's Bush. This new station was opened to serve the Franco British Exhibition that was taking place at Wood Lane. Trains were turned on the loop ready for their journey back towards Bank without the need for the driver to change ends. When Wood Lane bound trains departed from Shepherd's Bush, the westbound track passed over the top of the eastbound track with trains travelling around the loop in a counter-clockwise direction. At the east end of the line, an extension from Bank to Liverpool Street was opened on 28 July 1912. Back at the west end of the line, an extension over the tracks of the Great Western Railway's Ealing & Shepherd's Bush

91303 leads an eastbound Central Line service into Notting Hill Gate on 20 November 2016.

A train of 1992 Tube Stock with 91161 at the rear departs from Leytonstone towards Epping on 31 October 2015.

Railway to Ealing Broadway saw the opening out of the Wood Lane loop, resulting in trains coming off the loop on the right hand side. The standard practice is for trains to run on the left hand side, so a flyover was built close to Wormwood Scrubs prison which reverted the tracks back to left hand running. This arrangement can still be seen today at White City station where right hand running still prevails. There are other locations on the London Underground where right hand running takes place, but this is below ground and is not so visible.

Further expansion came in the form of the '1935-1940 New Works Programme', which saw the Central Line extended. Although work began in the 1930s, their completion was delayed by the war. At the west end, a new line ran to West Ruislip which diverged from the Ealing Broadway line at North Acton Junction. This opened to Greenford on 30 June 1947, and to West Ruislip on 21 November 1948.

At the east end, the Central Line was extended partly in new tube tunnel, but mostly over former LNER tracks to Hainault, Woodford, Epping and Ongar. Work on the tunnel sections between Liverpool Street and Stratford, Stratford and Leyton and Leytonstone and Newbury Park were largely complete when war broke out, and the latter section was converted into an underground secret aircraft components factory. The partially complete Bethnal Green station was used as an air raid shelter and became the scene of a terrible disaster which resulted in the loss of 173 lives (see page 104). Work resumed on the extension after the war; Liverpool Street to Stratford was the first part opened, on 4 December 1946, with Stratford to Leytonstone next on 5 May 1947. Part of this section was originally opened by the Eastern Counties Railway on 22 August 1856, so actually pre-dates the rest of the Underground. Central Line trains could be seen alongside LNER steam trains at Leytonstone for a short time until the next section to Woodford was transferred from the LNER to the Central Line on 14 December 1947. The new tunnel from Leytonstone to Newbury Park opened on the same day. The Newbury Park to Hainault section saw the last LNER steam services in November 1947. From December 1947, Central Line trains used the line to run empty between Newbury Park and the new Central Line depot at Hainault, with passenger services being introduced from 31 May 1948. Beyond Hainault, the line forms a loop, joining up with the Epping line to the east of Woodford. Central Line trains were introduced between Hainault and Woodford from 21

November 1948. On the same date, the next section east of Woodford as far as Loughton also became part of the Central Line. The final section from Loughton to Epping and Ongar became part of the Central Line from 25 September 1949. Initially, the Epping to Ongar section was not electrified, and although part of London Underground from the same date as Epping, services were operated by a hired-in British Railways steam train and carriages until 1957 when the line was finally electrified. Low patronage of the Epping to Ongar line eventually led to its closure on 30 September 1994. Thankfully it has survived and is now a preserved railway (see eorailway.co.uk). The line is still connected to the Central Line at Epping, with E&OR trains able to run to within a few hundred yards of the Central Line, although they mostly work between North Weald and Ongar with a connecting vintage bus service to and from Epping station on operating days.

THE ROUTE AND OPERATIONS

The Central Line passes horizontally through Central London serving the West End, the shopping district around Bond Street and Oxford Street and also the City of London. It runs out into the suburbs at each end, reaching as far as Epping in the east and West Ruislip in the west. The journey between West Ruislip and Epping is a distance of 34 miles, the longest single journey possible on the Underground without changing trains, taking 85 minutes. The line is worked by a fleet of 1992 Tube Stock trains built by ABB in Derby, formed into 8-car formations (see page 51). The whole of the Central Line is operated automatically using a system of ATO and ATP (see page 10).

Service patterns (not including Night Tube) are a mix of journeys over the full length of the line together with others working shorter journeys to concentrate more trains through Central London. The majority operate between Epping and West Ruislip, between Ealing Broadway and Hainault (via Newbury Park) and between Ealing Broadway and Woodford (via Hainault). The bulk of shorter workings run between White City and Newbury Park and between Loughton and Northolt, with some reversing at Debden and North Acton during peak hours. In addition, should the service be disrupted for any reason, there are a number of locations where trains can be reversed which currently do not have trains timetabled to reverse there. These include reversing sidings at Liverpool Street and Marble Arch and crossovers at Queensway and Bethnal Green. The reversing siding at the closed British Museum station (situated west of Holborn) was removed during 2016.

Outside of traffic hours, trains stable in sidings at Woodford and Loughton at the east end, and at White City at the west end, as well as at the two main depots at Hainault and Ruislip. Some trains, which are entering or leaving Ruislip and Hainault depots, start or finish their journeys at Ruislip Gardens and Grange Hill respectively. Several trains stable in Loughton sidings, some of which start and finish their day by running in service between Loughton and Epping and vice versa. The maximum number of trains required in service is 78, which occurs during both the morning and evening peaks.

Part of the Central Line operates continuously from start of traffic on Friday through to the close of traffic on Sunday night as part of Night Tube. This requires just 14 trains and operates between Ealing Broadway and Hainault (via Newbury Park) and Loughton (via Woodford). More details on page 6.

First trains:
0510 Epping to West Ruislip 0634 (Mon-Sat)
0642 Epping to West Ruislip 0807 (Sun)
0523 West Ruislip to Epping 0646 (Mon-Sat)
0656 West Ruislip to Epping 0822 (Sun)

Last trains:
2345 Epping to West Ruislip 0110 (Mon-Sat)
2257 Epping to West Ruislip 0028 (Sun)
2353 West Ruislip to Epping 0116 (Mon-Sat)
2258 West Ruislip to Epping 0022 (Sun)

Note: The above trains are the first and last to travel the full length of the line. There are other shorter workings before and after those listed above, and at weekends there is a continuous service through the night between Ealing Broadway and Hainault / Loughton.

STANMORE
CANONS PARK
QUEENSBURY
KINGSBURY
WEMBLEY PARK

Neasden Metropolitan Line Depot (Jubilee Line Stabling point)

NEASDEN
DOLLIS HILL
WILLESDEN GREEN
KILBURN
WEST HAMPSTEAD
FINCHLEY ROAD
SWISS COTTAGE
ST. JOHN'S WOOD

Connection with Bakerloo Line (used by engineering trains only)

BAKER STREET
BOND STREET
GREEN PARK

Charing Cross (disused)

WESTMINSTER
WATERLOO
SOUTHWARK
LONDON BRIDGE
BERMONDSEY
CANADA WATER
CANARY WHARF
NORTH GREENWICH
CANNING TOWN
WEST HAM

Stratford Market Depot

STRATFORD

JUBILEE LINE

Overview:

Route: Stanmore to Stratford

Night Tube: Stanmore to Stratford

Route type: Tube

First Section Opened: Stanmore to Wembley Park, opened by the Metropolitan Railway on 10 December 1932

Method of train operation: Automatic

Signalling: Transmission Based Train Control 'moving block' system (TBTC)

Direction of route: Northbound / Southbound between Stanmore and Green Park and Eastbound / Westbound between Green Park and Stratford

Route length: 22.5 miles

Number of stations: 27

Trains: 1996 Tube Stock

Max number of trains required: 58 (morning and evening peaks)

Depot: Stratford Market

Stabling points: Stanmore / Neasden

HISTORY

The Jubilee Line opened in 1979, but its history goes back further than that as part of the route shares its history with that of the Metropolitan Line. The section between Finchley Road and Wembley Park was opened in stages by the Metropolitan Railway between 30 June 1879 and 2 August 1880. The branch from Wembley Park to Stanmore, which today is operated solely as a part of the Jubilee Line, was opened by the Metropolitan Railway on 10 December 1932. The traffic generated by the Stanmore branch, combined with other Metropolitan trains serving Uxbridge, Watford, Chesham, Amersham, Aylesbury and beyond, caused a bottleneck on the two track section between Finchley Road and Baker Street. To relieve the pressure, as part of the '1935-1940 New Works Programme', a new line, consisting of a pair of tracks in tube tunnel, was built between Finchley Road and Baker Street, where it joined the Bakerloo. The new line opened as part of the Bakerloo Line on 20 November 1939, while the Stanmore branch was transferred from the Metropolitan to the Bakerloo on the same day. Two new stations were also opened on the new tube line, at Swiss Cottage and St John's Wood, which allowed the Metropolitan stations between Finchley Road and Baker Street at Lords, Marlborough Road and Swiss Cottage to be closed. Although the transfer of Stanmore trains to the Bakerloo Line helped to relieve the bottleneck between Finchley Road and Baker Street, another bottleneck was

96023 leads a Stanmore to Stratford service as it climbs towards Wembley Park, having just passed beneath the southbound tracks of the Metropolitan Line. This location is known as Stanmore Junction and is where the Jubilee's branch from Stanmore joins the formation of the Metropolitan Line. The two tracks on the left of the picture are the northbound Metropolitan fast and the northbound Metropolitan local. 4 December 2016.

generated over time. This was due to the fact that while southbound Bakerloo Line trains from the Watford Junction branch and the Stanmore branch had their own platforms at Baker Street, northbound trains heading for both branches had to share one platform.

Several proposals for a new tube line from Baker Street through the West End to serve a destination in south east London were put forward under the title of 'Fleet Line'. Eventually, a terminus well short of south east London at Charing Cross was decided upon. Building began in 1971, including the boring and construction of a new northbound platform at Baker Street to relieve the bottleneck. Although incomplete in 1977 when HM Queen Elizabeth II celebrated her Silver Jubilee, it was named the Jubilee Line, and was officially opened by the Prince of Wales on 30 April 1979, with public services starting the following day. On the same day, the Bakerloo Line's Stanmore branch was transferred to the Jubilee Line, and the new Jubilee Line operated between Stanmore and Charing Cross, leaving the Bakerloo with just the Elephant & Castle to Watford Junction route. Although the Jubilee and Bakerloo lines operate separately through Baker Street today, they are still physically linked, although this is only used for stock movements and by engineering trains.

Throughout the 1980s, the steady development of the Docklands area in the east end of London created a need for better transport links with central London. The only Underground line to serve the heart of Docklands was the East London Line (now part of the London Overground network), but this did not run directly into the City. An extension to the Jubilee Line was built, passing through Westminster, Waterloo, North Greenwich, Canary Wharf, Canning Town and West Ham to Stratford, opening in stages during 1999, with through running over the entire route from 20 November 1999. Known as the Jubilee Line Extension (JLE), it branched off the existing line to the south of Green Park, thus avoiding the Charing Cross terminus which closed on 19 November 1999. Charing Cross is still used to reverse trains (out of service), to stable engineering trains and for filming purposes.

THE ROUTE AND OPERATIONS

The Jubilee Line is operated by a fleet of 1996 Tube Stock trains (see page 57) which are formed of 7 cars. They operate in automatic mode using the Thales Transmission Based Control System (see page 10). The TBTC system was introduced in two stages, firstly between Dollis Hill and Stratford (including Charing Cross) on 29 December 2010, with the second stage between Dollis Hill and Stanmore going live on 26 June 2011.

The main depot is at Stratford Market. It was constructed as part of the JLE project and took over from Neasden Depot, which the Jubilee had shared with the Metropolitan until the opening of Stratford Market. Jubilee Line trains still use Neasden as a stabling point, along with a fan of sidings adjacent to Stanmore station. Trains coming into service from Neasden Depot can reach the Jubilee Line via an underpass at the north end of the depot (which is also used by Metropolitan Line trains coming into service). At the south end of the depot, trains entering or exiting Neasden Depot do so via a flat junction, which takes them across the southbound Metropolitan Line track at the north end of Neasden station. Engineering trains also use this flat junction to reach the Jubilee Line. It is possible that a wrongly routed Metropolitan Line train could access the Jubilee Line so there are a number of fixed train stops on the southbound Jubilee track immediately south of the platforms at Neasden as a safety measure. Jubilee Line trains, being signalled automatically using the TBTC system are not fitted with tripcocks, so pass over the fixed train stops, but a wrongly routed Metropolitan Line train's tripcock would strike the fixed train stops and be brought to a halt.

The Jubilee Line is a northbound / southbound railway between Stanmore and Green Park, but the JLE between Green Park and Stratford is an eastbound / westbound railway. The signage reflects this, which can be confusing to passengers who may board a westbound service on the JLE and alight from a northbound train further up the line (and vice versa). The JLE is out in the open between Stratford and just south of the station at Canning Town, and runs parallel with the Docklands Light Railway along this section. From Canning Town to Finchley Road, the Jubilee Line

This view taken at Southwark station clearly shows the platform layout with the platform edge doors (PEDs) along the left hand side of the photograph.

is in tube tunnel. All of the stations in tube tunnel on the JLE are fitted with platform edge doors (PEDs), which remain closed until a train is stationary in the platform and in line with the doors, at which point the PEDs open simultaneously with the doors on the train. The stations at Green Park and Bond Street and the northbound platform at Baker Street, were built in the 1970s, and together with the southbound platform at Baker Street (which dates from the 1930s), all have a similar style, being clad in bright colours. The tube tunnel stations at St John's Wood and Swiss Cottage both opened in 1939 and still retain their 'art deco' period feel from that time. Emerging into daylight at Finchley Road, the Jubilee Line rises up between the northbound and southbound tracks of the Metropolitan Line, and there is cross platform interchange between the two lines. Between Finchley Road and Wembley Park, the Metropolitan runs non-stop, with the Jubilee Line calling at all stations, these being West Hampstead, Kilburn, Willesden Green, Dollis Hill and Neasden. Only Willesden Green and Neasden have platform faces adjacent to the Metropolitan Line tracks, although under normal circumstances, Metropolitan Line trains pass straight through. West Hampstead, Kilburn and Dollis Hill are all island platforms. To the north of Wembley Park is Stanmore Junction where the tracks of the Jubilee dive down to pass beneath the southbound tracks of the Metropolitan and head towards the northern terminus at Stanmore. There are three intermediate stations on the Stanmore branch at Kingsbury, Queensbury and Canons Park. Stanmore is a terminus station consisting of three platforms.

Under normal operating conditions, the majority of trains operate over the full length of the route between Stanmore and Stratford. Some trains work shorter journeys, most of which reverse at either, Wembley Park, Willesden Green or North Greenwich. It is also possible to reverse trains at Canary Wharf, West Hampstead, Green Park (running empty to and from Charing Cross to reverse), Waterloo and London Bridge, but this only occurs during service disruption. Some trains coming out of or going into Stratford Market depot enter or leave passenger service at West Ham.

The maximum number of trains in service at one time is 58. This occurs both in the morning and evening peaks on a Monday to Friday and allows a peak service of 30 trains per hour in both directions to be operated.

On the night of 7/8 October, the Jubilee Line joined the Night Tube network (see page 6), which consists of a 10 minute interval service over the entire length of the line and requires 14 trains.

First Trains:
0515 Stratford to Stanmore 0611 (Mon-Fri)
0523 Stanmore to Stratford (Mon-Fri)

Last Trains:
0011 Stratford to Stanmore 0109 (Mon-Thu)
0013 Stanmore to Stratford 0111 (Mon-Thu)
2337 Stratford to Stanmore 0034 (Sun)
2326 Stanmore to Stratford 0025 (Sun)

Note: *The above trains are the first and last to travel the full length of the line. There are other shorter workings before and after those listed above. Earlier trains through Central London to Stratford on a Monday to Friday are offered by the 0505 and 0522 ex Wembley Park, and the 0512 and 0532 ex Neasden, which run ahead of the first train from Stanmore (having entered service from Neasden Depot).*

There are no last trains on a Friday or Saturday night, and no first trains on a Saturday or Sunday morning as the entire line has a continuous Night Tube service.

Where it states 'Mon-Thu' on the last trains section, the 'Thu' refers to the end of Thursday's traffic, so the 0011 and 0013 departures are actually at the very beginning of Friday.

96020 leads a Stanmore bound train into St John's Wood station on 20 February 2016.

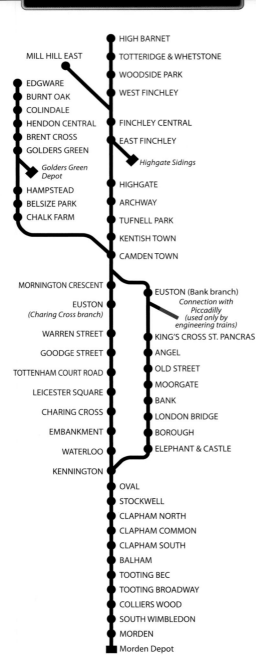

MILL HILL EAST

EDGWARE
BURNT OAK
COLINDALE
HENDON CENTRAL
BRENT CROSS
GOLDERS GREEN

Golders Green Depot

HAMPSTEAD
BELSIZE PARK
CHALK FARM

MORNINGTON CRESCENT
EUSTON
(Charing Cross branch)
WARREN STREET
GOODGE STREET
TOTTENHAM COURT ROAD
LEICESTER SQUARE
CHARING CROSS
EMBANKMENT
WATERLOO
KENNINGTON

HIGH BARNET
TOTTERIDGE & WHETSTONE
WOODSIDE PARK
WEST FINCHLEY
FINCHLEY CENTRAL
EAST FINCHLEY
Highgate Sidings
HIGHGATE
ARCHWAY
TUFNELL PARK
KENTISH TOWN
CAMDEN TOWN
EUSTON (Bank branch)
Connection with Piccadilly (used only by engineering trains)
KING'S CROSS ST. PANCRAS
ANGEL
OLD STREET
MOORGATE
BANK
LONDON BRIDGE
BOROUGH
ELEPHANT & CASTLE

OVAL
STOCKWELL
CLAPHAM NORTH
CLAPHAM COMMON
CLAPHAM SOUTH
BALHAM
TOOTING BEC
TOOTING BROADWAY
COLLIERS WOOD
SOUTH WIMBLEDON
MORDEN
Morden Depot

NORTHERN LINE

Overview:

Route: Edgware, High Barnet and Mill Hill East to Morden via Charing Cross or Bank

Night Tube: Morden to Edgware / High Barnet via Charing Cross

Route type: Tube

First section opened: King William Street to Stockwell, opened by the City & South London Railway on 18 December 1890

Method of train operation: Automatic

Signalling: Transmission Based Train Control 'moving block' system (TBTC)

Direction of route: Northbound / Southbound

Route length: 36 miles

Number of stations: 50

Trains: 1995 Tube Stock

Max number of trains required: 96 (morning and evening peaks)

Depots: Golders Green and Morden

Stabling points: Edgware / High Barnet / Highgate

HISTORY

The Northern Line owes its history to the development of two underground railways: the City & South London Railway (C&SLR) and the Charing Cross, Euston & Hampstead Railway (CCE&HR). The C&SLR was formally opened by the Prince of Wales (later to become King Edward VII) on 4 November 1890 between Stockwell and King William Street, although it did not open to the public until 18 December of the same year. Not only was this the first deep level tube railway (as opposed to the underground railways already built by the cut and cover method), but it was also the first underground railway to be powered by electricity. Early trains were hauled by electric locomotives and consisted of high sided carriages with small windows which soon gained the nickname 'padded cells'. One of these, together with electric locomotive number 13 can be seen at the London Transport Museum in Covent Garden. The first extension of the C&SLR also resulted in the first closure, as a northern extension to Moorgate Street (now called Moorgate) opened on 25 February 1900 and bypassed the terminus the terminus at King William Street which had closed the previous day. The next extension was at the south end of the line to Clapham Common (opened 3 June 1900), followed by a northern extension to Angel (opened 17 November 1901), which was then further extended as far as Euston (opened 12 May 1907).

The CCE&HR opened a line from Charing Cross to Camden Town where it split, with one line going to Highgate (now called Archway), and the other going to Golders Green. This line soon became known as 'The Hampstead Tube'. The first extension to CCE&HR opened on 6 April 1914 when it was extended one stop at the south end to the station which is today known as Embankment. Initially named Charing Cross (Embankment), and concurrent with the opening of this station, the existing CCE&HR station called Charing Cross was renamed Charing Cross (Strand). The new Charing Cross (Embankment) station featured a single platform on a balloon shaped loop which turned southbound trains back north without the need to reverse (the original single platform is today's northbound platform at Embankment).

Being the first deep level tube railway, the C&SLR had built its tunnels to a smaller diameter than the size subsequently adopted by other tube railways. The C&SLR set about enlarging its tunnels to match. Moorgate to Clapham Common was closed between 28 November 1923 and 1 December 1924, and Moorgate to Euston was closed between August 1922 and April 1924 while the work was done. The reopening of the Moorgate to Euston section coincided with the opening, on 20 April 1924, of an extension from Euston to Camden Town where the C&SLR joined up with the Hampstead & Highgate Line (previously known as the CCE&HR).

Extension beyond Golders Green took the line to Edgware in two stages, with the line opening to Hendon Central on 19 November 1923, and between Hendon Central and Edgware on 18 August 1924. On 13 September 1926, the C&SLR opened the Morden extension from Clapham Common to Morden. On the same day, the Hampstead and Highgate Line extended southwards from Charing Cross (today's Embankment) to join up with the C&SLR at Kennington. In so doing, the balloon shaped loop was abandoned and a new southbound platform built on a straight alignment, while the original curved platform on the outside of part of the loop became the northbound platform.

With the C&SLR and the former CCE&HR now connected at Camden Town and Kennington, and with two routes through Central London, plus the two northern branches, the two railways began to function as one, although both maintained separate legal existences. On 1 July 1933, the two companies were acquired by the London Passenger Transport Board, although it was not until 28 August 1937 that the line was given the name Northern Line.

The '1935-1940 New Works Programme' saw the opening on 3 July 1939 of an extension of the Highgate branch to East Finchley. From there, the Northern Line took over the LNER tracks to High Barnet with tube trains working through from 14 April 1940. The Northern also took over the first part of the LNER's Edgware branch between Finchley Central and Mill Hill East. Its main purpose was to serve the barracks close to Mill Hill East station and it opened to tube trains on 18 May 1941. The plan was that the branch to Edgware from Finchley Central would eventually be electrified, and also extended beyond Edgware to Bushey Heath as part of a wider programme of expansion. This would also include the electrification and transfer to the Underground of the line south of East Finchley to Finsbury Park (from where Northern Line trains would be able to reach Moorgate via the former Great Northern & City Railway) and the branch from Highgate to Alexandra Palace. The war put a stop to these works, with the final stage completed being the electrification through to Mill Hill East. After the war, finances and new green belt boundaries saw the project abandoned. Freight trains continued to run beyond Mill Hill East over the non-electrified line to Edgware until 1964, after which the line between Mill Hill East and Edgware was lifted.

Also part of the Northern Line's history is the Great Northern & City Railway. The GN&CR was opened between Finsbury Park and Moorgate on 14 February 1904. Taken over by the Metropolitan Railway on 1 September 1913, it was then operated as part of the Northern Line from 1939, with the eventual aim, as stated above, of it becoming a part of the Northern Line. This would have allowed trains to run from Moorgate via Finsbury Park to Alexandra Palace, East Finchley, Edgware, High

Barnet and Bushey Heath. However, these plans were abandoned and the former GN&CR became a part of the Northern Line but remained isolated from the rest of the line, becoming known as the Northern City Line. It was closed between Finsbury Park and Drayton Park on 3 October 1964 to allow for the construction of the (then) new Victoria Line. The section between Moorgate and Old Street closed on 6 September 1975, with the remaining section between Old Street and Drayton Park closing on 4 October 1975. The line later re-opened as part of British Rail operated by class 313 EMUs. Today it remains a part of Network Rail and is still served by class 313 EMUs which operate between Moorgate and Letchworth / Welwyn Garden City.

51587 leads a High Barnet bound train into Archway station on 19 June 2016. Opened as Highgate on 22 June 1907, this was one of the two northern termini of the Charing Cross, Euston & Hampstead Railway (the other being at Golders Green). The station was renamed Archway (Highgate) in June 1939, and then renamed to just Archway in December 1947.

ROUTE AND OPERATIONS

The Northern Line is operated by a fleet of 1995 Tube Stock built by Alsthom (see page 54). All trains are formed of six cars and operate in automatic mode using Thales Transmission Based Train Control System (TBTC). The TBTC system was introduced in stages with the whole line being converted by 1 June 2014.

The line has two main depots, at Golders Green and Morden. Both are operated by Alsthom, who look after the Northern's fleet as part of a supply and maintenance contract. Morden Depot is situated to the south of Morden station and is the most southerly location reached by the entire Underground. There are also three stabling points at Edgware, High Barnet and Highgate. The latter is located on the former LNER line to Finsbury Park to the south of East Finchley station and is accessed via the two tracks that pass through the centre platforms at East Finchley.

The Northern Line is unique in having two branches through central London which serve the City of London (Bank branch) and the West End (Charing Cross branch). They separate at Camden Town in the north and at Kennington in the south. Camden Town is really the hub of the Northern and is where the High Barnet, Edgware, Bank and Charing Cross branches all come together, and it is possible for trains from either the High Barnet or Edgware branches to continue via either the Charing Cross or Bank branches and vice versa.

Most of the Northern is in tube tunnel. At the south end, Morden station is located in a cutting with trains entering tunnel just a short distance from the north end of the platform, with the first few hundred yards being cut and cover before it becomes tube tunnel. Travelling north, the Northern emerges into daylight on the approach to Golders Green on the Edgware branch, and on the approach to East Finchley on the High Barnet branch. A train travelling between the High Barnet branch and Morden via Bank (and vice versa), will be in tunnel for just over 17 miles, the longest continuous tunnel on the Underground.

The bulk of services operate between Edgware and Morden (via Bank), Edgware and Kennington (via Charing Cross), High Barnet and Morden (via Bank) and High Barnet and Kennington (via Charing Cross). The Mill Hill East branch operates as a shuttle service to and from Finchley Central for most of the day, but does have a number of through trains to and from both Morden and Kennington during the morning and evening peaks. Mill Hill East is also served by through trains at the start and end of traffic. At the start of traffic, several trains leave Highgate Sidings and work in passenger service from East Finchley to Mill Hill East, and then form a southbound service from there. At the end of traffic, several trains operate through from Morden or Kennington to Mill Hill East, and then form a service to East Finchley from there and then run empty into Highgate Sidings. The bulk of trains on the Charing Cross branch reverse at Kennington via a balloon shaped loop which enables them to reverse without the need for the driver to change ends. Trains arrive from the north in platform 2, de-train, then proceed around the loop and arrive into platform 1 to form a northbound service. There is also a reversing siding which can be reached by trains from either the Bank branch or the Charing Cross branch, and trains exiting the siding can also access both branches. During peak hours, and at the start and end of traffic, several Charing Cross branch trains run to and from Morden. There are of course variations at the start and end of service which see trains starting and ending their journeys at Golders Green and East Finchley in order to exit / enter Golders Green Depot and Highgate Sidings respectively. A maximum of 96 trains are needed for service during the morning and evening peaks.

From the night of 18/19 November 2016, part of the Northern Line joined the Night Tube network. A total of 19 trains are required to operate the service which between High Barnet / Edgware and Morden via Charing Cross. Night Tube does not operate over the Mill Hill East and Bank branches. More details about Night Tube can be found on page 6.

First trains:
First trains via Charing Cross:
0515 Morden to High Barnet 0617 (Mon-Fri)
0522 Edgware to Morden 0624 (Mon-Fri)

Last trains:
Last trains via Charing Cross:
0033 Kennington to Edgware 0112 (Mon-Thu)
2337 Kennington to Edgware 0016 (Sun)
0001 Edgware to Morden 0102 (Mon-Thu)
2310 Edgware to Morden 0020 (Sun)

First trains via Bank:
0518 Morden to Edgware 0621 (Mon-Sat)
0655 Morden to High Barnet 0804 (Sun)
0522 High Barnet to Morden 0630 (Mon-Sat)
0655 Edgware to Morden 0800 (Sun

Last trains via Bank:
0005 Morden to High Barnet 0115 (Mon-Thu+Sat)
0003 Morden to High Barnet 0115 (Fri)
2310 Morden to High Barnet 0019 (Sun)
0000 High Barnet to Morden 0107 (Mon-Thu)
0000 High Barnet to Morden 0113 (Fri)
0000 High Barnet to Morden 0114 (Sat)
2308 High Barnet to Morden 0023 (Sun)

Note: The above trains are the first and last to serve the entire length of the Edgware and High Barnet branches, as well as the Bank and Charing Cross branches. There are other shorter workings before and after those listed above. Night Tube gives a continuous service over the Charing Cross branch from start of traffic on Friday until close of traffic on Sunday, so there are no first and last trains during this period.

Last trains shown as just after midnight are at the end of the previous day's traffic, so for example, the 0003 Morden to High Barnet on a Friday is at the end of Friday's traffic and is actually at the very start of Saturday.

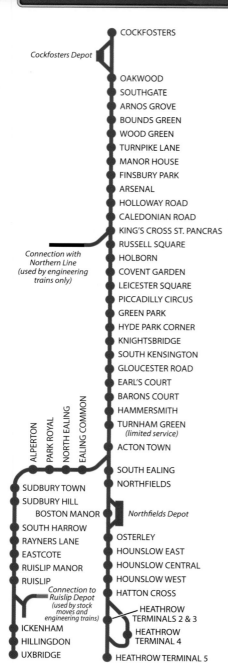

COCKFOSTERS

Cockfosters Depot

OAKWOOD
SOUTHGATE
ARNOS GROVE
BOUNDS GREEN
WOOD GREEN
TURNPIKE LANE
MANOR HOUSE
FINSBURY PARK
ARSENAL
HOLLOWAY ROAD
CALEDONIAN ROAD
KING'S CROSS ST. PANCRAS
RUSSELL SQUARE

Connection with
Northern Line
(used by engineering
trains only)

HOLBORN
COVENT GARDEN
LEICESTER SQUARE
PICCADILLY CIRCUS
GREEN PARK
HYDE PARK CORNER
KNIGHTSBRIDGE
SOUTH KENSINGTON
GLOUCESTER ROAD
EARL'S COURT
BARONS COURT
HAMMERSMITH
TURNHAM GREEN
(limited service)
ACTON TOWN

SOUTH EALING
NORTHFIELDS

ALPERTON
PARK ROYAL
NORTH EALING
EALING COMMON

SUDBURY TOWN
SUDBURY HILL
BOSTON MANOR
SOUTH HARROW
RAYNERS LANE
EASTCOTE
RUISLIP MANOR
RUISLIP

Northfields Depot

OSTERLEY
HOUNSLOW EAST
HOUNSLOW CENTRAL
HOUNSLOW WEST
HATTON CROSS

Connection to
Ruislip Depot
(used by stock
moves and
engineering trains)

ICKENHAM
HILLINGDON
UXBRIDGE

HEATHROW
TERMINALS 2 & 3
HEATHROW
TERMINAL 4
HEATHROW TERMINAL 5

PICCADILLY LINE

Overview:

Route: Cockfosters to Heathrow and Uxbridge

Night Tube: Cockfosters to Heathrow Terminal 5

Route type: Tube

First section opened: Finsbury Park to Hammersmith opened by the Great Northern, Piccadilly & Brompton Railway on 15 December 1906

Method of train operation: Manually driven

Signalling: Colour light signals protected by train stops

Direction of route: Eastbound / Westbound

Route length: 44.3 miles

Number of stations: 53

Trains: 1973 Tube Stock

Max number of trains required: 78 (morning peak)

Depots: Cockfosters and Northfields

Stabling points: Arnos Grove / South Harrow / Uxbridge

HISTORY

The first section of what we know today as the Piccadilly Line was opened by the Great Northern, Piccadilly & Brompton Railway between Finsbury Park and Hammersmith on 15 December 1906. A short branch from Holborn to Strand (later renamed Aldwych) was opened on 30 November 1907. From 4 July 1932, the Piccadilly took over District Railway services to South Harrow, with the District still operating between South Harrow and Uxbridge until the Piccadilly also took over this section on 23 October 1933. Piccadilly trains used the centre pair of tracks west of Hammersmith to give a non-stop service between Hammersmith and Acton Town, parallel with District trains which called at all stations. This arrangement along this stretch of railway still exists to this day. The Piccadilly also took over the Hounslow branch from the District, with Piccadilly Line trains running to Northfields from 9 January 1933, and to Hounslow West from 13 March 1933. District Line trains continued to serve the Hounslow branch at rush hours alongside those of the Piccadilly Line until they were finally withdrawn in 1964.

The east end of the Piccadilly was extended beyond Finsbury Park to Cockfosters. It opened in stages during 1932 and 1933 with the first part to Arnos

Two trains of 1973 Tube Stock pass each other on top of Arnos Park Viaduct on 27 August 2016. The lead unit of the train closest to the camera is 112-512-312.

Grove opening on 19 September 1932. Following the completion of the impressive Arnos Park Viaduct and a short tunnel section through Southgate, the line was extended to Enfield West (later renamed Oakwood) on 13 March 1933 and finally to Cockfosters on 31 July 1933.

The first section of an extension to serve Heathrow Airport, from Hounslow West to Hatton Cross, was opened on 19 July 1975, with the next part to Heathrow Central opened on 16 December 1977. Expansion of the airport saw the construction of a single track loop to serve a new station called Heathrow Terminal 4. This was opened on 12 April 1986. At the same time, Heathrow Central was renamed Heathrow Terminals 1,2 & 3 and was transformed from a terminus station into a through station. A new terminus station serving Heathrow Terminal 5 was opened on a short branch to the west of Heathrow Terminals 1, 2 & 3 on 27 March 2008. Since 2016, Heathrow Terminals 1, 2 & 3 has been renamed on the Underground map to just Heathrow Terminals 2 & 3, reflecting the fact that Terminal 1 has been knocked down to make way for development of Terminal 2. The name change has yet to be reflected on station signage and train destination displays.

The Holborn to Aldwych branch was closed on 30 September 1994 (the same day as the Central Line's Epping to Ongar line). The branch is still in situ and is used for training and filming purposes.

THE ROUTE AND OPERATIONS

The Piccadilly Line is operated by a fleet of 1973 Tube Stock trains built by Metro-Cammell of Birmingham (see page 49). Trains are formed of six cars which are made up of two 3-car units. The line is signalled throughout with colour light signals protected by train stops and trains are driven manually.

The Piccadilly Line is operated by a mixture of services, most running end to end with some shorter workings to concentrate more trains on the central London area. On the Heathrow branch, most trains work through to either Heathrow Terminal 5 via Heathrow Terminals 2 & 3, or they go to Heathrow Terminal 4 and call at Heathrow Terminals 2 & 3 on their way back to central London. There are also trains scheduled to terminate at Northfields and reverse in Northfields Depot. On the Uxbridge branch, some trains terminate at Rayners Lane and reverse via the centre reversing siding at the west end of the station, while others continue through to Uxbridge supplementing the Metropolitan Line which also operates to and from Uxbridge. It is also possible for Piccadilly trains to reverse at Ruislip using the siding which engineering trains use when leaving Ruislip Depot, although Piccadilly Line trains only tend to reverse here at times of disruption. In the eastbound direction, trains can be reversed at Acton Town using one of three sidings (21-23) to the east of the station, and several are booked to reverse here at the start and end of traffic to get them to or from Northfields depot.

At the east end of the line, the majority of trains run through to the terminus at Cockfosters, but some terminate at Arnos Grove throughout the course of the day. Trains entering or leaving service via the west end of Cockfosters Depot start or finish their journeys at Oakwood. The majority of these are at the beginning and end of traffic, but others do this during the day. At the start of traffic, several trains are booked to enter service towards Heathrow via the west end of Northfields Depot and these enter passenger service at Osterley. Trains which stable at South Harrow either run empty to Rayners Lane, reverse and enter service from there, or enter service at South Harrow. At the end of traffic, they terminate at Rayners Lane and run empty to South Harrow.

There are a number of other locations where trains can reverse which can be used at times of service disruption. As well as several crossovers, there are centre reversing sidings at Wood Green, Hammersmith and the closed Down Street station. The latter actually has a train booked to reverse there on Monday to Saturday nights, when an empty train from Arnos Grove reverses in there and then forms a 0025 passenger service from Green Park to Oakwood.

Between Hounslow West and Hatton Cross, the Heathrow branch emerges from tunnel to climb up and over the River Crane. Here we see the Night Tube liveried train of 1973 Tube Stock heading east and passing over the River Crane which is roughly level with the end of the train furthest from the camera. 5 June 2016.

The Piccadilly Line's central section is in tube tunnel from just east of Barons Court to a point roughly half way between Bounds Green and Arnos Grove. There is a tunnel section of roughly half a mile in length which includes Southgate station. The Heathrow branch is in a mix of tube and cut and cover tunnel west of Hounslow West station with the exception of a short stretch where the line climbs to pass over the top of the River Crane, before descending back into tunnel. The remainder of the Piccadilly Line is in the open air.

The Piccadilly shares sections with other Underground lines: with the Metropolitan between Rayners Lane and Uxbridge and with the District Line between Barons Court and just west of Ealing Common where it turns away to Ealing Broadway at Hanger Lane Junction. The Piccadilly runs non-stop between Hammersmith and Acton Town, while District Line trains call at Ravenscourt Park, Stamford Brook, Turnham Green and Chiswick Park. This section is four tracks wide, and as a rule the District Line trains run on the two outer tracks (local lines) with the Piccadilly using the two centre tracks (fast lines), although Piccadilly trains can run on the local lines when needed. Piccadilly Line trains call at Turnham Green at the beginning and end of traffic to provide better connections with District Line services. Trains also call here throughout the night during the Night Tube service. Trains call from the start of traffic until 0650 Mondays to Fridays, through the night until 0650 on Saturdays, and through the night until 0745 on Sundays. Piccadilly Line trains call here after 2230 every evening.

The Piccadilly Line joined the Night Tube service from the night of 16/17 December 2016. It requires 21 trains and operates between Cockfosters and Heathrow Terminal 5 via Heathrow Terminals 2 & 3. For more details of Night Tube, see page 6.

First trains:
0509 Cockfosters to Heathrow Terminal 5 0640 (Mon-Fri)
0518 Boston Manor to Cockfosters 0629 (Mon-Fri)*

Last trains:
2354 Cockfosters to Heathrow Terminals 2 & 3 0121 (Mon-Fri)
2300 Cockfosters to Heathrow Terminals 2 & 3 0026 (Sun)
2342 Heathrow Terminal 5 to Cockfosters 0114 (Mon-Fri)
2325 Heathrow Terminal 5 to Cockfosters 0056 (Sun)

Note: *The above trains are the first and last to travel through the core central section of the line through central London. There are other shorter workings before and after those listed above. A continuous service operates between Cockfosters and Heathrow Terminal 5 from start of traffic Friday morning until end of traffic Sunday night as part of Night Tube.*

*This train exits Northfields Depot at the west end and uses the crossover to gain the eastbound line.

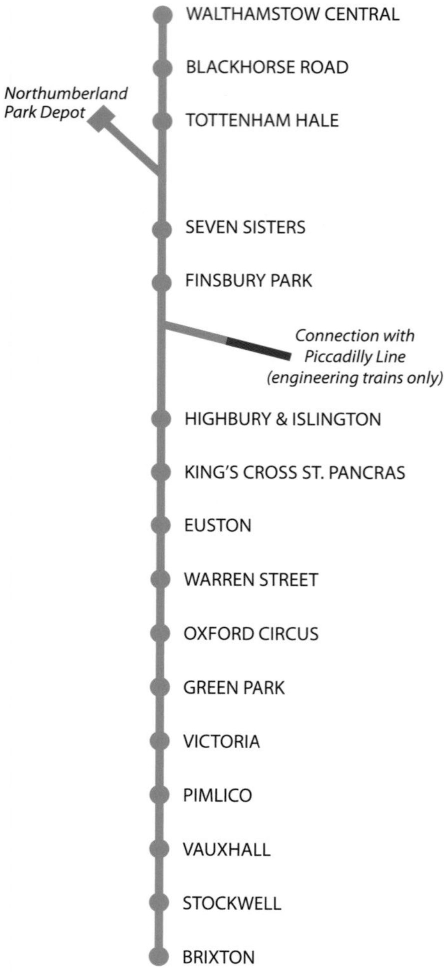

VICTORIA LINE

Overview:

Route: Walthamstow Central to Brixton

Night Tube: Walthamstow Central to Brixton

Route type: Tube

First section opened: Walthamstow Central to Highbury & Islington opened by London Transport on 1 September 1968

Method of train operation: Automatic

Signalling: Invensys Distance to Go (Radio)

Direction of route: Northbound / Southbound

Route length: 13.3 miles

Number of stations: 16

Trains: 2009 Tube Stock

Max number of trains required: 39 (morning and evening peaks)

Depot: Northumberland Park

Stabling points: Walthamstow Central / Brixton / Victoria

HISTORY

The Victoria Line was built by London Transport to relieve congestion on other lines in central London. The planned route was from Walthamstow Central to Victoria, but an extension southwards to Brixton was also later authorised. Construction began in 1962 and the first section, between Walthamstow Central and Highbury & Islington, opened to passengers on 1 September 1968. The next section to Warren Street opened on 1 December 1968, and the entire line to Victoria was opened by HM Queen Elizabeth II on 7 March 1969. The extension to Brixton was opened on 23 July 1971, although one station on this section, at Pimlico, did not open until 14 September 1972. The Victoria Line was the first underground railway in the world that was built to feature automatic operation. It has been operated automatically since opening (automatic operation was trialled between Hainault and Woodford on the Central Line prior to the opening of the Victoria Line). The first trains were 1967 Tube Stock which operated automatically by receiving codes from the track. These were replaced in 2011 by the current trains of 2009 Tube Stock and the signalling system upgraded.

WALTHAMSTOW CENTRAL

BLACKHORSE ROAD

Northumberland Park Depot

TOTTENHAM HALE

SEVEN SISTERS

FINSBURY PARK

Connection with Piccadilly Line (engineering trains only)

HIGHBURY & ISLINGTON

KING'S CROSS ST. PANCRAS

EUSTON

WARREN STREET

OXFORD CIRCUS

GREEN PARK

VICTORIA

PIMLICO

VAUXHALL

STOCKWELL

BRIXTON

A train of 2009 Tube Stock led by 11072 arrives at Blackhorse Road with a Brixton to Walthamstow Central service on 30 December 2016. The seat recess with tile motif can be seen on the left hand side of the photograph.

THE ROUTE AND OPERATIONS

The Victoria Line is worked by a fleet of 2009 Tube Stock built by Bombardier in Derby (see page 59). Trains operate in automatic mode using the Invensys DTG-R system (see page 10). A maximum of 39 are required for service, which is reached in both the morning and evening peaks.

Since the publication of the 2016 Guide Book, there have been two notable changes to the way in which the Victoria Line operates. The most noticeable was the introduction of the Night Tube service on the night of 19/20 August, which includes the whole of the line. The second was the introduction of a new timetable in May 2016 that saw trains operate end to end, with short workings to and from Seven Sisters eliminated except for trains entering or leaving service. This increased the number of trains serving stations between Seven Sisters and Walthamstow Central by over 30%. Previously, northbound trains which terminated at Seven Sisters continued as a staff service to Northumberland Park Depot, while southbound trains starting at Seven Sisters arrived there as a staff special from Northumberland Park Depot. The staff trains are now mostly worked as a shuttle between Northumberland Park Depot and Seven Sisters platform 4.

Northumberland Park Depot is the Victoria Line's only depot and is where the bulk of the fleet stable outside of traffic hours. A few trains stable at other locations when Night Tube is not in operation as follows: Walthamstow Central (2 trains), Victoria Siding (1) and Brixton (3). Centre reversing sidings exist at King's Cross St Pancras (single siding) and Victoria (2 sidings – numbered 22 and 23). The King's Cross St Pancras siding is normally only used at times of disruption, although a train is booked to reverse there every Saturday and Sunday early morning to keep the rails free from rust. The Victoria Sidings have a train booked to stable overnight in number 22 siding Monday to Thursday nights and Sunday night, plus the same train that uses the King's Cross St Pancras siding on Saturday and Sunday mornings also enters Victoria's 23 siding to keep the rails rust free.

Northumberland Park Depot is the only part of the Victoria Line above ground, the entire passenger route from Walthamstow Central to Brixton being below ground. Most of the underground stations have a very similar appearance, each displaying its own individual tile motif in the seat recesses along the platforms. There are however a few notable exceptions: the southbound platforms at Finsbury Park and Highbury & Islington are both former Great Northern & City Railway platforms and are built to a much larger overall bore size than the rest of the platform tunnels on the line.

First trains:
0526 Brixton to Walthamstow Central 0558 (Mon-Fri)
0525 Walthamstow Central to Brixton 0557 (Mon-Fri)

Last trains:
0028 Brixton to Walthamstow Central 0102 (Mon-Thu)
2352 Brixton to Walthamstow Central 0024 (Sun)
0010 Walthamstow Central to Brixton 0049 (Mon-Thu)
2329 Walthamstow Central to Brixton 0003 (Sun)

Note: *The above trains are the first and last to travel the entire length of the line. There are other shorter workings before and after those listed above. A continuous service operates over the entire length of the line from start of traffic on Friday morning until end of traffic on Sunday night as part of the Night Tube service.*

Last trains shown as just after midnight are at the end of the previous day's traffic, so for example, the 0028 Brixton to Walthamstow Central on a Thursday is at the end of Thursday's traffic and is actually at the very start of Friday.

A clearer view of the seat recess tiled motif at Blackhorse Road which depicts a black horse which has been elongated to look like a road.

WATERLOO & CITY LINE

Overview:

BANK

WATERLOO

Waterloo Depot

Route: Waterloo to Bank

Night Tube: Not applicable

Route type: Tube

First section opened: Waterloo to Bank (then called City), opened by the Waterloo & City Railway Company on 8 August 1898

Method of train operation: Manually driven

Signalling: Colour light signals protected by train stops

Direction of route: Eastbound / Westbound

Route length: 1.5 miles

Number of stations: 2

Trains: 1992 Tube Stock

Max number of trains required (peak times): 5

Depot: Waterloo

Stabling point: Bank

HISTORY

Formally opened by the Duke of Cambridge on 11 July 1898, there was a slight delay before the Waterloo & City Railway opened to the public on 8 August 1898. Built to connect the London & South Western Railway's Waterloo terminus with the City of London, and operated from the outset by the L&SWR, it was not fully absorbed by them until the first day of 1907. Ownership passed to the Southern Railway (along with the rest of the L&SWR) in 1923, and the railways were nationalised in 1948. The line remained a part of British Rail (latterly under BR's Network SouthEast banner) until 1994 when it was sold to London Underground. Its last day as a part of BR was 31 March 1994, with London Underground taking over from 5 April 1994. It was also converted from the Southern's third rail system to the London Underground four rail system to coincide with the introduction of new class 482 trains (1992 Tube Stock) towards the end of BR's ownership of the line.

When opened, what we now know as the Bank terminus was called City, which gave the railway the unusual distinction of having every station name included in its title. The City terminus had been connected below ground by passenger subways with the City & South London Railway (Northern Line) and the Central London Railway (Central Line) at Bank since those lines had opened, but it was not renamed to Bank until October 1940.

The fact that the Waterloo & City was a part of BR until 1994 is reflected by there being no physical connection to the rest of the Underground network. Until the building of the now disused Eurostar terminal at Waterloo, Waterloo & City trains had to leave the line for maintenance via a lift alongside Waterloo station. Since the Eurostar terminal was built over the site of the lift, any train needing to leave the Waterloo & City has to be craned out.

THE ROUTE AND OPERATIONS

The service is provided by trains of 1992 Tube Stock, similar to those on the Central Line, but of only four cars in length, which are driven manually in accordance with colour light signals fitted with train stops.

With only two stations, operations are quite straight forward. The depot is situated at the Waterloo end of the line beyond the platforms. There are two platforms, number 25 is pick up only and number 26 is set down only. A train entering service will draw forward into platform 25, pick up passengers and then run to Bank. On the approach to Bank, there is a scissors crossover which gives access to the two platforms (numbered 7 and 8). At busy times, at both Waterloo and Bank, the driver of the previous train takes out the next one to reduce the turn round time (known as stepping back). At quieter times, the driver takes out the same train that he brought in. After departing from Bank, trains run directly to platform 26 at Waterloo, which is set down only. Once everybody has detrained, the train will move forward into Waterloo depot to reverse.

The route of the Waterloo & City takes it beneath the times just to the west of Blackfriars Bridge. It then turns to the east and runs parallel with the District and Circle lines (albeit at a deeper level) to the terminus at Bank.

The main reason for the existence of this line is to connect the Waterloo mainline terminus with the City of London. There is little need for the railway when the City is quiet. For this reason, the line is closed on Sundays and Bank Holidays.

A maximum of five trains are required during the morning and evening peaks on Mondays to Fridays, with three providing the service outside the peaks on Mondays to Fridays and all day on Saturday. Train maintenance is carried out at Waterloo and all bar one train stables there outside traffic hours – the other stables in a platform at Bank.all bar one train is stabled at Waterloo. One train stables in one of the platforms at Bank.

First trains:
0615 Waterloo to Bank 0620 (Mon-Fri)
0800 Waterloo to Bank 0805 (Sat)
0621 Bank to Waterloo 0626 (Mon-Fri)
0802 Bank to Waterloo 0807 (Sat)
0802 Bank to Waterloo 0807 (Sat)

Last trains:
0020 Waterloo to Bank 0025 (Mon-Sat)
0026 Bank to Waterloo 0031 (Mon-Sat)

A train of 1992 Tube Stock led by 65507 arrives at Bank with a service from Waterloo. Note the British Rail Network SouthEast logos along the platform edge, partly obscured by the yellow line. 3 September 2016.

TUBE STOCK TRAINS

The following information and abbreviations apply:

DM – Driving motor (powered vehicle with a driving cab at one end)

NDM – Non-driving motor (powered vehicle with no driving cab)

UNDM – Uncoupling non-driving motor (powered vehicle with no driving cab but fitted with controls at one end to allow uncoupling and shunting)

T – Trailer (vehicle with no motors and no cabs)

Trains have an 'A' end and a 'D' end. On the Bakerloo, Victoria, Waterloo & City and Jubilee lines, trains always face the same way as there is nowhere on those lines where trains can become turned. Bakerloo trains always have the 'A' car facing south, but on the Victoria, Waterloo & City and Jubilee lines, the 'A' car faces either north or west.

The 1995 Tube Stock trains on the Northern Line are turned each time they go round the Kennington loop. The Hainault loop at the east end of the Central Line causes the 1992 Tube Stock to become turned so it is designed to be fully reversible and runs with an 'A' car (DM) at both ends. When in service, each train is allocated a three digit reporting number, from which that train's duty can be identified. The number is designated at the start of its duty and is displayed digitally on the front and rear, either as part of the destination display, or in a separate display in the cab window (as per the 1972 Tube Stock).

1972 TUBE STOCK

Year of manufacture: 1972-1974

Built by: Metro-Cammell, Birmingham

Entry into service: 1972

Lines used on: Bakerloo

Number of cars per train: 7

Train formation: DM-T-T-DM+UNDM-T-DM
　　　　　　　　　　plus one train formed DM-T-T-UNDM+UNDM-T-DM

The 1972 Stock was first introduced to the Northern Line in 1972. The first batch of trains became known as the 1972 MkI Stock, and they were eventually joined by a later batch intended for eventual use on the Jubilee Line, which became known as the 1972 MkII Stock. The 1972 Tube Stock were built as a crew operated (driver and guard) version of the now withdrawn automatic 1967 Tube Stock which was built for the opening of the Victoria Line and the two types were externally almost identical. Prior to refurbishment and application of the corporate red, white and blue London Underground livery, the 1972 MkII Tube Stock could be distinguished from the 1972 MkI Tube Stock, as they had red painted passenger doors, while the MkI Tube Stock's doors were unpainted. After use on both the Northern and Jubilee lines, the 1972 MkII Tube Stock were moved to the Bakerloo Line. Amongst the MkII cars are a number of MkI cars which have been incorporated into the MkII fleet and renumbered. Although they are pretty much identical, look out for black handles on the ventilation grilles and internal panels with a black pattern instead of brown inside some of the ex-MkI cars. Don't be too surprised to see the occasional blue ventilation grille handle or grab rail, no doubt spare parts obtained from the withdrawn Victoria Line 1967 Tube Stock fleet.

The 1972 Tube Stock trains are formed of two units back to back: a 4-car unit at the south end and a 3-car unit at the north end. All of the 4-car units have a DM at both ends, except one which has a UNDM instead; it is numbered out of sequence (3299-4299-4399-3399) to highlight to operational staff that it is different.

The 1972 Tube Stock is now the oldest type in regular passenger use on the Underground. Replacement is likely to come in the form of the 'New Tube for London', but this is likely to be some

A train of 1972 MkII Tube Stock working a Harrow & Wealdstone to Elephant & Castle service heads south from Kensal Green with unit 3535-4535-3435 at the rear on 25 September 2016.

years away (2033 has been suggested). As the 1972 Tube Stock will have to soldier on for a few more years yet, they are undergoing life extension works at Acton Works. This has mostly involved repairs to rotten areas of the under-frames and new flooring, while from 2016 the trains have also been receiving a new design of seat moquette (pictured above).

Top: *An interior view of DM 3366 showing the Bakerloo Line's new seat moquette which was introduced from 2016.*

Bottom: *A close up of one of the ventilation grilles in UNDM 3443, showing the two handles which were originally from a Victoria Line 1967 Tube Stock car. Despite best efforts to paint them in the Bakerloo's brown house colour, the paint has worn off, revealing the Victoria Line blue.*

1972 MkII Tube Stock (Bakerloo Line)
4-car 'A' end units (south facing)

DM	T	T	DM	DM	T	T	DM	DM	T	T	DM	DM	T	T	DM
3231	4231	4331	3331	3240	4240	4340	3340	3250	4250	4350	3350	3260	4260	4360	3360
3232	4232	4332	3332	3241	4241	4341	3341	3251	4251	4351	3351	3261	4261	4361	3361
3233	4233	4333	3333	3242	4242	4342	3342	3252	4252	4352	3352	3262	4262	4362	3362
3234	4234	4334	3334	3243	4243	4343	3343	3253	4253	4353	3353	3263	4263	4363	3363
3235	4235	4335	3335	3244	4244	4344	3344	3254	4254	4354	3354	3264*	4264*	4364*	3364*
3236	4236	4336	3336	3245	4245	4345	3345	3255	4255	4355	3355	3265*	4265*	4365*	3365*
3237	4237	4337	3337	3246	4246	4346	3346	3256	4256	4356	3356	3266*	4266*	4366	3366
3238	4238	4338	3338	3247	4247	4347	3347	3258	4258	4358	3358	3267*	4267*	4367*	3367*
3239	4239	4339	3339	3248	4248	4348	3348	3259	4259	4359	3359				

DM	T	T	UNDM
3299	4299	4399	3399

3-car 'D' end units (north facing)

UNDM	T	DM	UNDM	T	DM	UNDM	T	DM	UNDM	T	DM	UNDM	T	DM
3431	4531	3531	3438	4538	3538	3446	4546	3546	3453	4553	3553	3460	4560	3560
3432	4532	3532	3440	4540	3540	3447	4547	3547	3454	4554	3554	3461	4561	3561
3433	4533	3533	3441	4541	3541	3448	4548	3548	3455	4555	3555	3462	4562	3562
3434	4534	3534	3442	4542	3542	3449	4549	3549	3456	4556	3556	3463	4563	3563
3435	4535	3535	3443	4543	3543	3450	4550	3550	3457	4557	3557	3464*	4564*	3564*
3436	4536	3536	3444	4544	3544	3451	4551	3551	3458	4558	3558	3465*	4565*	3565*
3437	4537	3537	3445	4545	3545	3452	4552	3552	3459	4559	3559	3466*	4566*	3566*
												3467*	4567*	3567*

* 1972 MkI stock cars renumbered

1973 TUBE STOCK

Year of manufacture: 1974-1977
Built by: Metro-Cammell, Birmingham
Entry into service: 1975
Lines used on: Piccadilly
Number of cars per train: 6
Train formation: DM-T-UNDM+UNDM-T-DM or DM-T-DM+UNDM-T-DM
or DM-T-UNDM+DM-T-DM or DM-T-DM+DM-T-DM

A late running Piccadilly Line service has been terminated short of its destination (Uxbridge) at Ruislip and is entering the Ruislip Siding to reverse. The line bearing to the right goes to Ruislip Depot and is used by stock movements and engineering trains. The unit at the head of this train is double ended 3-car set 859-658-858. 6 November 2016.

The first train of 1973 Stock entered service in 1975. Built to coincide with the extension of the Piccadilly Line to Heathrow Airport, their interiors were designed to cope with airport passenger traffic and they have a large space to accommodate luggage adjacent to the doors. Each train is made up of two 3-car units, the bulk of which are single ended and have a UNDM on the inner end. There are also 21 double ended units with a DM at both ends to give operational flexibility. These can be identified by the strips along the corners of the cab ends which are used to mount the inter-car barriers when that cab is formed into the middle of a train (see above picture).

Due to the Heathrow Terminal 4 loop, trains are frequently turned and the 'A' and 'D' ends of trains can face in either direction. The 1973 Stock fleet was refurbished between 1995 and 2000 and is expected to last into the 2020s when replacement is anticipated to come in the form of the 'New Tube for London'.

Interior view of DM 162 looking towards the cab end. The luggage areas can be identified by the perch seats in the centre of the car.

1973 Tube Stock (Piccadilly Line)
3-car 'A' end units

DM	T	UNDM	DM	T	UNDM	DM	T	UNDM	DM	T	UNDM	DM	T	UNDM	DM	T	UNDM
100	500	300	128	528	328	154	554	354	182	582	382	210	610	410	236	636	436
102	502	302	130	530	330	156	556	356	184	584	384	212	612	412	238	638	438
104	504	304	132	532	332	158	558	358	186	586	386	214	614	414	240	640	440
106	506	306	134	534	334	160	560	360	188	588	388	216	616	416	242	642	442
110	510	310	136	536	336	162	562	362	190	590	390	218	618	418	244	644	444
112	512	312	138	538	338	164	564	364	192	592	392	220	620	420	246	646	446
116	516	316	140	540	340	168	568	368	194	594	394	222	622	422	248	648	448
118	518	318	142	542	342	170	570	370	196	596	396	224	624	424	250	650	450
120	520	320	144	544	344	172	572	372	198	598	398	226	626	426	252	652	452
122	522	322	146	546	346	174	574	374	200	600	400	228	628	428			
124	524	324	148	548	348	176	576	376	202	602	402	230	630	430			
126	526	326	150	550	350	178	578	378	206	606	406	232	632	432			
			152	552	352	180	580	380	208	608	408	234	634	434			

1973 Tube Stock (Piccadilly Line)
3-car 'D' end units

UNDM	T	DM	UNDM	T	DM	UNDM	T	DM	UNDM	T	DM	UNDM	T	DM	UNDM	T	DM
301	501	101	327	527	127	353	553	153	379	579	179	405	605	205	431	631	231
303	503	103	329	529	129	355	555	155	381	581	181	407	607	207	433	633	233
305	505	105	331	531	131	357	557	157	383	583	183	409	609	209	435	635	235
307	507	107	333	533	133	359	559	159	385	585	185	411	611	211	437	637	237
309	509	109	335	535	135	361	561	161	387	587	187	413	613	213	439	639	239
311	511	111	337	537	137	363	563	163	389	589	189	415	615	215	441	641	241
313	513	113	339	539	139	365	565	165	391	591	191	417	617	217	443	643	243
315	515	115	341	541	141	367	567	167	393	593	193	419	619	219	445	645	245
317	517	117	343	543	143	369	569	169	395	595	195	421	621	221	447	647	247
319	519	119	345	545	145	371	571	171	397	597	197	423	623	223	449	649	249
321	521	121	347	547	147	373	573	173	399	599	199	425	625	225	451	651	251
323	523	123	349	549	149	375	575	175	401	601	201	427	627	227	453	653	253
325	525	125	351	551	151	377	577	177	403	603	203	429	629	229			

1973 Tube Stock (Piccadilly Line)
3-car double ended units

DM	T	DM	DM	T	DM	DM	T	DM	DM	T	DM	DM	T	DM	DM	T	DM
854	654	855	862	662	863	870	670	871	878	678	879	886	686	887	896	696	897
856	656	857	864	664	865	872	672	873	880	680	881	890	690	891			
858	658	859	866	666	867	874	674	875	882	682	883	892	692	893			
860	660	861	868	668	869	876	676	877	884	684	885	894	694	895			

1992 TUBE STOCK

Year of manufacture: 1991-1994
Built by: BREL (Adtranz), Derby
Entry into service: 1993 (on both the Central and Waterloo & City)
Lines used on: Central and Waterloo & City
Number of cars per train: 8 (Central) / 4 (Waterloo & City)
Train formation: See explanation below

91233 leads an eastbound Central Line service into Lancaster Gate on 30 December 2016.

Three prototype trains (known as 1986 Tube Stock) were tested on London Underground in the late 1980s, and the 1992 Tube Stock was the result. Built by ABB (now Bombardier and formerly British Rail Engineering Ltd) in Derby, they were introduced to the Central Line from 1993 to replace the driver and guard operated 1962 Tube Stock. British Rail (Network SouthEast) tagged five 4-car sets onto the order to replace the class 487 units then in use on the Waterloo & City Line (which at the time was not a part of the London Underground). The Waterloo & City Line units were designated class 482 and were finished in a version of the Network SouthEast red, white and blue livery. The Waterloo & City became a part of London Underground in 1994; the class 482s were painted in the standard LU red, white and blue livery in 2006 and are now known as 1992 Tube Stock. The Waterloo & City is totally isolated from the rest of the London Underground network, so there is no scope for two fleets to ever operate together. On the Central Line, the 1992 Tube Stock runs as 8-car trains made up of four 2-car units. The fleet is designed to be totally reversible and 2-car units can be formed as A+B, B+C or B+D (A = DM / B and C = NDM / D = de-icing NDM). These 2-car units can be formed into any of 36 different combinations to make up an 8-car train, so long as the 'A' cars are at the outer ends. On the Waterloo & City Line, trains are formed DM-NDM+NDM-DM.

The Central Line is an automatic railway on which the 1992 Tube Stock operates with the Automatic Train Operation (ATO) driving the trains and the Automatic Train Protection (ATP) picking up codes in the track to determine target speeds. They can also run in coded manual, where the Train Operator drives the train manually but obeys the target speeds set by the ATP. There is also a restricted manual mode where it is driven manually, restricted to 11mph, with the ATP isolated and the train operator obeying trackside signals. Waterloo & City Line trains are driven manually as the line is fitted with colour light signals and train stops. As there are only two stations, the trains have fixed destinations displayed on the cab fronts: Bank on one end and Waterloo on the other.

During 2011 and 2012, the Central Line fleet underwent a refresh and received new saloon windows, seat moquette, internal lighting and modified cab fronts.

1992 Tube Stock (Central Line)
2-car A-B units

DM(A)	NDM(B)	DM(A)	NDM(B)	DM(A)	NDM(B)	DM(A)	NDM(B)	DM(A)	NDM(B)	DM(A)	NDM(B)	DM(A)	NDM(B)
91001	92001	91057	92057	91113	92113	91169	92169	91225	92225	91281	92281	91337	92337
91003	92003	91059	92059	91115	92115	91171	92171	91227	92227	91283	92283	91339	92339
91005	92005	91061	92061	91117	92117	91173	92173	91229	92229	91285	92285	91341	92341
91007	92007	91063	92063	91119	92119	91175	92175	91231	92231	91287	92287	91343	92343
91009	92009	91065	92065	91121	92121	91177	92177	91233	92233	91289	92289	91345	92345
91011	92011	91067	92067	91123	92123	91179	92179	91235	92235	91291	92291	91347	92347
91013	92013	91069	92069	91125	92125	91181	92181	91237	92237	91293	92293	91349	92349
91015	92015	91071	92071	91127	92127	91183	92183	91239	92239	91295	92295		
91017	92017	91073	92073	91129	92129	91185	92185	91241	92241	91297	92297		
91019	92019	91075	92075	91131	92131	91187	92187	91243	92243	91299	92299		
91021	92021	91077	92077	91133	92133	91189	92189	91245	92245	91301	92301		
91023	92023	91079	92079	91135	92135	91191	92191	91247	92247	91303	92303		
91025	92025	91081	92081	91137	92137	91193	92193	91249	92249	91305	92305		
91027	92027	91083	92083	91139	92139	91195	92195	91251	92251	91307	92307		
91029	92029	91085	92085	91141	92141	91197	92197	91253	92253	91309	92309		
91031	92031	91087	92087	91143	92143	91199	92199	91255	92255	91311	92311		
91033	92033	91089	92089	91145	92145	91201	92201	91257	92257	91313	92313		
91035	92035	91091	92091	91147	92147	91203	92203	91259	92259	91315	92315		
91037	92037	91093	92093	91149	92149	91205	92205	91261	92261	91317	92317		
91039	92039	91095	92095	91151	92151	91207	92207	91263	92263	91319	92319		
91041	92041	91097	92097	91153	92153	91209	92209	91265	92265	91321	92321		
91043	92043	91099	92099	91155	92155	91211	92211	91267	92267	91323	92323		
91045	92045	91101	92101	91157	92157	91213	92213	91269	92269	91325	92325		
91047	92047	91103	92103	91159	92159	91215	92215	91271	92271	91327	92327		
91049	92049	91105	92105	91161	92161	91217	92217	91273	92273	91329	92329		
91051	92051	91107	92107	91163	92163	91219	92219	91275	92275	91331	92331		
91053	92053	91109	92109	91165	92165	91221	92221	91277	92277	91333	92333		
91055	92055	91111	92111	91167	92167	91223	92223	91279	92279	91335	92335		

1992 Tube Stock (Central Line)
2-car B-C units

NDM(B)	NDM (C)	NDM(B)	NDM (C)	NDM(B)	NDM (C)	NDM(B)	NDM (C)	NDM(B)	NDM (C)	NDM(B)	NDM (C)	NDM(B)	NDM (C)
92002	93002	92042	93042	92082	93082	92122	93122	92162	93162	92202	93202	92242	93242
92004	93004	92044	93044	92084	93084	92124	93124	92164	93164	92204	93204	92244	93244
92006	93006	92046	93046	92086	93086	92126	93126	92166	93166	92206	93206	92246	93246
92008	93008	92048	93048	92088	93088	92128	93128	92168	93168	92208	93208	92248	93248
92010	93010	92050	93050	92090	93090	92130	93130	92170	93170	92210	93210	92250	93250
92012	93012	92052	93052	92092	93092	92132	93132	92172	93172	92212	93212	92252	93252
92014	93014	92054	93054	92094	93094	92134	93134	92174	93174	92214	93214	92254	93254
92016	93016	92056	93056	92096	93096	92136	93136	92176	93176	92216	93216	92256	93256
92018	93018	92058	93058	92098	93098	92138	93138	92178	93178	92218	93218	92258	93258
92020	93020	92060	93060	92100	93100	92140	93140	92180	93180	92220	93220	92260	93260
92022	93022	92062	93062	92102	93102	92142	93142	92182	93182	92222	93222	92262	93262
92024	93024	92064	93064	92104	93104	92144	93144	92184	93184	92224	93224	92264	93264
92026	93026	92066	93066	92106	93106	92146	93146	92186	93186	92226	93226	92266	93266
92028	93028	92068	93068	92108	93108	92148	93148	92188	93188	92228	93228		
92030	93030	92070	93070	92110	93110	92150	93150	92190	93190	92230	93230		
92032	93032	92072	93072	92112	93112	92152	93152	92192	93192	92232	93232		
92034	93034	92074	93074	92114	93114	92154	93154	92194	93194	92234	93234		
92036	93036	92076	93076	92116	93116	92156	93156	92196	93196	92236	93236		
92038	93038	92078	93078	92118	93118	92158	93158	92198	93198	92238	93238		
92040	93040	92080	93080	92120	93120	92160	93160	92200	93200	92240	93240		

A Bank to Waterloo service on the Waterloo & City line arrives at its destination led by 65504 on 12 March 2016.

1992 Tube Stock (Central Line)

2-car B-D de-icing units

NDM(B)	NDM (D)	NDM(B)	NDM (D)	NDM(B)	NDM (D)	NDM(B)	NDM (D)	NDM(B)	NDM (D)	NDM(B)	NDM (D)	NDM(B)	NDM (D)
92402	93402	92412	93412	92422	93422	92432	93432	92442	93442	92452	93452	92462	93462
92404	93404	92414	93414	92424	93424	92434	93434	92444	93444	92454	93454	92464	93464
92406	93406	92416	93416	92426	93426	92436	93436	92446	93446	92456	93456		
92408	93408	92418	93418	92428	93428	92438	93438	92448	93448	92458	93458		
92410	93410	92420	93420	92430	93430	92440	93440	92450	93450	92460	93460		

1992 Tube Stock (Waterloo & City Line)

2-car units (facing Bank)		2-car units (facing Waterloo)	
DM	NDM	NDM	DM
65501	67501	67502	65502
65503	67503	67504	65504
65505	67505	67506	65506
65507	67507	67508	65508
65509	67509	67510	65510

1995 TUBE STOCK

Year of manufacture: 1996-1999
Built by: Alsthom Transportation, Birmingham
Entry into service: 1998
Lines used on: Northern
Number of cars per train: 6
Train formation: DM-T-UNDM+UNDM-T-DM

The 1995 Tube Stock was introduced to the Northern Line from 1998 onwards to replace the older crew operated (driver and guard) trains of 1959 Tube Stock and 1972 Tube Stock, eventually eradicating the older stock by January 2000. When first introduced, the 1995 Tube Stock was manually driven, as at that time the Northern Line was signalled entirely with colour light signals protected by train stops. The signalling has since been upgraded to the Thales Transmission Based Train Control 'moving block' system (TBTC), and since 2014, the 1995 Tube Stock has operated automatically, and the trackside colour light signals on the Northern Line have been made redundant.

Although designated as 1995 Tube Stock, they were in fact built from 1996 onwards alongside the Jubilee Line's 1996 Tube Stock. These two types are almost identical in appearance but are very different beneath the skin. The 1995 Tube Stock has Alsthom's 'Onyx' three phase Insulated Gate Bipolar Transistor system (IGBT) which makes a very different sound to the traction package on the 1996 Tube Stock which employs Gate Turn Off Thyristors (GTOs).

The internal layout is also different, with the 1996 Tube Stock having perch seats alongside the doors and the 1995 Tube Stock having tip up seats. The 1995 Tube Stock went through a 'refresh' programme, completed in 2015, during which their cabs and interiors were refurbished and LED destination displays fitted.

Interior view of 'D' end driving motor 51517, clearly showing the tip up seats adjacent to the doors.

A High Barnet to Morden (via Bank) service arrives at Tufnell Park with 51682 leading on 19 June 2016.

1995 Tube Stock (Northern Line)
3-car 'D' end units

DM	T	UNDM	DM	T	UNDM	DM	T	UNDM	DM	T	UNDM	DM	T	UNDM
51501	52501	53501	51539	52539	53539	51577	52577	53577	51615	52615	53615	51653	52653	53653
51503	52503	53503	51541	52541	53541	51579	52579	53579	51617	52617	53617	51655	52655	53655
51505	52505	53505	51543	52543	53543	51581	52581	53581	51619	52619	53619	51657	52657	53657
51507	52507	53507	51545	52545	53545	51583	52583	53583	51621	52621	53621	51659	52659	53659
51509	52509	53509	51547	52547	53547	51585	52585	53585	51623	52623	53623	51661	52661	53661
51511	52511	53511	51549	52549	53549	51587	52587	53587	51625	52625	53625	51663	52663	53663
51513	52513	53513	51551	52551	53551	51589	52589	53589	51627	52627	53627	51665	52665	53665
51515	52515	53515	51553	52553	53553	51591	52591	53591	51629	52629	53629	51667	52667	53667
51517	52517	53517	51555	52555	53555	51593	52593	53593	51631	52631	53631	51669	52669	53669
51519	52519	53519	51557	52557	53557	51595	52595	53595	51633	52633	53633	51671	52671	53671
51521	52521	53521	51559	52559	53559	51597	52597	53597	51635	52635	53635	51673	52673	53673
51523	52523	53523	51561	52561	53561	51599	52599	53599	51637	52637	53637	51675	52675	53675
51525	52525	53525	51563	52563	53563	51601	52601	53601	51639	52639	53639	51677	52677	53677
51527	52527	53527	51565	52565	53565	51603	52603	53603	51641	52641	53641	51679	52679	53679
51529	52529	53529	51567	52567	53567	51605	52605	53605	51643	52643	53643	51681	52681	53681
51531	52531	53531	51569	52569	53569	51607	52607	53607	51645	52645	53645	51683	52683	53683
51533	52533	53533	51571	52571	53571	51609	52609	53609	51647	52647	53647	51685	52685	53685
51535	52535	53535	51573	52573	53573	51611	52611	53611	51649	52649	53649			
51537	52537	53537	51575	52575	53575	51613	52613	53613	51651	52651	53651			

1995 Tube Stock (Northern Line)
3-car 'A' end units

UNDM	T	DM	UNDM	T	DM	UNDM	T	DM	UNDM	T	DM	UNDM	T	DM
53502	52502	51502	53540	52540	51540	53578	52578	51578	53616	52616	51616	53654	52654	51654
53504	52504	51504	53542	52542	51542	53580	52580	51580	53618	52618	51618	53656	52656	51656
53506	52506	51506	53544	52544	51544	53582	52582	51582	53620	52620	51620	53658	52658	51658
53508	52508	51508	53546	52546	51546	53584	52584	51584	53622	52622	51622	53660	52660	51660
53510	52510	51510	53548	52548	51548	53586	52586	51586	53624	52624	51624	53662	52662	51662
53512	52512	51512	53550	52550	51550	53588	52588	51588	53626	52626	51626	53664	52664	51664
53514	52514	51514	53552	52552	51552	53590	52590	51590	53628	52628	51628	53666	52666	51666
53516	52516	51516	53554	52554	51554	53592	52592	51592	53630	52630	51630	53668	52668	51668
53518	52518	51518	53556	52556	51556	53594	52594	51594	53632	52632	51632	53670	52670	51670
53520	52520	51520	53558	52558	51558	53596	52596	51596	53634	52634	51634	53672	52672	51672
53522	52522	51522	53560	52560	51560	53598	52598	51598	53636	52636	51636	53674	52674	51674
53524	52524	51524	53562	52562	51562	53600	52600	51600	53638	52638	51638	53676	52676	51676
53526	52526	51526	53564	52564	51564	53602	52602	51602	53640	52640	51640	53678	52678	51678
53528	52528	51528	53566	52566	51566	53604	52604	51604	53642	52642	51642	53680	52680	51680
53530	52530	51530	53568	52568	51568	53606	52606	51606	53644	52644	51644	53682	52682	51682
53532	52532	51532	53570	52570	51570	53608	52608	51608	53646	52646	51646	53684	52684	51684
53534	52534	51534	53572	52572	51572	53610	52610	51610	53648	52648	51648	53686	52686	51686
53536	52536	51536	53574	52574	51574	53612	52612	51612	53650	52650	51650			
53538	52538	51538	53576	52576	51576	53614	52614	51614	53652	52652	51652			

1995 Tube Stock (Northern Line)
3-car 'D' end de-icing units

DM	T	UNDM	DM	T	UNDM	DM	T	UNDM	DM	T	UNDM	DM	T	UNDM
51701	52701	53701	51707	52707	53707	51713	52713	53713	51719	52719	53719	51725	52725	53725
51703	52703	53703	51709	52709	53709	51715	52715	53715	51721	52721	53721			
51705	52705	53705	51711	52711	53711	51717	52717	53717	51723	52723	53723			

1995 Tube Stock (Northern Line)
3-car 'A' end de-icing units

UNDM	T	DM	UNDM	T	DM	UNDM	T	DM	UNDM	T	DM	UNDM	T	DM
53702	52702	51702	53708	52708	51708	53714	52714	51714	53720	52720	51720	53726	52726	51726
53704	52704	51704	53710	52710	51710	53716	52716	51716	53722	52722	51722			
53706	52706	51706	53712	52712	51712	53718	52718	51718	53724	52724	51724			

1996 TUBE STOCK

Year of manufacture: 1996-1999 and 2005-2006
Built by: Alsthom Transportation, Birmingham
Entry into service: 1997
Lines used on: Jubilee
Number of cars per train: 7
Train formation: DM-T-UNDM+UNDM-T-T-DM

96009 leads the 0534 Stanmore to Stratford Night Tube service into Kingsbury on Sunday morning 6 November 2016. The generous height of the overbridge here reflects the fact that this section was originally part of the Metropolitan Railway and was built to accommodate full size trains.

When the Jubilee Line Extension (JLE) was being constructed, the original plan was to build a new fleet of 1996 Tube Stock trains to supplement the 1983 Tube Stock trains which were already serving the Jubilee Line between Stanmore and Charing Cross. Some of these had been delivered as recently as 1988, so were still considered to be relatively new and the 1996 Tube Stock was designed to resemble the 1983 Tube Stock, so that the line would appear to have a uniform fleet. In the event, the new trains completely replaced the 1983 Tube Stock, as the older trains were deemed unsuitable for operation over the new line, mainly because of the single leaf doors which caused extended station dwell times, especially in the peak hours. So, the introduction of the 1996 Tube Stock saw the withdrawal of the 1983 Tube Stock, which found no further use elsewhere on the Underground. The 1996 Tube Stock entered service between December 1997 and July 2001 as 6-car trains. In 2005/6 new trailers were delivered to bring the fleet up to seven cars, together with four additional trains which were delivered as 7-car trains.

Externally very similar to the Northern Line's 1995 Tube Stock which was built alongside it, the 1996 Tube Stock has a very different traction package using Gate Turn Off Thyristors (GTOs) similar to the equipment used on class 465 Networker EMUs. This gives the 1996 Tube Stock a very distinctive sound which changes tone as the train accelerates or decelerates, whereas the 1995 Tube Stock has a slightly quieter and more constant tone.

When first introduced, the Jubilee Line was still fitted with colour light signals protected by train stops and trains were driven manually. The line has since been resignalled using the Transmission Based Train Control 'moving block' system (TBTC), which was implemented in two stages, Dollis Hill to Stratford and Charing Cross (29 December 2010) and Dollis Hill to Stanmore (26 June 2011).

1996 Tube Stock (Jubilee Line)
3-car 'A' end units

DM	T	UNDM	DM	T	UNDM	DM	T	UNDM	DM	T	UNDM	DM	T	UNDM
96002	96202	96402	96028	96228	96428	96054	96254	96454	96080	96880	96480	96106	96906	96506
96004	96204	96404	96030	96230	96430	96056	96256	96456	96082	96882	96482	96108	96908	96508
96006	96206	96406	96032	96232	96432	96058	96258	96458	96084	96884	96484	96110	96910	96510
96008	96208	96408	96034	96234	96434	96060	96260	96460	96086	96886	96486	96112	96912	96512
96010	96210	96410	96036	96236	96436	96062	96262	96462	96088	96888	96488	96114	96914	96514
96012	96212	96412	96038	96238	96438	96064	96264	96464	96090	96890	96490	96116	96916	96516
96014	96214	96414	96040	96240	96440	96066	96266	96466	96092	96892	96492	96118	96918	96518
96016	96216	96416	96042	96242	96442	96068	96268	96468	96094	96894	96494	96120	96320	96520
96018	96218	96418	96044	96244	96444	96070	96270	96470	96096	96896	96496	96122	96322	96522
96020	96220	96420	96046	96246	96446	96072	96272	96472	96098	96898	96498	96124	96324	96524
96022	96222	96422	96048	96248	96448	96074	96274	96474	96100	96900	96500	96126	96326	96526
96024	96224	96424	96050	96250	96450	96076	96276	96476	96102	96902	96502			
96026	96226	96426	96052	96252	96452	96078	96278	96478	96104	96904	96504			

1996 Tube Stock (Jubilee Line)
4-car 'D' end units

UNDM	T	T	DM	UNDM	T	T	DM	UNDM	T	T	DM	UNDM	T	T	DM
96401	96601	96201	96001	96433	96633	96233	96033	96465	96665	96265	96065	96497	96697	96297	96097
96403	96603	96203	96003	96435	96635	96235	96035	96467	96667	96267	96067	96499	96699	96299	96099
96405	96605	96205	96005	96437	96637	96237	96037	96469	96669	96269	96069	96501	96701	96301	96101
96407	96607	96207	96007	96439	96639	96239	96039	96471	96671	96271	96071	96503	96703	96303	96103
96409	96609	96209	96009	96441	96641	96241	96041	96473	96673	96273	96073	96505	96705	96305	96105
96411	96611	96211	96011	96443	96643	96243	96043	96475	96675	96275	96075	96507	96707	96307	96107
96413	96613	96213	96013	96445	96645	96245	96045	96477	96677	96277	96077	96509	96709	96309	96109
96415	96615	96215	96015	96447	96647	96247	96047	96479	96679	96279	96079	96511	96711	96311	96111
96417	96617	96217	96017	96449	96649	96249	96049	96481	96681	96281	96081	96513	96713	96313	96113
96419	96619	96219	96019	96451	96651	96251	96051	96483	96683	96283	96083	96515	96715	96315	96115
96421	96621	96221	96021	96453	96653	96253	96053	96485	96685	96285	96085	96517	96717	96317	96117
96423	96623	96223	96023	96455	96655	96255	96055	96487	96687	96287	96087	96519	96719	96319	96119
96425	96625	96225	96025	96457	96657	96257	96057	96489	96689	96289	96089	96521	96721	96321	96121
96427	96627	96227	96027	96459	96659	96259	96059	96491	96691	96291	96091	96523	96723	96323	96123
96429	96629	96229	96029	96461	96661	96261	96061	96493	96693	96293	96093	96525	96725	96325	96125
96431	96631	96231	96031	96463	96663	96263	96063	96495	96695	96295	96095				

The 1996 Tube Stock fleet is currently undergoing mid-life refurbishment at Stratford Market Depot, including new flooring, repainted / vinyl exteriors, new grab rails and the turquoise areas of the interiors replaced with white.

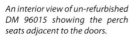

An interior view of un-refurbished DM 96015 showing the perch seats adjacent to the doors.

2009 TUBE STOCK

Year of manufacture: 2006-2011
Built by: Bombardier Transportation
Entry into service: 2009
Lines used on: Victoria
Number of cars per train: 8
Train formation: DM-T-NDM-UNDM+UNDM-NDM-T-DM

11018 brings up the rear of a departing southbound Victoria Line service at Euston, 20 August 2016 .

The 2009 Tube Stock was built to replace the 1967 Tube Stock which had operated on the Victoria Line since its opening in 1968. The first 2009 Tube Stock train appeared on the Underground in 2007, this being a pre-production train which underwent type testing on the line, followed in July 2009 by a second pre-production train. The 2009 Tube Stock is a very close relative of the Sub-Surface S Stock trains which was built alongside it at the Bombardier factory in Derby. By 2011, enough of the 2009 Tube Stock had entered traffic to allow the remaining 1967 Tube Stock trains to be withdrawn, and the last of this type ran on 30 June 2011.

The 2009 Tube Stock is 40mm wider than the 1967 Tube Stock it replaced. When the Victoria Line was built, the tunnel bores had a slightly larger diameter than those used on previous lines: the 2009 Tube Stock has been designed with this in mind, so with a thinner body shell and externally hung doors, there is much more room inside. It has allowed more room for standing passengers and also improved access for those with wheelchairs and pushchairs. Due to their larger overall size, the trains cannot leave the line by rail; it is connected to the rest of the Underground via the Piccadilly Line at Finsbury Park, but as they are too large to fit in the Piccadilly Line tube tunnels, if they need to leave the line, they have to do so by road haulage.

Internally, the trains are well equipped for carrying passengers with impaired mobility, with tip up seats creating space for wheelchairs and pushchairs and offset grab poles in the doorways which allow ample room for a wheelchair to pass through easily. Lighting at floor level by each door which illuminates when the doors are opened also aids passengers with a visual impairment.

The trains are operated automatically using the Invensys 'Distance to Go – Radio' (DTG-R) system of ATO/ATP. The Victoria Line has been an automatic railway ever since its inception, but the current system is more advanced than that used by the 1967 Tube Stock. As there was a period of changeover between the 1967 Tube Stock and the 2009 Tube Stock, the DTG-R had to work alongside the previous system until the old stock had been withdrawn.

An interior view of a 2009 Stock trailer car.

2009 Tube Stock (Victoria Line)

8-car units

DM (D)	T	NDM	UNDM	UNDM	NDM	T	DM(A)	DM (D)	T	NDM	UNDM	UNDM	NDM	T	DM(A)
11001	12001	13001	14001	14002	13002	12002	11002	11049	12049	13049	14049	14050	13050	12050	11050
11003	12003	13003	14003	14004	13004	12004	11004	11051	12051	13051	14051	14052	13052	12052	11052
11005	12005	13005	14005	14006	13006	12006	11006	11053	12053	13053	14053	14054	13054	12054	11054
11007	12007	13007	14007	14008	13008	12008	11008	11055	12055	13055	14055	14056	13056	12056	11056
11009	12009	13009	14009	14010	13010	12010	11010	11057	12057	13057	14057	14058	13058	12058	11058
11011	12011	13011	14011	14012	13012	12012	11012	11059	12059	13059	14059	14060	13060	12060	11060
11013	12013	13013	14013	14014	13014	12014	11014	11061	12061	13061	14061	14062	13062	12062	11062
11015	12015	13015	14015	14016	13016	12016	11016	11063	12063	13063	14063	14064	13064	12064	11064
11017	12017	13017	14017	14018	13018	12018	11018	11065	12065	13065	14065	14066	13066	12066	11066
11019	12019	13019	14019	14020	13020	12020	11020	11067	12067	13067	14067	14068	13068	12068	11068
11021	12021	13021	14021	14022	13022	12022	11022	11069	12069	13069	14069	14070	13070	12070	11070
11023	12023	13023	14023	14024	13024	12024	11024	11071	12071	13071	14071	14072	13072	12072	11072
11025	12025	13025	14025	14026	13026	12026	11026	11073	12073	13073	14073	14074	13074	12074	11074
11027	12027	13027	14027	14028	13028	12028	11028	11075	12075	13075	14075	14076	13076	12076	11076
11029	12029	13029	14029	14030	13030	12030	11030	11077	12077	13077	14077	14078	13078	12078	11078
11031	12031	13031	14031	14032	13032	12032	11032	11079	12079	13079	14079	14080	13080	12080	11080
11033	12033	13033	14033	14034	13034	12034	11034	11081	12081	13081	14081	14082	13082	12082	11082
11035	12035	13035	14035	14036	13036	12036	11036	11083	12083	13083	14083	14084	13084	12084	11084
11037	12037	13037	14037	14038	13038	12038	11038	11085	12085	13085	14085	14086	13086	12086	11086
11039	12039	13039	14039	14040	13040	12040	11040	11087	12087	13087	14087	14088	13088	12088	11088
11041	12041	13041	14041	14042	13042	12042	11042	11089	12089	13089	14089	14090	13090	12090	11090
11043	12043	13043	14043	14044	13044	12044	11044	11091	12091	13091	14091	14092	13092	12092	11092
11045	12045	13045	14045	14046	13046	12046	11046	11093	12093	13093	14093	14094	13094	12094	11094
11047	12047	13047	14047	14048	13048	12048	11048								

Sub-Surface Lines

AMERSHAM
CHESHAM
UXBRIDGE
HILLINGDON
ICKENHAM
CHALFONT & LATIMER
CHORLEYWOOD
RICKMANSWORTH

Connection to Ruislip Depot (used by stock moves and engineering trains)

WATFORD
CROXLEY
RUISLIP
RUISLIP MANOR
EASTCOTE
RAYNERS LANE
MOOR PARK
NORTHWOOD
NORTHWOOD HILLS
PINNER
NORTH HARROW

WEST HARROW

HARROW-ON-THE-HILL
NORTHWICK PARK
PRESTON ROAD
WEMBLEY PARK

Neasden Depot

FINCHLEY ROAD
BAKER STREET
GREAT PORTLAND STREET
EUSTON SQUARE
KING'S CROSS ST. PANCRAS
FARRINGDON
BARBICAN
MOORGATE
LIVERPOOL STREET
ALDGATE

METROPOLITAN LINE
Overview:
Route: Aldgate to Watford, Uxbridge, Chesham and Amersham

Night Tube: Not applicable

Route type: Sub-surface

First section opened: Baker Street Junction to Farringdon (opened as part of the Paddington Bishops Road to Farringdon Street line) opened by the Metropolitan Railway on 10 January 1863

Method of train operation: Manually driven

Signalling: Colour light signals protected by train stops

Direction of route: Northbound / Southbound between Baker Street and Amersham, Chesham and Watford plus Harrow to Rayners Lane sub gap) and Eastbound / Westbound between Aldgate and Baker Street Junction and between Rayners Lane sub gap and Uxbridge

Route length: 41.5 miles

Number of stations: 34

Trains: S Stock (8-car)

Max number of trains required: 49 (evening peak)

Depot: Neasden

Stabling points: Rickmansworth / Watford / Uxbridge

HISTORY
The Metropolitan Line today uses part of the world's first underground railway which was opened by the Metropolitan Railway between Paddington Bishop's Road and Farringdon Street on 10 January 1863. This was followed by an extension eastwards to Moorgate Street (now Moorgate), which was opened on 23 December 1865. The Metropolitan & St John's Wood Railway opened a single track line to Swiss Cottage on 13 April 1868 which diverged from the Metropolitan Railway's existing line at Baker Street, forming what we today know as Baker Street Junction.

A further extension eastwards to the Liverpool Street terminus of the Great Eastern Railway opened on 1 February 1875. It was a temporary arrangement, and the Metropolitan Railway opened the present day Liverpool Street sub-surface station (then called Bishopsgate) on 12

July of the same year. The current City terminus of the Metropolitan Line at Aldgate was then reached, opening on 18 November 1876. There was further extension beyond Aldgate, but that is best told as part of the history of the Circle Line, while this chapter concentrates on the sections of railway that make up today's Metropolitan Line.

Extension of the Metropolitan & St John's Wood Railway from Swiss Cottage to West Hampstead opened on 30 June 1879, followed by further extension to Willesden Green from 24 November 1879 and Harrow-on-the-Hill (then just called Harrow) from 2 August 1880. In 1882, ownership of the Metropolitan & St John's Wood Railway passed to the Metropolitan Railway and the single track tunnel section north of Baker Street was doubled to increase capacity. The Metropolitan Railway saw itself as a mainline railway and pushed itself further and further away from the capital. On 25 May 1885 an extension north of Harrow to Pinner opened, followed by Rickmansworth on 1 September 1887 and then to a terminus at Chesham which opened on 8 July 1889.

In 1891, the Metropolitan Railway absorbed the Aylesbury & Buckingham Railway and on 1 September 1892 a line between Chalfont Road (now Chalfont & Latimer) and Aylesbury South Junction was opened. This was followed in 1894 by a section from Aylesbury South Junction to Aylesbury North Junction which allowed MR trains to run through to Verney Junction, some 50 miles from London. In 1899, the Brill branch, which diverged from the MR's line at Quainton Road, was taken over by the MR.

On 4 July 1904, the Metropolitan Railway opened its line from Harrow-on-the-Hill to Uxbridge, initially with just one intermediate station at Ruislip. The branch to Watford was opened on 2 November 1925, diverging from the main line to the north of Moor Park (then called Moor Park & Sandy Lodge), followed on 10 December 1932 by the Stanmore branch. The Metropolitan Railway became part of London Transport in 1933. There then followed a period of contraction as the Brill branch closed in 1935 and Metropolitan trains ceased to run beyond Aylesbury to Verney Junction after July 1936.

The two track section between Finchley Road and Baker Street became very congested with trains serving the Metropolitan branches to and from Aylesbury (and beyond), Chesham, Watford, Uxbridge and Stanmore all converging upon it. To relieve the bottleneck, and as part of the '1935-1940 New Works Programme', a new tube tunnel was built parallel to the Baker Street to Finchley Road section, albeit at a deeper level. The new tube line surfaced at Finchley Road, which was remodelled to accommodate the new tracks and provide cross platform interchange between the two lines. The new tube tunnel line connected with the Bakerloo Line via a new junction at Baker Street, and this new line, together with the Stanmore branch were operated by the Bakerloo from 20 November 1939, at which point the Metropolitan ceased to serve Stanmore. The opening of the new section of tube tunnel also resulted in the closure of three stations on the Metropolitan between Baker Street and Finchley Road – Lords, Marlborough Road and Swiss Cottage - which were replaced by the new tube stations at St John's Wood and Swiss Cottage.

The Metropolitan Railway had been totally dependent on steam traction at its inception. Electrification was to follow, but for many years this only went as far as Rickmansworth, where steam traction took over to Chesham, Aylesbury and beyond. The line north of Rickmansworth was eventually electrified, but only as far as Amersham and Chesham and stations beyond Amersham were served only by British Railways after 9 September 1961. This left the Metropolitan Line as we find it today. There will be further changes in the future, as a new chord is being built to allow Watford trains to run to Watford Junction. This will see the closure of the current Watford Met station, which is likely to be reduced to a train stabling point. The latest estimate for completion of this line is 2020.

A southbound Metropolitan Line train formed of S8 set 21070-21069 is seen between Neasden and Dollis Hill. Metropolitan Line trains run non-stop along this stretch between Wembley Park and Finchley Road while Jubilee Line trains call at all stations. A Jubilee Line train of 1996 Tube Stock with 96045 on the rear can be seen heading north. The tracks here, left to right are, 'up and down' Chiltern lines in and out of Marylebone (Network Rail), northbound Metropolitan, southbound Jubilee and southbound Metropolitan. 11 September 2016.

THE ROUTE AND OPERATIONS

The line is worked by a fleet of 8-car S Stock trains constructed by Bombardier in Derby. Most are purpose built 8-car trains (known as type S8), but at the time of writing, there were also two which were formed of a 7-car set (known as type S7) into which an additional car has been inserted from another S7 set. This makes them up to 8-car trains, but they are known as type S7+1 to distinguish them from the S8 sets, as the S7+1 trains have a different internal layout and some slight technical differences. More details about the S Stock can be found on page 78.

The Metropolitan is signalled throughout with colour light signals protected by train stops, although work will be continuing throughout 2017 on installing a new signalling system that will eventually facilitate automatic operation. This is unlikely to become live during 2017 and trains will continue to be driven manually for the time being. A maximum of 49 trains are required for service during the evening peak.

The Metropolitan's main depot is at Neasden where all heavy maintenance is carried out. The majority of trains are stabled here outside of traffic hours, but there are also additional stabling points at Watford, Rickmansworth and Uxbridge.

At the London end of the route, trains usually terminate at either Baker Street or Aldgate. Those trains which run through to Aldgate supplement the Circle and Hammersmith & City Line services over the north side of the inner circle. From London, trains run to either, Watford, Chesham, Amersham or Uxbridge, with some shorter workings at the start and end of traffic which see trains terminating at Rickmansworth, Harrow-on-the-Hill and Wembley Park. The Metropolitan has always been known for its fast and semi-fast services; while there are fewer of these nowadays, some trains run fast or semi-fast southbound during the morning peak, and northbound in the evening peak. Northwards from Wembley Park, the Metropolitan's four tracks are northbound fast / northbound local / southbound local / southbound fast. The fast lines allow the stations at Preston Road and Northwick Park to be missed out. There are platforms on the fast lines at Wembley Park; some trains pass through while others call here. The Uxbridge branch diverges at Harrow-on-the-Hill, which is a major hub on the Metropolitan. There is also interchange here with Network Rail services operated by Chiltern Railways, which have been running alongside the Metropolitan since Finchley Road. North of Harrow-on-the-Hill, towards Watford, Amersham and Chesham, there are once again four tracks which are divided up as northbound main / southbound main / northbound local / southbound local. The Chiltern Railways services share the northbound and southbound main with the Metropolitan, and these two tracks miss out the stations at North Harrow, Pinner, Northwood Hills and Northwood which are only served by trains running on the local lines.

North of Moor Park at Watford South Junction, trains can either go straight on towards Rickmansworth, Chesham and Amersham, or bear right towards Watford. This is part of a triangular junction, the north curve of which is mainly used by empty stock workings, although a few passenger trains traverse it as follows:

0516 Chesham to Watford (Mon to Sat)

0049 Watford to Rickmansworth (Mon to Fri)*

0700 Rickmansworth to Watford (Sun)

0029 Watford to Rickmansworth (Sun)*

*These trains are at the end of traffic on the days denoted, for example the 0029 shown as Sunday is at the end of Sunday's traffic, although technically, it is Monday by the time the train runs.

Track and drainage work is currently taking place between Baker Street and Finchley Road on Monday, Tuesday and Wednesday nights, requiring the early closure of the Metropolitan Line between Aldgate and Wembley Park on these nights and a late start on Tuesday, Wednesday and Thursday mornings. This work and its associated closures are likely to continue until late 2018, although not on Bank Holidays or when there is a major event on at Wembley Stadium.

First trains:
0520 Baker Street to Uxbridge 0601 (Mon/Fri/Sat)
0553 Baker Street to Watford 0636 (Tue/Wed/Thu)
0512 Uxbridge to Aldgate 0609 (Mon-Sat)
0658 Baker Street to Uxbridge 0738 (Sun)
0636 Uxbridge to Aldgate 0735 (Sun)

Last Trains:
2232 Aldgate to Chesham 2345 (Mon-Wed)
2127 Uxbridge to Aldgate 2224 (Mon-Wed)
0043 Baker Street to Uxbridge 0122 (Thu-Sat)*
0003 Uxbridge to Baker Street 0043 (Thu-Sat)*
2359 Aldgate to Uxbridge 0059 (Sun)
2323 Chesham to Baker Street 0025 (Sun)

Note: *The above trains are the first and last to serve the central London stations at either Baker Street or Aldgate and the extremities of one of the Metropolitan's branches. There are other shorter workings before and after those listed above.*

*Where it states 'Thu-Sat' on the last trains section, trains just after midnight are part of the previous day's traffic, so the 0043 and 0003 departures are actually at the very beginning of Friday / Saturday / Sunday.

The 0814 Amersham to Aldgate is seen on the outskirts of Amersham shortly after starting its journey on 6 November 2016. The train is formed of one of the S7+1 sets, 21327-328.

HAMMERSMITH & CITY LINE

Overview:

HAMMERSMITH

GOLDHAWK ROAD

SHEPHERD'S BUSH MARKET

WOOD LANE

LATIMER ROAD

LADBROKE GROVE

WESTBOURNE PARK

ROYAL OAK

PADDINGTON

EDGWARE ROAD

BAKER STREET

GREAT PORTLAND STREET

EUSTON SQUARE

KING'S CROSS ST. PANCRAS

FARRINGDON

BARBICAN

MOORGATE

LIVERPOOL STREET

ALDGATE EAST

WHITECHAPEL

STEPNEY GREEN

MILE END

BOW ROAD

BROMLEY-BY-BOW

WEST HAM

PLAISTOW

UPTON PARK

EAST HAM

BARKING

Route: Hammersmith to Barking

Night Tube: Not applicable

Route type: Sub-surface

First section opened: Paddington Bishops Road to Farringdon Street opened by the Metropolitan Railway on 10 January 1863

Method of train operation: Manually driven

Signalling: Colour light signals protected by train stops

Direction of route: Eastbound / Westbound

Route length: 16 miles

Number of stations: 29

Trains: S Stock (7-car)

Max number of trains required: 33 (morning and evening peak - combined with Circle Line services)

Depots: Neasden / Ealing Common / Upminster (see notes in 'The Route and Operations')

Stabling points: Hammersmith / Barking / Upminster / Wembley Park / Aldgate / Edgware Road / Triangle Sidings

HISTORY

The Hammersmith & City Line operates over the Hammersmith branch, the top of the 'inner circle' and part of the District Line eastwards from Aldgate East to Barking and therefore shares its history with those lines. Part of this route includes the oldest underground railway in the world, which was opened by the Metropolitan Railway between Paddington Bishops Road and Farringdon Street on 10 January 1863.

The Hammersmith branch was a joint venture between the Metropolitan Railway and the Great Western Railway which opened on 13 June 1864. Operation of the line was initially in the hands of the GWR, but a year after opening, the Metropolitan took over services between Hammersmith and Addison Road (now Kensington Olympia), which was reached via a junction just west of Latimer Road station. The line between Latimer Road and Addison Road ceased operation in October 1940 after it suffered a direct hit during an air raid. Services never resumed but to this day traces of the junction can still be seen to the west of Latimer Road station.

In 1869, the London & South Western Railway opened a line from Addison Road to Richmond which came alongside the Hammersmith terminus and had its own station called Grove Road. A link was built between the H&C and the L&SWR's line to the north of Hammersmith station (known as Grove Road Junction), and some trains ran onto the

L&SWR from the H&C. This connection was taken out of service in 1916 along with the station at Hammersmith Grove Road. Traces of the former junction can still be seen to the north of Hammersmith station.

At the east end of what now forms the Hammersmith & City Line, the Metropolitan Railway had extended beyond Farringdon Street to Aldgate. In 1884, MR trains were extended via a curve to Aldgate East where they joined the tracks of the Metropolitan District Railway to St Mary's near Whitechapel. Here they turned off the MDR tracks, joined the East London Railway (now part of the London Overground network) and worked through to New Cross. From 1936, some Hammersmith trains were scheduled to run to Barking instead of the ELR; Hammersmith trains ceased running to and from the ELR in 1939.

On the Underground map, what we know today as the Hammersmith & City Line was a part of the Metropolitan Line. In 1989 it gained its own identity, becoming known as the Hammersmith & City Line; it has appeared on the Underground map in its own colour of salmon pink since 1990. The Hammersmith branch was served exclusively by Hammersmith & City Line trains until December 2009, at which point Circle Line services (running Hammersmith – Edgware Road – Victoria – Edgware Road and vice versa) also ran onto the Hammersmith branch to increase the frequency of service.

Aldgate East with S7 set 21545-546 waiting to depart and turn right towards Liverpool Street with a Hammersmith & City service for Edgware Road. The Hammersmith branch was closed for engineering works on this day, hence the train only going as far as Edgware Road. On the left is an Upminster bound District Line train of D Stock with 7030 on the rear. 20 August 2016.

THE ROUTE AND OPERATIONS

The Hammersmith & City Line is worked by 7-car trains of S Stock (designated as type S7) which operate across the Hammersmith & City, Circle and District lines with no dedicated fleet solely for the H&C. They are maintained by the depots which look after the S Stock fleet: Ealing Common and Upminster on the District Line and Neasden on the Metropolitan Line. Hammersmith depot is a stabling point for trains being used on the Circle and Hammersmith

& City lines outside traffic hours while others use Barking sidings at the east end of the route. Wembley Park sidings are only long enough for S7s and cannot accommodate the longer S8s which operate on the adjacent Metropolitan Line. In order to reach them, trains run empty from Baker Street to Harrow-on-the-Hill where they reverse, as northbound trains cannot cross the Jubilee Line, which lies between the northbound and southbound tracks of the Metropolitan between Finchley Road and Wembley Park. In the opposite direction, trains run empty directly to Baker Street. Close to the end of traffic, some run to Upminster Depot to stable, providing the unusual sight of trains leaving Hammersmith with Upminster as a destination as they carry passengers all the way to Upminster station. The reverse of this happens in the morning, when they leave Upminster Depot and enter passenger service at Upminster station with Hammersmith as their destination. Plaistow used to be a common reversing point for H&C trains, but today only sees a few reversing here towards the end of traffic (one Mon-Sat and three on Sun).

From Hammersmith to Westbourne Park, the line runs on top of brick viaducts giving passengers an interesting view down on to the colourful Shepherd's Bush Market and the former BBC Television studios (now being converted into luxury apartments) at Wood Lane. At Westbourne Park, the line comes alongside the Network Rail tracks of the Great Western Main Line just outside the Paddington terminus. The Underground tracks then dive down into Subway Tunnel, which takes them beneath the Network Rail tracks between Westbourne Park and Royal Oak, where they come alongside the western portal of the Elizabeth Line (Crossrail), which is still under construction. It then runs parallel to Paddington main line terminus, serving platforms 15 and 16. East of Paddington, H&C trains are joined by the Circle and District lines from High Street Kensington at Praed Street Junction and run around the top of the inner circle as far as Aldgate Junction where they branch to the left, then join the District Line at Aldgate East. From here, the tracks are shared between the Hammersmith & City and District lines all the way through to the end of the Hammersmith & City Line at Barking. The District continues beyond Barking to Upminster.

The maximum number of trains required for service is 33, which occurs in both the morning and evening peaks. This figure is slightly misleading however, as it also includes Circle Line trains since the two lines are jointly managed.

First trains:
0457 Hammersmith to Barking 0555 (Mon-Sat)
0707 Hammersmith to Barking 0806 (Sun)
0501 Barking to Hammersmith 0559 (Mon-Sat)
0626 Barking to Hammersmith 0725 (Sun)

Last Trains:
0014 Hammersmith to Barking 0111 (Mon-Sat)
2354 Hammersmith to Barking 0055 (Sun)
2345 Barking to Hammersmith 0044 (Mon-Sat)
2315 Barking to Hammersmith 0014 (Sun)

Note: The above trains are the first and last to serve the entire length of the line. There are other shorter workings before and after those listed above.

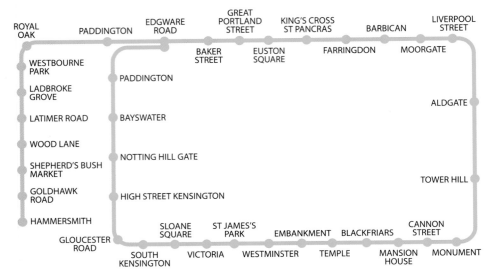

CIRCLE LINE

Overview:

Route: Hammersmith to Edgware Road, then via King's Cross St Pancras, Aldgate, Tower Hill, Victoria, High Street Kensington and Notting Hill Gate to Edgware Road

Night Tube: Not applicable

Route type: Sub-surface

First section opened: Paddington Bishops Road to Farringdon Street opened by the Metropolitan Railway on 10 January 1863

Method of train operation: Manually driven

Signalling: Colour light signals protected by train stops

Direction of route: Outer rail (clockwise) / Inner rail (counter-clockwise) and Eastbound / Westbound on the Hammersmith branch

Route length: 17 miles

Number of stations: 36

Trains: S Stock (7-car)

Max number of trains required (peak times): 33 (combined with Hammersmith & City Line services)

Depots: Neasden / Ealing Common / Upminster (see notes in 'The Route and Operations')

Stabling points: Hammersmith / Edgware Road / Barking / Moorgate / Triangle Sidings / Wembley Park / Upminster

HISTORY

The history of the Circle Line, like the Hammersmith & City and the Metropolitan, starts with the world's first underground railway, opened by the Metropolitan Railway between Paddington Bishops Road and Farringdon Street on 10 January 1863. As London's underground railways developed, a select committee recommended they should be linked together to form an 'inner circle' to link the termini of the mainline railway companies, as they had been prevented from building them too close to the centre of London. In 1868 the Metropolitan Railway built a line from Praed Street Junction (between Edgware Road and Paddington), passing through Bayswater and Notting Hill Gate to Brompton Gloucester Road (now just called Gloucester Road), which opened on 1 October 1868. It was extended to South Kensington where it met the Metropolitan District Railway's South Kensington to Westminster Bridge (now just called Westminster) line. The MR's short extension and the MDR's new line both opened on the same day, 24 December 1868. The MDR extended progressively eastwards, to Blackfriars (30 May 1870) and to Mansion House (3 July 1871). The MR and MDR now collectively formed a big 'C' around the capital. When the MR extended to Liverpool Street and then Aldgate (18 November 1876), the 'inner circle' was almost complete except for a gap between Aldgate and Mansion House.

The similarity in names between the Metropolitan Railway and the Metropolitan District Railway was no coincidence, as it had been the intention that the two companies would eventually merge. Instead they became bitter rivals with a reluctance to complete the 'inner circle'; it eventually took an Act of Parliament to force them to do so.

On 25 September 1882, the MR was extended to a station called Tower of London, which was on the site of the current Tower Hill station. On 6 October 1884 the MDR extended eastwards to Whitechapel, completing the 'inner circle'. The MR's Tower of London station was closed on 12 October 1884 and replaced by Mark Lane, just a short distance to the west. The clockwise service was operated by the MR, with a mix of MR and MDR trains running the anti-clockwise service.

Although the 'inner circle' was completed in 1884, the Circle Line did not appear as a separate colour on the Underground map until 1949. It operated as a complete circle until 13 December 2009 when the Hammersmith branch was incorporated to increase the frequency of trains on the Hammersmith branch.

21551 is at the rear of a High Street Kensington bound Circle Line train at Embankment, 29 October 2016. Engineering work north of High Street Kensington saw all trains terminate there on this day.

THE ROUTE AND OPERATIONS

The Circle Line is operated by the 7-car S Stock trains (S7) which run across the Circle, Hammersmith & City and District lines; there is no dedicated fleet specifically for the Circle Line. Therefore the H&C's trains are maintained with the rest of the S7 fleet at Ealing Common and Upminster on the District Line and Neasden on the Metropolitan Line. Circle Line train operation is managed jointly with the Hammersmith & City Line, with a maximum requirement of 33 trains across both lines, which occurs in both the morning and evening peaks.

For many years services on the Circle Line simply ran in circuits around London. On 13 December 2009, the Hammersmith branch was incorporated, increasing frequency between Edgware Road and Hammersmith, so it now resembles something more akin to a tea cup than a circle. Trains run from Hammersmith to Edgware Road, then around the outer rail of the 'inner circle' via Liverpool Street, Aldgate, Victoria and High Street Kensington, to terminate at Edgware Road (usually in platform 2). The same journey is made in reverse on the inner rail back to Edgware Road and then to Hammersmith.

At the start and end of each day, there are some variations in the workings in order to get trains to the various stabling points. Perhaps the most unusual of which is on a Saturday night when the 2251 from Hammersmith goes around the outer rail, and then instead of terminating at Edgware Road, carries on around the top of the 'inner circle' and becomes a service for Upminster, where it terminates and proceeds into Upminster Depot.

A Circle Line train spends most of its journey sharing tracks with other lines. The Hammersmith branch and the top of the 'inner circle' are shared with the Hammersmith & City Line and also with the Metropolitan Line from Baker Street Junction to Aldgate. Two stretches are shared with the District Line: the south side of the 'inner circle' from Minories Junction (between Aldgate and Tower Hill) to Gloucester Road and from High Street Kensington to Edgware Road. The Circle has exclusive use of the tracks at just two locations: the curve between Gloucester Road and High Street Kensington and also through Aldgate to Minories Junction. The Hammersmith & City turns away towards Aldgate East to the north of Aldgate station and although the Metropolitan Line serves Aldgate, it uses the middle platforms (2 and 3), while only the Circle uses the outer platforms (1 and 4) and the short section between Aldgate station and Minories Junction where the District joins.

First trains:
0446 Hammersmith to Edgware Road 0603 (Mon-Sat)
0621 Hammersmith to Edgware Road 0735 (Sun)
0528 Edgware Road to Hammersmith 0639 (Mon-Sat)
0707 Edgware Road to Hammersmith 0819 (Sun)

Last trains:
2331 Hammersmith to Edgware Road 0042 (Mon-Sat)
2311 Hammersmith to Edgware Road 0022 (Sun)
2350 Edgware Road to Hammersmith 0059 (Mon-Sat)
2330 Edgware Road to Hammersmith 0039 (Sun)

Note: *The above trains are the first and last to serve the entire Hammersmith branch and complete circuit of the 'inner circle'. There are other shorter workings before and after those listed above.*

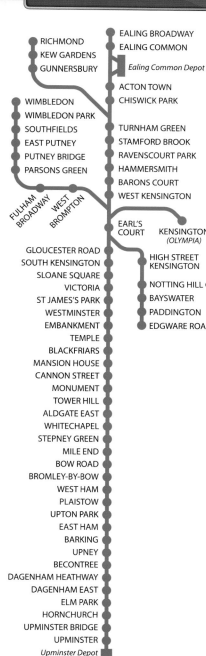

DISTRICT LINE

Overview:

Route: Upminster to Ealing Broadway with branches to Richmond, Wimbledon, Kensington (Olympia), High Street Kensington and Edgware Road

Night Tube: Not applicable

Route type: Sub-surface

First section opened: South Kensington to Westminster Bridge opened by the Metropolitan District Railway on 24 December 1868

Method of train operation: Manually driven

Signalling: Colour light signals protected by train stops

Direction of route: Eastbound / Westbound

Route length: 40 miles

Number of stations: 60

Trains: S Stock (7-car) / D Stock (6-car)

Max number of trains required: 76 (evening peak)

Depots: Upminster and Ealing Common

Stabling points: Lillie Bridge / Parsons Green / Barking / Triangle Sidings / Richmond / High Street Kensington

HISTORY

The Metropolitan District Railway opened a line from South Kensington to Westminster Bridge (now called Westminster) on 24 December 1868. A westward extension to West Brompton opened on 12 April 1869, then the east end of the line was extended, initially to Blackfriars (opened on 30 May 1870) and then to Mansion House (opened on 3 July 1871). On the same day, a short spur off the West Brompton line from Earl's Court round to High Street Kensington also opened. Another branch off the West Brompton line took the MDR to Addison Road (now Kensington Olympia), opening on 1 February 1872. A further extension through West Kensington to Hammersmith was opened on 9 September 1874.

On 1 June 1877, a short link was opened west of Hammersmith, which connected the MDR to the London & South Western Railway's Addison Road to Richmond line which had opened to mainline trains on 1 January 1869. The two lines came together at Studland Road Junction which is just a short distance to the west of Hammersmith station. This allowed MDR trains to run through to Richmond. It should be noted that the LSWR's line towards Addison Road, which also connected to the Hammersmith & City Railway, was closed on 3 June 1916 and the track removed in 1932; however, much of the brick viaduct which formed part of the junction is still in situ and can be seen from the train.

On 1 July 1879 the MDR opened a line to Ealing Broadway which branched off the L&SWR's line at Turnham Green. The West Brompton branch was extended as far as the River Thames, opening to Putney Bridge & Fulham (now just called Putney Bridge) on 1 March 1880. A spur to Hounslow Town opened on 1 May 1883, diverging from the Ealing Broadway branch at Acton Town (then called Mill Hill Park). However, after a line bypassing Hounslow Town opened to Hounslow Barracks on 21 July 1884, Hounslow Town became a terminus on a short branch, which closed on 31 March 1886.

When the MDR extended from Mansion House to Whitechapel on 6 October 1884, it connected with the Metropolitan Railway at Tower of London and the 'inner circle' was completed. From March 1883 to September 1885, the District Railway (as the MDR had become more commonly known by then), operated trains over Great Western Railway tracks beyond Ealing Broadway to Windsor.

The L&SWR opened a line from Wimbledon and built Fulham Rail Bridge over the River Thames which allowed them to join up with the District Railway's Putney Bridge & Fulham branch. The District had running powers over this line and the first District train ran through to Wimbledon on

A westbound District Line train formed of S Stock climbs away from Hammersmith towards Ravenscourt Park station (visible in the background) on 3 September 2016. The disused brick viaduct which once formed part of Studland Road Junction dominates the centre of the picture.

3 June 1889. The Underground kept its running powers until it took over the route from British Rail in 1994. The signalling west of East Putney is still controlled by Network Rail, while the track is maintained by London Underground. Mainline trains still operate on this route today, albeit only empty stock workings to and from Wimbledon Depot.

The District began operating to East Ham from 2 June 1902 following the construction of a link to the London, Tilbury & Southend Railway at Campbell Road Junction. Some trains also continued along the LT&SR to Upminster until 30 September 1905. At the west end of the District, a very short branch opened on 13 June 1905 from Mill Hill Park to South Acton. The Hounslow Town branch also re-opened, this time with a spur allowing trains to arrive into the terminus from the east and then depart to the west to Hounslow Barracks. Hounslow Town re-opened on 1 March 1903 but closed again on 1 May 1909. A line to South Harrow opened on 28 June 1903. The eventual aim was Uxbridge and a short extension was opened from South Harrow to Rayners Lane, where the District joined the tracks of the Metropolitan, over which it obtained running rights. District trains ran through to Uxbridge from 1 March 1910.

Widening of the track formation at the east end of the line saw District trains segregated from those of the LT&SR and the line was electrified through to Barking from July 1908. In 1932, the London Midland & Scottish Railway (successors to the LT&SR) added a new pair of electrified tracks between Barking and Upminster for exclusive use by District trains. This allowed the LMS to speed up their own services with the District trains segregated and making most of the station stops on this stretch of railway.

There was then a period of contraction for the District; first of all the Piccadilly Line took over Acton Town to South Harrow from 4 July 1932. District Line trains still operated a shuttle service between South Harrow and Uxbridge until that section was also taken over by the Piccadilly from 23 October 1933. In March 1933, the Piccadilly also took over most of the services to Hounslow West (the former Hounslow Barracks station, which had been renamed in 1925), although the District still operated some peak hour services until 1964. The branch from Acton Town to South Acton closed on 28 February 1959, leaving the District Line as we find it today.

THE ROUTE AND OPERATIONS

At the end of January 2017, the District still had eight operational trains of D Stock; these are being replaced by new 7-car S Stock trains (designated type S7) which now work the majority of services. The D Stock trains are expected to dwindle further and there may well be fewer than eight by the time this book appears in print. The latest estimates are May 2017 for the total removal of the type from District Line services, at which point the entire sub-surface railway will be operated by S Stock. The S7 fleet covers all services on the Hammersmith & City, Circle and District lines, so once the D Stock is withdrawn, the District will not have a train fleet dedicated only to its services.

The District Line has more stations than any other Underground line (60) and runs east to west across London. Upminster Depot is the most easterly point reached by the entire Underground, while Upminster station is the furthest east an Underground train in passenger service can reach. The section from Upminster to Barking is on segregated tracks built by the LMS in 1932 and runs parallel with the Network Rail line in and out of Fenchurch Street as far as Campbell Road Junction (just west of Bromley-by-Bow). West of Barking, the District shares tracks with Hammersmith & City Line services as far as Aldgate East where the H&C turns right towards Liverpool Street, and the District turns left and joins the Circle Line at Minories Junction. The District then share tracks with the Circle Line along the bottom section of the 'inner circle' through Mansion House, Westminster and Victoria to Gloucester Road, where the Circle Line turns towards High Street Kensington. The District continues to Earl's Court, which is considered to be the hub of the District Line, and from where there are branches to High Street

Kensington and Edgware Road, Wimbledon, Richmond and Ealing Broadway. Between West Kensington and Barons Court, the Piccadilly Line emerges from tube tunnel between the eastbound and westbound tracks of the District and parallels it all the way to Acton Town. Along this stretch, the District calls at all stations while the Piccadilly runs non-stop (some Piccadilly trains do call at Turnham Green at the start and end of traffic and during Night Tube). At Turnham Green, the Richmond branch diverges away from the Ealing Broadway route then

A Wimbledon to Tower Hill service formed of D Stock arrives at Temple led by 7057 on 22 October 2016.

joins Network Rail tracks at Gunnersbury Junction for the run to Richmond. Ealing Broadway bound trains share tracks with the Piccadilly's Uxbridge branch as far as Hangar Lane Junction where they branch off and drop down into the terminus at Ealing Broadway.

Services over the District Line are a mixture of full length workings plus some shorter journeys. Most travel over the whole route from Upminster to either Richmond or Ealing Broadway, while others run between Wimbledon and Edgware Road, Wimbledon and Tower Hill, Wimbledon and Barking and Kensington (Olympia) and High Street Kensington. This latter service usually only operates at weekends or Bank Holidays or when there is an exhibition taking place at Olympia. A few trains also operate between Wimbledon and Dagenham East during peak hours. The central platform at Mansion House, that was used for one train each morning, and for use at times of disruption, had its track removed along with the associated crossover, during the weekend of 8/9 October 2016, so Mansion House can no longer be used to reverse trains.

The maximum number of trains required for service is 76, which occurs during the evening peaks. An unusual pair of workings operates on a Sunday morning, with the 0537 and 0557 departures from Upminster both scheduled to reverse at Aldgate East via the crossover east of the station.

The D Stock is only maintained at the line's two main depots at Upminster and Ealing Common, but the S Stock which is replacing them is in a common user fleet, and so will also receive attention at Neasden when necessary. In addition to the main depots, trains engaged on District Line duties also stable at Richmond, Lillie Bridge, Parsons Green, Triangle Sidings, High Street Kensington and Barking.

A train of S Stock with 21487 at the rear passes beneath the tracks of the Piccadilly Line and the District's Ealing Broadway branch near Chiswick Park station with a train from Richmond. It will join the line that it is passing beneath on the approach to Turnham Green. The track on the right is the Richmond bound track which diverged from the Ealing Broadway line at Turnham Green.

First trains:
0453 Upminster to Richmond 0622 (Mon-Sat)
0609 Upminster to Richmond 0738 (Sun)
0451 Ealing Broadway to Upminster 0621 (Mon-Sat)
0617 Ealing Broadway to Upminster 0748 (Sun)

Last trains:
2341 Upminster to Ealing Broadway 0112 (Mon-Sat)
2307 Upminster to Ealing Broadway 0038 (Sun)
0003 Richmond to Upminster 0133 (Mon-Sat)
2329 Richmond to Upminster 0100 (Sun)

Note: *The above trains are the first and last to serve the entire length of the District Line. There are other shorter workings before and after those listed above.*

Surface Stock Trains

SURFACE STOCK TRAINS

The following information and abbreviations apply:

DM – Driving motor (powered vehicle with a driving cab at one end)

UNDM – Uncoupling non-driving motor (powered vehicle with no driving cab but fitted with controls at one end to allow uncoupling and shunting)

T – Trailer (vehicle with no motors and no cabs)

M1 – Non-driving motor car (powered vehicle with no driving cab)

M2 – Non-driving motor car (powered vehicle with no driving cab)

MS – Motor shoe (powered vehicle fitted with semi-permanent couplings allowing trains to be split for maintenance

Trains have an 'A' end and a 'D' end. The D Stock on the District Line always faces the same way with the 'A' end facing west and the 'D' end facing east. As the 7-car S Stock trains (S7) are members of a pool covering the Hammersmith & City, Circle and District lines, they can become turned depending on what routes they take and where they stable. The 8-car S Stock trains on the Metropolitan Line can also become turned if they work round the Watford North Curve.

On entering service, each train is allocated a three digit reporting number. Displayed on the front and rear of the train, it is used to identify its duty in the working timetable. The D Stock fleet is fitted with holders, into which plates are slotted to display the number, while the S Stock shows it on its digital destination display.

The S Stock 'M' cars are known as either 'M1' or 'M2', purely to denote their position within the train: M1 cars being next to the DMs and the M2 cars being next to the MS cars.

S STOCK

Year of manufacture: 2009 to 2016

Built by: Bombardier Transportation, Derby

Entry into service: 2010

Lines used on: Metropolitan, Circle, Hammersmith & City and District lines

Number of cars per train: 7 (S7) and 8 (S8 and S7+1)

Train formation: DM-M1-M2-MS-MS-M2-M1-DM (S8 and S7+1)

DM-M1-M2-MS-MS-M1-DM (S7)

The S Stock has been introduced across the entire sub-surface network, replacing the A Stock on the Metropolitan Line, the C Stock on the Hammersmith & City, Circle and District lines, and has now almost replaced the D Stock fleet on the District Line too. Once the last of the D Stock has been phased out, the entire sub-surface network will be operated by S Stock trains.

Built by Bombardier in Derby, the last S Stock trains to be constructed rolled off the production line during summer 2016. Although the entire fleet has been constructed, two trains (21467-468, and 21547-548) have yet to be delivered. At the start of 2017, both were based at the Asfordby Test Centre in Leicestershire, and were being used for tests associated with Automatic Train Operation (ATO). 21467-468 has been fitted with a very crude prototype version of the ATO equipment, whereas 21547-548 is the first of the fleet to receive the finished system. The entire fleet of S Stock trains will need to return to Derby over the course of the next two years to have the ATO equipment installed (and also receive other engineering modifications).

The S Stock is air conditioned, the first on the Underground to have this feature from new (although a car was converted as an experiment as long ago as 1935). The trains also have an open plan interior rather than individual cars separated by emergency doors as on all other Underground trains, so passengers can walk through the interior from one end to the other. This has a number of

An Uxbridge to Baker Street Metropolitan Line service led by 21071 heads south from Harrow-on-the-Hill, paralleled by 165035 which is working an Aylesbury Vale Parkway to London Marylebone Chiltern Railways service. 3 May 2016.

advantages: the area which would have been occupied by the car ends and the emergency inter-car doors is used as an additional standing area, thus increasing capacity. There is greater passenger security and people are able to walk through to the nearest available opening doors at stations with short platforms.

The S Stock trains are longer than those which they have replaced, and where possible, platforms have been lengthened to accommodate them. There are some places where this has not been possible, the west side of the Circle Line for example, where the retaining walls would have had to be moved in order to lengthen the platforms. Where platforms are shorter than the S Stock, they pull up with each end of the train beyond the ends of the platforms. The doors which are not lined up with the platforms do not open and passengers can walk through the train to the nearest available opening door. A 'Door not in use' sign illuminates shortly after leaving the previous station and localised announcements inside the train stating that 'doors will not open here' are repeated several times prior to the train arriving at the station with the short platforms.

The S Stock trains come in two distinct types: the 8-car S8 and the 7-car S7. The S7 sets operate from a common pool on the Circle, Hammersmith & City

A close up of 21547 whilst in transit from Bombardier in Derby to the Asfordby Test Centre. The grey pod above the windscreen is one of the antennas for the ATO (there is another located on the opposite side of the destination display). In due course, all S Stock trains will have this equipment.

An unusual picture of ATO test train 21467-21468 being hauled by class 08 diesel shunter 08892 from Asfordby Test Centre to Old Dalby for ATO tests on 3 October 2016.

and District lines. Their seating is all longitudinal, leaving a lot of room for standing passengers, as they mostly work on lines where many short journeys are made. The S8 sets are dedicated to the Metropolitan Line and differ internally from the S7s; their partially transverse seating reflects the nature of this outer suburban railway, where average journey lengths are longer so extra seating capacity is provided.

There is a third type, known as the S7+1. Three S7 sets were boosted to 8-car trains for use on the Metropolitan Line by having an extra car added which had been borrowed from another S7 set. Initially, this was done to cover for S8s which had to return to Derby for engineering modifications. It had been the intention that these sets would all revert to their standard S7 configuration, however the plan is now for one S7+1 to be used when the Croxley Link to Watford Junction is opened, with another to cover for S8 sets returning to Derby for the fitting of ATO equipment. The third train returned to Derby where it was reverted to a 7-car train which has since been returned to London Underground. An additional set was constructed to replace the S7+1 which will remain on the Metropolitan as the 'Croxley Link train', taking the order from 191 to 192. At the same time, two additional cars were built to replace those borrowed from S7 sets, so that the two S7 sets, each with a car missing, could be delivered as 7-car trains.

Interior view of a DM (21008) of an S8 set, showing the mix of longitudinal and transverse seating.

S Stock, 8-car (S8) Metropolitan Line

DM (D)	M	M	MS	MS	M	M	DM(A)	DM (D)	M	M	MS	MS	M	M	DM(A)
21001	22001	23001	24001	24002	25002	22002	21002	21059	22059	23059	24059	24060	23060	22060	21060
21003	22003	23003	24003	24004	25004	22004	21004	21061	22061	23061	24061	24062	23062	22062	21062
21005	22005	23005	24005	24006	25006	22006	21006	21063	22063	23063	24063	24064	23064	22064	21064
21007	22007	23007	24007	24008	25008	22008	21008	21065	22065	23065	24065	24066	23066	22066	21066
21009	22009	23009	24009	24010	25010	22010	21010	21067	22067	23067	24067	24068	23068	22068	21068
21011	22011	23011	24011	24012	25012	22012	21012	21069	22069	23069	24069	24070	23070	22070	21070
21013	22013	23013	24013	24014	25014	22014	21014	21071	22071	23071	24071	24072	23072	22072	21072
21015	22015	23015	24015	24016	25016	22016	21016	21073	22073	23073	24073	24074	23074	22074	21074
21017	22017	23017	24017	24018	25018	22018	21018	21075	22075	23075	24075	24076	23076	22076	21076
21019	22019	23019	24019	24020	25020	22020	21020	21077	22077	23077	24077	24078	23078	22078	21078
21021	22021	23021	24021	24022	25022	22022	21022	21079	22079	23079	24079	24080	23080	22080	21080
21023	22023	23023	24023	24024	25024	22024	21024	21081	22081	23081	24081	24082	23082	22082	21082
21025	22025	23025	24025	24026	25026	22026	21026	21083	22083	23083	24083	24084	23084	22084	21084
21027	22027	23027	24027	24028	25028	22028	21028	21085	22085	23085	24085	24086	23086	22086	21086
21029	22029	23029	24029	24030	25030	22030	21030	21087	22087	23087	24087	24088	23088	22088	21088
21031	22031	23031	24031	24032	25032	22032	21032	21089	22089	23089	24089	24090	23090	22090	21090
21033	22033	23033	24033	24034	25034	22034	21034	21091	22091	23091	24091	24092	23092	22092	21092
21035	22035	23035	24035	24036	25036	22036	21036	21093	22093	23093	24093	24094	23094	22094	21094
21037	22037	23037	24037	24038	25038	22038	21038	21095	22095	23095	24095	24096	23096	22096	21096
21039	22039	23039	24039	24040	25040	22040	21040	21097	22097	23097	24097	24098	23098	22098	21098
21041	22041	23041	24041	24042	25042	22042	21042	21099	22099	23099	24099	24100	23100	22100	21100
21043	22043	23043	24043	24044	25044	22044	21044	21101	22101	23101	24101	24102	23102	22102	21102
21045	22045	23045	24045	24046	25046	22046	21046	21103	22103	23103	24103	24104	23104	22104	21104
21047	22047	23047	24047	24048	25048	22048	21048	21105	22105	23105	24105	24106	23106	22106	21106
21049	22049	23049	24049	24050	25050	22050	21050	21107	22107	23107	24107	24108	23108	22108	21108
21051	22051	23051	24051	24052	25052	22052	21052	21109	22109	23109	24109	24110	23110	22110	21110
21053	22053	23053	24053	24054	25054	22054	21054	21111	22111	23111	24111	24112	23112	22112	21112
21055	22055	23055	24055	24056	25056	22056	21056	21113	22113	23113	24113	24114	23114	22114	21114
21057	22057	23057	24057	24058	25058	22058	21058	21115	22115	23115	24115	24116	23116	22116	21116

S Stock, 8-car (S7+1) Metropolitan Line)

DM (D)	M	M	MS	MS	M	M	DM(A)
21323	22323	25384	24323	24324	25324	22324	21324
21327	22327	25386	24327	24328	25328	22328	21328

S Stock, 7-car (S7) Circle, District and Hammersmith & City lines

DM(D)	M	MS	MS	M	M	DM(A)	DM(D)	M	MS	MS	M	M	DM(A)
21301	22301	24301	24302	25302	22302	21302	21333	22333	24333	24334	25334	22334	21334
21303	22303	24303	24304	25304	22304	21304	21335	22335	24335	24336	25336	22336	21336
21305	22305	24305	24306	25306	22306	21306	21337	22337	24337	24338	25338	22338	21338
21307	22307	24307	24308	25308	22308	21308	21339	22339	24339	24340	25340	22340	21340
21309	22309	24309	24310	25310	22310	21310	21341	22341	24341	24342	25342	22342	21342
21311	22311	24311	24312	25312	22312	21312	21343	22343	24343	24344	25344	22344	21344
21313	22313	24313	24314	25314	22314	21314	21345	22345	24345	24346	25346	22346	21346
21315	22315	24315	24316	25316	22316	21316	21347	22347	24347	24348	25348	22348	21348
21317	22317	24317	24318	25318	22318	21318	21349	22349	24349	24350	25350	22350	21350
21319	22319	24319	24320	25320	22320	21320	21351	22351	24351	24352	25352	22352	21352
21311	22311	24311	24312	25312	22312	21312	21353	22353	24353	24354	25354	22354	21354
21313	22313	24313	24314	25314	22314	21314	21355	22355	24355	24356	25356	22356	21356
21315	22315	24315	24316	25316	22316	21316	21357	22357	24357	24358	25358	22358	21358
21317	22317	24317	24318	25318	22318	21318	21359	22359	24359	24360	25360	22360	21360
21319	22319	24319	24320	25320	22320	21320	21361	22361	24361	24362	25362	22362	21362
21321	22321	24321	24322	25322	22322	21322	21363	22363	24363	24364	25364	22364	21364
21325	22325	24325	24326	25326	22326	21326	21365	22365	24365	24366	25366	22366	21366
21329	22329	24329	24330	25330	22330	21330	21367	22367	24367	24368	25368	22368	21368
21331	22331	24331	24332	25332	22332	21332	21369	22369	24369	24370	25370	22370	21370

S Stock

S Stock, 7-car (S7) Circle, District and Hammersmith & City lines

DM(D)	M	MS	MS	M	M	DM(A)	DM(D)	M	MS	MS	M	M	DM(A)
21371	22371	24371	24372	25372	22372	21372	21471	22471	24471	24472	23472	22472	21472
21373	22373	24373	24374	25374	22374	21374	21473	22473	24473	24474	23474	22474	21474
21375	22375	24375	24376	25376	22376	21376	21475	22475	24475	24476	23476	22476	21476
21377	22377	24377	24378	25378	22378	21378	21477	22477	24477	24478	23478	22478	21478
21379	22379	24379	24380	25380	22380	21380	21479	22479	24479	24480	23480	22480	21480
21381	22381	24381	24382	25382	22382	21382	21481	22481	24481	24482	23482	22482	21482
21383	22383	24383	24384	*23384**	22384	21384	21483	22483	24483	24484	23484	22484	21484
21385	22385	24385	24386	*23386**	22386	21386	21485	22485	24485	24486	23486	22486	21486
21387	22387	24387	24388	23388	22388	21388	21487	22487	24487	24488	23488	22488	21488
21389	22389	24389	24390	23390	22390	21390	21489	22489	24489	24490	23490	22490	21490
21391	22391	24391	24392	23392	22392	21392	21491	22491	24491	24492	23492	22492	21492
21393	22393	24393	24394	23394	22394	21394	21493	22493	24493	24494	23494	22494	21494
21395	22395	24395	24396	23396	22396	21396	21495	22495	24495	24496	23496	22496	21496
21397	22397	24397	24398	23398	22398	21398	21497	22497	24497	24498	23498	22498	21498
21399	22399	24399	24400	23400	22400	21400	21499	22499	24499	24500	23500	22500	21500
21401	22401	24401	24402	23402	22402	21402	21501	22501	24501	24502	23502	22502	21502
21403	22403	24403	24404	23404	22404	21404	21503	22503	24503	24504	23504	22504	21504
21405	22405	24405	24406	23406	22406	21406	21505	22505	24505	24506	23506	22506	21506
21407	22407	24407	24408	23408	22408	21408	21507	22507	24507	24508	23508	22508	21508
21409	22409	24409	24410	23410	22410	21410	21509	22509	24509	24510	23510	22510	21510
21411	22411	24411	24412	23412	22412	21412	21511	22511	24511	24512	23512	22512	21512
21413	22413	24413	24414	23414	22414	21414	21513	22513	24513	24514	23514	22514	21514
21415	22415	24415	24416	23416	22416	21416	21515	22515	24515	24516	23516	22516	21516
21417	22417	24417	24418	23418	22418	21418	21517	22517	24517	24518	23518	22518	21518
21419	22419	24419	24420	23420	22420	21420	21519	22519	24519	24520	23520	22520	21520
21421	22421	24421	24422	23422	22422	21422	21521	22521	24521	24522	23522	22522	21522
21423	22423	24423	24424	23424	22424	21424	21523	22523	24523	24524	23524	22524	21524
21425	22425	24425	24426	23426	22426	21426	21525	22525	24525	24526	23526	22526	21526
21427	22427	24427	24428	23428	22428	21428	21527	22527	24527	24528	23528	22528	21528
21429	22429	24429	24430	23430	22430	21430	21529	22529	24529	24530	23530	22530	21530
21431	22431	24431	24432	23432	22432	21432	21531	22531	24531	24532	23532	22532	21532
21433	22433	24433	24434	23434	22434	21434	21533	22533	24533	24534	23534	22534	21534
21435	22435	24435	24436	23436	22436	21436	21535	22535	24535	24536	23536	22536	21536
21437	22437	24437	24438	23438	22438	21438	21537	22537	24537	24538	23538	22538	21538
21439	22439	24439	24440	23440	22440	21440	21539	22539	24539	24540	23540	22540	21540
21441	22441	24441	24442	23442	22442	21442	21541	22541	24541	24542	23542	22542	21542
21443	22443	24443	24444	23444	22444	21444	21543	22543	24543	24544	23544	22544	21544
21445	22445	24445	24446	23446	22446	21446	21545	22545	24545	24546	23546	22546	21546
21447	22447	24447	24448	23448	22448	21448	*21547*	*22547*	*24547*	*24548*	*23548*	*22548*	*21548*
21449	22449	24449	24450	23450	22450	21450	21549	22549	24549	24550	23550	22550	21550
21451	22451	24451	24452	23452	22452	21452	21551	22551	24551	24552	23552	22552	21552
21453	22453	24453	24454	23454	22454	21454	21553	22553	24553	24554	23554	22554	21554
21455	22455	24455	24456	23456	22456	21456	21555	22555	24555	24556	23556	22556	21556
21457	22457	24457	24458	23458	22458	21458	21557	22557	24557	24558	23558	22558	21558
21459	22459	24459	24460	23460	22460	21460	21559	22559	24559	24560	23560	22560	21560
21461	22461	24461	24462	23462	22462	21462	21561	22561	24561	24562	23562	22562	21562
21463	22463	24463	24464	23464	22464	21464	21563	22563	24563	24564	23564	22564	21564
21465	22465	24465	24466	23466	22466	21466	21565	22565	24565	24566	23566	22566	21566
21467	*22467*	*24467*	*24468*	*23468*	*22468*	*21468*	21567	22567	24567	24568	23568	22568	21568
21469	22469	24469	24470	23470	22470	21470							

*Newly built M cars to replace those used to make the two S7+1 trains

The two trains in italics and highlighted had yet to be delivered to London Underground (Jan 2017)

D STOCK

Year of manufacture: 1978-1981
Built by: Metro-Cammell, Birmingham
Entry into service: 1980
Lines used on: District
Number of cars per train: 6
Train formation: DM-T-UNDM+UNDM-T-DM or DM-T-UNDM+DM-T-DM
or DM-T-DM+UNDM-T-DM or DM-T-DM+DM-T-DM

More commonly known as D Stock, these are also sometimes referred to as D78 Stock (1978 being the intended year of introduction). They have always been associated with the District Line and can work all of its routes except for the section north of High Street Kensington, where they are too long for the short platforms at Notting Hill Gate, Bayswater and Paddington. Services over this route were provided by the shorter C Stock trains until their withdrawal in 2014; 7-car S Stock trains are now used, which are also too long for these platforms, but their open plan interiors and selective door opening allow passengers to walk through to the nearest available opening door.

The D Stock runs as 6-car trains formed of two 3-car units coupled together. The fleet originally consisted of 150 units (75 trains), most of which were single ended with a DM at one end and a UNDM at the other. A small number of units were also built with a DM at both ends which offered greater operational flexibility. All units, whether single or double ended, are formed with a trailer car in the middle. 6-car trains can be formed of two single ended units (provided one is west facing and the other is east facing), two double ended units or a single ended unit with a double ended unit. The double ended units can be easily identified as the DMs have inter-car barrier fixings for use when that cab is formed in the middle of a train.

The D Stock fleet is being replaced by new 7-car S Stock on all District Line services. At the end of January 2017 the fleet was down to just eight trains; the latest estimate for total withdrawal was looking likely to be May 2017 although this does not spell the end for the D Stock. Four units have been sent to Acton to be converted into two 5-car Rail Adhesion Trains for use laying Sandite on the railhead to assist adhesion in the autumn leaf fall season. The first of these trains was released from Acton Works in autumn 2016 and spent several weeks making trial runs on the Metropolitan Line and the Rayners Lane to Acton Town section of the Piccadilly Line. It is also expected that a unit or two may be retained for Emergency Response Unit (ERU) training.

Most of the withdrawn D Stock is being sold to a company called Vivarail for further use (see page 95). Once withdrawn, the vehicles are either sent to Long Marston (for Vivarail) or to Booth's of Rotherham for scrap. Vivarail are not taking any of the UNDM cars, which are being scrapped as well as some of the trailers.

D Stock											
West Facing Units											
DM (A)	T	UNDM	DM (A)	T	UNDM	DM (A)	T	UNDM	DM (A)	T	UNDM
7012	17012	8012	7018	17018	8018	7032	17032	8032	7070	17070	8070
7016	17016	8016	7030	17030	8030	7046	17046	8046			

East Facing Units											
UNDM	T	DM (D)	UNDM	T	DM (D)	UNDM	T	DM (D)	UNDM	T	DM (D)
8007	17007	7007	8057	17057	7057	8095	17095	7095	8115	17115	7115
8037	17037	7037									

Double Ended Units											
DM	T	DM	DM	T	DM	DM	T	DM	DM	T	DM
7502	17502	7503	7526	17526	7527	7532	17532	7533	7534	17534	7535

This picture of the western approach to Acton Town station has three trains of D Stock visible. On the left, 7525 brings up the rear of an Ealing Broadway bound train which is climbing up to cross over the top of the Piccadilly's Heathrow branch. In the centre, in the far distance there is an unidentified D Stock stabled on Ealing Common Depot, while on the right and the main subject of the picture, 7121 approaches with the 1328 Ealing Broadway to Upminster service. A Piccadilly Line train of 1973 Tube Stock can also be seen approaching on the Heathrow branch in the distance. 4 April 2016.

Engineering Trains, Heritage Operations & Redundant Stock

ENGINEERING TRAINS

As one of the most intensively used railways in the world, there are very limited hours during which engineers and other staff can gain access for cleaning, routine maintenance, inspections, changing adverts, station refurbishments, rail replacement and many other tasks. With the exception of the lines which form the Night Tube network on Friday / Saturday and Saturday / Sunday nights, the London Underground shuts down each night for a period of about 4-5 hours, during which this work is done. Some tasks can be performed by a team arriving in a van at a location. Other tasks may require the use of special trains or for large / heavy equipment and materials to be delivered by train. London Underground has a fleet of engineering vehicles for this purpose, which most of the travelling public will rarely see. Some have been purpose built for their work, while others were converted from redundant stock to perform a specific task.

In addition to the overnight maintenance, some larger engineering jobs, including track replacement, re-signalling and drainage, are undertaken over longer periods (usually weekends), when sections of line are closed. While inconvenient for the traveller, these shut downs are aimed at improving the Underground network and represent a welcome investment in the infrastructure.

Battery locomotive L22 passes through Turnham Green at the start of traffic on 14 December 2016 as it heads back to Ruislip Depot with a train of empty rail carriers.

Battery Locomotives

Forming the backbone of the engineering fleet are 29 battery locomotives which are used in the main to haul engineering trains around the system. They are in fact battery-electric locomotives as they can draw power from the conductor rails or from their 320V onboard batteries. The usual method of operation is to travel to the worksite on electric power, then the power is switched off and the loco performs any movements using battery power. They all have an almost identical design, but were constructed in three batches by two different manufacturers. The oldest are L20-L32, built by Metro-Cammell in Birmingham in 1964/65. The next batch was L15-L19, built by Metro-Cammell in 1969/1970, with the third batch being L44-L54 which were built by BREL Doncaster in 1973/74. All are to tube gauge and have tripcocks for use on lines with colour light signalling protected by train stops. Several are also fitted with the Central Line ATP system and / or

BREL Doncaster built L52 is seen at Wimbledon waiting to be called into an engineering possession at East Putney. This loco is one of four that have no buffers at their 'A' end.

the TBTC system used on the Jubilee and Northern lines. None have yet received the DTG-R system so any engineering train accessing the Victoria Line has to do so once there are no other trains moving on the line.

Like most other Underground trains, the battery locos have an 'A' end and a 'D' end. Four of the BREL locomotives (L50-L53) have had their buffers and screw / buckeye couplings removed from their 'A' end to facilitate their use on long welded rail trains where they would couple to the train using the Ward coupler on their 'A' end. This long welded rail train is no longer in use, but the locos can still be used to haul any type of engineering train provided that the 'D' end is coupled to the train.

BREL Doncaster built L52 is seen at Wimbledon waiting to be called into an engineering possession at East Putney. This loco is one of four which have no buffers at their 'A' end.

Engineering trains are usually top and tailed (i.e.: a loco on each end of the train). This makes reversing en route quick and easy and also assists at the worksite itself as the train may need to be split to access equipment or materials being carried.

Internal views of battery loco L18 showing the inside of the battery and equipment compartment and the 'A' end cab.

The battery loco fleet is currently undergoing life extension modifications, which involves fitting new batteries, revised cabs with the side doors plated over and crew access moved to the door in the centre of the cab front. For safety reasons, railings are then fitted to the ends of the loco to make entering and exiting the cab through the centre door safe and easy. New, more powerful headlights and working lights have also been fitted to the ends of the locos. They are all also being upgraded to work on 750V dc as well as 630V dc, as several lines are to have their power upgraded. Battery locomotives recharge from the traction current, but only while stationary.

Schöma Locomotives

IIn 2000, Transplant inherited a fleet of 14 diesel locomotives which had hauled construction trains during the building of the Jubilee Line Extension. Produced by Schöma in 1995, their 500hp diesel engines were fitted with exhaust scrubbers to help keep emissions down and allow their use in sub-surface tunnels (but not tube tunnels). At the end of 2014 locos 2 and 5 were sent to Clayton Equipment in Burton-on-Trent for conversion into battery locomotives. Others followed, leaving only four of the type still powered by diesel (1, 3, 9 and 12). Those converted to battery power have yet to be used in anger and stand out of use at Ruislip Depot and Highgate Sidings. The intention was that the Schöma battery locos would operate in pairs alongside the existing battery loco fleet as unlike the older vehicles, the Schöma locos can recharge their batteries while moving on electric power.

The diesel powered Schöma locos still see occasional use. Here loco number 3 is standing on the east end of Fulham Rail Bridge with an engineering train during a possession to remodel the track through Putney Bridge on 29 May 2016.

Asset Inspection Train

Formed of a mix of 1967 Tube Stock and 1972 MkI Tube Stock vehicles, the AIT is intended for use monitoring track and other trackside equipment. The project to get this train into service is currently on hold for technical reasons and it is not known if or when it will enter service.

Track Recording Train

This train consists of two former 1960 Tube Stock driving motors and a former 1973 Tube Stock trailer car. It is used to monitor the condition of the track using recording equipment housed in the trailer. The train is tripcock-fitted for use on conventionally signalled lines and also has the Central Line's ATP system. It does not have TBTC or DTG-R so any use on the Victoria, Jubilee and Northern lines has to be done under controlled conditions (a possession), usually outside of traffic hours.

The Track Recording Car has buckeye couplers at a height which makes them compatible with trains on Network Rail, thus allowing the trailer car to be hauled over Network Rail if needed. The cab ends of the 1960 Tube Stock DMs have standard tube height drawgear, with Network Rail-height buckeye couplers at the non-driving end (to match the centre car). There has been much talk of this train being replaced by the AIT, but as this project is now on hold, the Track Recording Train (TRT) appears to be safe, at least for the immediate future.

The Track Recording Train is seen heading north from Queen's Park while recording on the Bakerloo Line. L132 is nearest the camera. A southbound Bakerloo Line train of 1972 Stock can also be seen entering the station. 25 November 2015.

Rail Adhesion Trains

The autumn leaf fall season causes problems at both ends of the Central Line and the north end of the Metropolitan Line. Wet leaves which are crushed by the weight of a train become a dangerous slimy substance which can cause trains to slip when accelerating and skid when braking. To combat this, the Underground has some Rail Adhesion Trains (RATs) which apply a sticky paste known as Sandite to the railhead to improve adhesion. These only operate during the autumn, usually from the start of October through until December. The two Central Line trains are formed of 1962 Tube Stock cars (and one 1959 Tube Stock car). A 5-car train works at the west end of the Central between West Ruislip, White City and Ealing Broadway, with an 8-car train running at the east end of the Central between Newbury Park, Hainault, Woodford, Leytonstone and Epping. On the Metropolitan Line, during the 2016 season, a 4-car train of A Stock, into which Rail Adhesion Car 6036 was inserted, operated between Neasden Depot, Uxbridge, Watford, Chesham and Amersham. Following reports of poor adhesion on the Piccadilly Line south of Rayners Lane, the A Stock RAT also made frequent visits to this line during autumn 2016.

For 2017, the A Stock RAT is expected to be replaced by a new Rail Adhesion Train formed of redundant D Stock, which was on trial during autumn 2016 and should replace the A Stock from the start of the 2017 autumn season. The A Stock is expected to be kept in reserve at Neasden during the 2017 autumn season.

Interior view of the Sandite car (2440) of the 1962 Tube Stock Central Line west end 'RAT'. The Central Line route maps, still in place from its passenger service days will be noted.

Track Maintenance Machines

Transplant have three tube gauge track maintenance machines (TMM771-TMM773) built in 1980 by Plasser & Theurer and one full size points and crossings machine (TMM774) built by Franz Plasser in 2007. Two new machines numbered TMM775 and TMM776, both to full loading gauge, were delivered from Matisa at the start of 2016.

TMM771 parked at Willesden Green during an engineering possession on the Metropolitan Line, 12 March 2016.

Rail Grinders and Rail Millers

Used for correcting the profile of the railhead, these machines are owned by contractors such as Schweerbau and Speno and are not part of the Transplant fleet. A recent visitor to the Underground has been a Schweerbau RGS rail grinder which is powered by two Schöma-built diesel locomotives (see below), not too dissimilar to those provided for the JLE construction. As these trains are hired in when required, and not part of the LU fleet, they do not appear in the stock lists in this book. However, for details of the Schweerbau trains, their website is worth a visit. **http://www.schweerbau.de/en/**

The Schweerbau RGS rail grinder is seen parked at Moorgate on 10 January 2017.

Non-powered Vehicles

A large and varied fleet of wagons is available for forming into engineering trains to perform an array of tasks. These include ballast hoppers, general purpose wagons, rail carriers, spoil and ballast wagons, flat wagons, drum wagons, well wagons and cranes. Some vehicles have been adapted for specific jobs while others are for general use (see stock lists on page 93).

General Purpose wagon GP940 is seen at Baker Street carrying spoil from an engineering possession. The train is being hauled by battery loco L16 and is waiting for a clear road to proceed on to the Circle Line at Baker Street Junction. 20 February 2016.

ENGINEERING TRAIN WORKINGS

As the London Underground is dominated by multiple unit trains, the sight of a locomotive hauling a train of wagons turns a few heads as they pass through stations. They are also of particular interest to railway enthusiasts who would like to see them and take video or photographs. They are however, a little elusive, but this guide book offers the following tips for tracking them down. For the first time since the London Underground Guide was first published in 2014, there is a working which runs regularly to the same pattern that is easy to see.

The engineering fleet is based at Ruislip Depot, from where trains are despatched to worksites. Located at the west end of the Central Line, trains to any worksite on the Central Line can depart from the south end of the depot close to Ruislip Gardens and reach anywhere on the Central Line from there. At the west side of the depot, a connecting spur runs down to Ruislip Siding (see picture on page 49), which is adjacent to the Metropolitan and Piccadilly line's Uxbridge branch. From there, trains can depart onto the Uxbridge branch towards Rayners Lane, where they can turn left towards Harrow-on-the-Hill or right towards Acton Town. For overnight engineering jobs, trains usually leave Ruislip Depot towards the end of traffic on Monday through to Thursday nights, usually from about 2300 onwards. By visiting the stations between Ruislip Siding and Rayners Lane (Ruislip / Ruislip Manor / Eastcote and Rayners Lane), there is a good chance you will see an engineering train. They return at the start of traffic the following day; how late they return will depend on where they have come from, but they can be seen passing between Rayners Lane and Ruislip Siding any time between the start of traffic and about 7am. Engineering trains need to arrive at their worksite almost immediately behind the last passenger service and depart just before the first passenger service the following day in order to have maximum time on site. As a general rule, the further away from Ruislip the worksite is, the earlier the outward train will depart and the later it will return. A word of warning though; while on some nights five or more trains depart from Ruislip, on others there can be very few or none at all. Sometimes on a Friday night a procession of trains will depart to support a weekend long possession. Check the TfL website for weekend closure notices for clues as to when and where these may run. Trains returning from weekend engineering possessions often do so during daylight, but these are far less predictable than the inbound workings as they essentially leave when they are ready to do so.

Rayners Lane Junction (at the east end of the station) is key to the routing of engineering trains. From here, turning right towards Acton Town gives access to the entire Sub-Surface network and the whole Piccadilly Line, from which trains can also reach the Northern and Victoria lines. Northern Line bound trains run to King's Cross St Pancras on the Piccadilly Line, where they reverse and turn off onto the King's Cross loop. This line joins the Northern Line's Bank branch between King's Cross St Pancras and Euston; trains can proceed northbound through Euston towards Camden Town, or they can pass through the Euston loop and enter the southbound platform to reverse and head south. Victoria Line-bound engineering trains travel along the Piccadilly Line to Finsbury Park where they cross over onto the Victoria Line.

Turning left at Rayners Lane Junction provides access to the entire Sub-Surface network and also the Jubilee Line via the junction adjacent to the south end of Neasden Depot. To reach the Bakerloo Line, trains have to first reach the Jubilee Line and run to Baker Street where they can cross over.

As already mentioned in the Metropolitan Line section of this book, during 2017 and through to late 2018, the tunnels between Finchley Road and Baker Street are undergoing track replacement and drainage works, so this section will close early to passenger trains on Monday, Tuesday and Wednesday nights during this period. A special engineering train conveying a railvac and a cement mixer is used for this work; it leaves Ruislip Depot at about 2130 on Monday, Tuesday and Wednesday nights, passing through Ruislip, Rayners Lane, Harrow-on-the-Hill and Wembley Park to reach Finchley Road. Although the Metropolitan Line is closed south of Wembley Park at this time, the Jubilee Line is still open, making this train very easy to see. This was the approximate time for this train when this book went to press; it is not guaranteed to work as stated above, as operational circumstances may dictate otherwise, but it is quite likely. It may not run when there is an event on at Wembley Stadium, or on Bank Holidays.

Battery Locomotives

L15 (Metro-Cammell 1970)	L30 (Metro-Cammell 1965)*
L16 (Metro-Cammell 1970)**	L31 (Metro-Cammell 1965)*
L17 (Metro-Cammell 1970)*	L32 (Metro-Cammell 1965)*
L18 (Metro-Cammell 1970)*	L44 (BREL Doncaster 1974)*
L19 (Metro-Cammell 1970)*	L45 (BREL Doncaster 1974)**
L20 (Metro-Cammell 1964)	L46 (BREL Doncaster 1974)*
L21 (Metro-Cammell 1964)	L47 (BREL Doncaster 1974)*
L22 (Metro-Cammell 1965)*	L48 (BREL Doncaster 1974)
L23 (Metro-Cammell 1965)*	L49 (BREL Doncaster 1974)*
L24 (Metro-Cammell 1965)*	L50 (BREL Doncaster 1974)*
L25 (Metro-Cammell 1965)*	L51 (BREL Doncaster 1974)*
L26 (Metro-Cammell 1965)*	L52 (BREL Doncaster 1974)
L27 (Metro-Cammell 1965)*	L53 (BREL Doncaster 1974)*
L28 (Metro-Cammell 1965)*	L54 (BREL Doncaster 1974)
L29 (Metro-Cammell 1965)*	

*Refurbished with modified cab ends

** Undergoing refurbishment

General Purpose Wagons (ex JLE)

JLE1	JLE3	JLE5	JLE7	JLE9	JLE11	JLE13
JLE2	JLE4	JLE6	JLE8	JLE10	JLE12	JLE14
						JLE15

Bogie Well Wagon (ex JLE)

JLE16	JLE17	JLE18
		JLE19

Cable Drum Wagon (ex JLE)

JLE20	JLE21	JLE22
		JLE23

Spoil and Ballast Wagons (ex BR Turbot)

SB231	SB240	SB249	SB258	SB267	SB276	SB285
SB232	SB241	SB250	SB259	SB268	SB277	SB286
SB233	SB242	SB251	SB260	SB269	SB278	SB287
SB234	SB243	SB252	SB261	SB270	SB279	SB288
SB235	SB244	SB253	SB262	SB271	SB280	SB289
SB236	SB245	SB254	SB263	SB272	SB281	SB290
SB237	SB246	SB255	SB264	SB273	SB282	
SB238	SB247	SB256	SB265	SB274	SB283	
SB239	SB248	SB257	SB266	SB275	SB284	

Rail Wagons

RW495	RW505	RW506

Diesel Hydraulic Crane

C623	C625	C626
C624		

Diesel Hydraulic Crane (Twin Jib)

TRM627	TRM628

Cement Mixer (mounted on a former FEA wagon)

CM932

Deep Well Cable Drum Wagon

CW1053	CW1054	CW1055

Cement Mixer Wagons

CM950	CM952	CM954
CM951	CM953	CM955

A60/A62 Stock

DM(A)	T	T	DM(D)	Notes
5110	6110	6111	5111	
5112	6112	6113	5113	Acton Works (spare)
5234	6234	6235	5235	
	6036			Rail Adhesion Car
	6132			Acton Works (stored)

Schöma Diesel Locomotives

1 (Britta Lotta)	9 (Debora)	12 (Melanie)
3 (Claire)		

Schöma Battery Electric Locomotives

2 (Nikki)	7 (Annemarie)	11 (Joan)
4 (Pam)	8 (Emma)	13 (Michele)
5 (Sophie)	10 (Clementine)	14 (Carol)
6 (Denise)		

Track Maintenance Machines

TMM771	Plasser Theurer 1980	
TMM772	Plasser Theurer 1980	
TMM773	Plasser Theurer 1980	Named 'Alan Jenkins'
TMM774	Franz Plasser 2007	
TMM775	Matisa 2016	
TMM776	Matisa 2016	

Hopper Wagons

HW201	HW204	HW207	HW210	HW213	HW216	HW219
HW202	HW205	HW208	HW211	HW214	HW217	HW220
HW203	HW206	HW209	HW212	HW215	HW218	HW221
						HW222

Rail Wagons

RW801	RW805	RW809	RW813	RW817	RW821	RW825
RW802	RW806	RW810	RW814	RW818	RW822	RW826
RW803	RW807	RW811	RW815	RW819	RW823	
RW804	RW808	RW812	RW816	RW820	RW824	

High Deck Wagons

HD871	HD872	HD873	HD874	HD875	HD876

General Purpose Wagons

GP901	GP909	GP917	GP925	GP933	GP941
GP902	GP910	GP918	GP926	GP934	
GP903	GP911	GP919	GP927	GP935	
GP904	GP912	GP920	GP928	GP936	
GP905	GP913	GP921	GP929	GP937	
GP906	GP914	GP922	GP930	GP938	
GP907	GP915	GP923	GP931	GP939	
GP908	GP916	GP924	GP932	GP940	

Match Wagons

MW956	MW957	MW958	MW959	MW960	MW961

D Stock Rail Adhesion Trains

DM	UNDM	T	UNDM	DM
7010	8123	17010	8010	7123
7040	8107	17040	8040	7107

1962 Stock (*1959 Stock)										
DM(A)	T	NDM	DM(D)	DM(A)	T	NDM	T	NDM	DM(D)	Notes
1406	2682	9125*	1681	1682		9577	2406		1407	8-car Sandite 1
1570		9691			2440			9441	1441	5-car Sandite 2
1690			1691					9459		Acton Works (Spare)

Track Recording Train	
L132	Ex 1960 Stock DM 3901
TRC666	Ex 1973 Stock trailer 514
L133	Ex 1960 Stock DM 3905

1972 MkI Stock / 1967 Stock* Asset Inspection Train					
DM(A)	T	DM(D)	DM(A)	T	DM(D)
3213	4213	3179*	3079*	4313	3313

1967 Stock				
DM(A)	T	T	DM(D)	Notes
3060	4060	4160	3160	Acton Works
3061	4061	4161	3161	Acton Works
3067	4067	4167	3167	London Road (ambience training vehicles)
3075	4075	4175	3175	Acton Works
3022			3122	Acton Works
3007			3107	Acton Works

1972 MkI/MkII Stock					
DM(A)	T	T	DM(D)	UNDM	Notes
3202	4202	4302	3302		Acton Works (used for shunting)
	4511			3411	Hainault depot (stored)
3229	4229	4329	3329		Aldwych

1973 Stock		
T	DM(D)	Notes
566	366	Northfields

HERITAGE OPERATIONS

Although the London Underground's main reason for existence is to move millions of people, it has always recognised its history. This is very apparent in many of the stations, quite a few of which have been sympathetically restored; some are even listed buildings. The London Transport Museum in Covent Garden is well worth a visit and includes diverse items relating to the Underground, and other transport modes such as buses and trams. Not everything that the LTM owns can be accommodated at Covent Garden and they also have a large storage depot at Acton which stages occasional open days (usually 2-3 per year). The museum depot can also be visited by appointment – see their website for details (www.ltmuseum.co.uk).

In conjunction with Transport for London, the London Transport Museum occasionally operates special heritage trains on parts of the Underground network. At the time of writing, there were plans for some heritage steam trips during 2017. Details of any forthcoming heritage train trips are usually advertised on the London Transport Museum website.

Stock which may be used on heritage train trips are as follows:

1938 Tube Stock – 10012-012256-12048-11012 (currently under repair at Acton Works)
Metropolitan Vickers Electric locomotive number 12 'Sarah Siddons'
Ex-BR 4TC set – 70823, 71163, 76297 and 76324
Ex-GWR 'Prairie' tank L150 (GWR 5521 – hired in as required)
Metropolitan Railway 'E' class No.1 (hired in as required)
Metropolitan Ashbury's coaches 368, 387, 394 and 412 (hired in)
Metropolitan Railway milk van No.4

Metropolitan Railway 'Jubilee' coach 353

THE VIVARAIL D-TRAIN

While this guide book is all about the London Underground, in order to tell the complete story of the withdrawal of the D Stock, it is necessary to include a page about the Vivarail D-Train.

Vivarail have developed an idea to create new trains for potential use on Network Rail, using recycled bodies, bogies and motors from withdrawn D Stock, fitted with diesel engine modules, generator sets, new electronics and new traction equipment. The idea behind the engine modules is that they can be removed and replaced easily at the trackside, reducing the need for trains to return to a depot (which could be some distance from where it is working). A range of interiors has been designed to suit the requirements of every route they may serve. The diesel engines are controlled by 'Start / Stop' technology which shuts them down when the train is stationary, thus saving fuel and reducing emissions.

Due to the pending withdrawal from service of the 4-wheeled 'Pacer' trains, there will be a shortage of diesel multiple units and Vivarail believes that their D-Train offers a cost effective solution to this problem.

The first train underwent a series of runs on the test track at Long Marston during 2016 then was moved to Tyseley for trials on Network Rail towards the end of the year. The first run took place on the evening of 28 November 2016, consisting of two return trips to Leamington Spa with it formed as a 2-car set. After several weeks of similar trial runs, during which time a trailer car was added, the train was moved to Nuneaton for crew training with a view to it being introduced into passenger service on the London Midland operated Coventry to Nuneaton line. A technical issue prevented

any crew training trips from taking place and the train returned to Tyseley for the Christmas break. During a journey back to Nuneaton on 30 December 2016, a diesel engine module caught fire at Kenilworth on the Leamington Spa to Coventry line. While this was a serious incident, causing a temporary closure of the line, damage to the train was mostly confined to the module itself. The plan to introduce this train to the Coventry to Nuneaton line has now been dropped, mainly due to the delay caused by the fire conflicting with the LM franchise expiring in October 2017.

Running as a 2-car set, 230001, led by DM(A) 300001, pauses at Dorridge while working a 5Z30 2209 Leamington Spa to Tyseley test run on 28 November 2016. Your author can confirm that beneath the sound of the diesel engines, this train still sounds like D Stock!

The current prototype D-Train is formed as follows:
Network Rail unit number 230001
DM(A) 300001 (ex 7058)
Trailer 300201 (ex 17128)
DM(B) 300101 (ex 7511)

230001 passes through platform 1 at Dorridge as it accelerates away from a booked pathing stop in Dorridge Up Passenger Loop while working a 5Z26 2111 Tyseley Up & Down Through Sidings to Leamington Spa test run on 29 November 2016. DM(B) 300101 (ex 7511) is leading.

A-Z OF STATIONS

Acton Town ● District ● Piccadilly (zone 3)
Opened 1 July 1879 as Mill Hill Park.
Renamed Acton Town 1 March 1910.

Acton Town is a busy four platform station served by both the District and Piccadilly lines. It was served initially by the Metropolitan District Railway's Ealing Broadway branch, with the Piccadilly Line also serving the station from 4 July 1932. At street level it has a fine example of a Charles Holden-designed 'brick box with concrete lid' station building which dates from 1932. To the west lies the junction where the Piccadilly's Heathrow branch diverges away from the Ealing Broadway and Uxbridge branches of the District and Piccadilly. Adjacent to this junction are the District's Ealing Common depot and the Acton store of the London Transport Museum (which holds a few open days per year and is well worth a visit). At one time, Acton Town had a fifth platform which served a short branch to South Acton and was operated by a single motor car; it is still there, minus track and mostly hidden by advertising boards opposite platform 4. The branch opened on 13 June 1905 and closed on 28 February 1959.

At the east end of the station, three reversing sidings are situated between the westbound and eastbound tracks. On the south side of the line at this point is London Underground's Acton Works, which is accessed via a connection with the westbound local track adjacent to platform 1.

Aldgate ○ Circle ● Metropolitan (zone 1)
Opened 18 November 1876.

Aldgate is situated in a triangle of lines at the eastern edge of the Circle Line. Aldgate has four platforms made up of two islands, the outer faces of which are served exclusively by the Circle Line (outer rail platform 1 and inner rail platform 4). The two centre tracks which serve platforms 2 and 3 are dead end roads which form the City terminus of the Metropolitan Line. Immediately to the north of the platforms is Aldgate North Junction where Hammersmith & City Line trains leave the Circle Line and head to Aldgate East and on to Barking. At the south end of the station is Minories Junction where the District Line leaves the Circle Line to head to Aldgate East, where it is joined by the Hammersmith & City Line from Aldgate North Junction. This makes Aldgate the only station from which you can see trains from all four of the sub-surface lines.

Aldgate East ● District ○ Hammersmith & City (zone 1)
Original station opened 6 October 1884 and closed 30 October 1938.
Current station opened 31 October 1938.

The original station at Aldgate East opened as part of the Metropolitan District Railway's extension to Whitechapel, but it closed on 30 October 1938 and was replaced by the current station which opened the following day. The reason for re-siting was to allow the enlargement of the Aldgate triangle as part of the '1935-40 New Works Programme'. The new station, being further to the east than the original, was close enough to the next station at St Mary's, that this station was closed on the same day that the original Aldgate East station closed.

Alperton ● Piccadilly (zone 4)
Opened 28 June 1903 as Perivale-Alperton.
Renamed Alperton 7 October 1910.

Located on the Piccadilly's Uxbridge branch, Alperton was opened by the Metropolitan District Railway. The station building is a later Charles Holden designed brick, reinforced concrete and glass affair dating from 1931, situated at street level with the platforms and track high above the street. At one time, Alperton had an escalator up to the eastbound platform; it is no longer in use and is not visible, being located behind a brick wall and a locked door.

Amersham ● Metropolitan (zone 9)
Opened 1 September 1892 as Amersham.
Renamed Amersham & Chesham Bois 12 March 1922 and renamed back to Amersham circa 1934.
Opened by the Metropolitan Railway as part of that railway's extension from Chalfont & Latimer to Aylesbury, Amersham is today a terminus for Metropolitan Line trains. The tracks continue beyond Amersham, minus conductor rails, and this route is served by Chiltern Railway's trains which operate between London Marylebone and Aylesbury, which also call at Amersham. The boundary between London Underground and Network Rail is to the west of Amersham at Mantles Wood. Metropolitan Line trains usually arrive at Amersham and proceed into one of two sidings to reverse. Although Chesham station is the most westerly location that passengers can travel to on the Underground, the sidings at Amersham are very slightly further west and are therefore the most westerly point on the Underground.

Angel ● Northern (zone 1)
Opened 17 November 1901.
Opened by the City & South London Railway, Angel station was the northern terminus of the C&SLR until the railway was further extended to Euston from 12 May 1907. When built, Angel had both the northbound and southbound tracks in one station tunnel either side of a central island platform. This arrangement existed until an upgrade in the 1990s which diverted the northbound track into a new platform tunnel and the space it occupied in what is now the southbound tunnel was filled in to create an extra wide platform. A new station building and escalators down to platform level were also built as part of the upgrade; the upper flight of escalators are today the longest on the entire Underground with a vertical rise of just over 27 metres and a length of 60 metres.

Archway ● Northern (zones 2 and 3)
Opened 22 June 1907 as Highgate.
Renamed Archway (Highgate) 11 June 1939, and renamed Archway in December 1947.
Opened by the Charing Cross, Euston & Hampstead Railway as Highgate, this was originally a terminus. It became a through station from 3 July 1939 when the line was extended to join the LNER at East Finchley. To the north of the platforms there is a centre reversing siding to turn northbound trains back south, which is only used at times of service disruption.

Arnos Grove ● Piccadilly (zone 4)
Opened 19 September 1932.
The Charles Holden designed station building here, was based on the design of the public library building in Stockholm, Sweden. Built in 1932, it performed the role of a terminus until the next stage of the extension opened to Oakwood on 13 March 1933. There are three tracks; the central one has a platform face on both sides and is used mostly by trains which are timetabled to reverse here, although it is also a through road. To the south are seven sidings which are used to stable trains outside traffic hours. To the east the line crosses the Pymmes Brook Valley on the 34 arch Arnos Park Viaduct (see picture on page 37).

Arnos Grove station with its Charles Holden designed cylindrical brick station building.

Arsenal ● Piccadilly (zone 2)

Opened 15 December 1906 as Gillespie Road.
Renamed Arsenal (Highbury Hill) 31 October 1932. Suffix gradually dropped around 1960 to leave the station named just Arsenal.

This is the only station on the London Underground to be named after a football club, although it was originally called Gillespie Road, a name still displayed on replica tiles on the platforms. There are no lifts or escalators here; access to the platforms is via a sloping walkway from the entrance.

The sloping walkway from the entrance down to the platforms at Arsenal.

Baker Street ● Metropolitan ● Circle ● Hammersmith & City ● Bakerloo ● Jubilee (zone 1)

Opened 10 January 1863 (Hammersmith & City and Circle lines), 13 April 1868 (Metropolitan Line), 10 March 1906 (Bakerloo Line) and 1 May 1979 (Jubilee Line).

The Baker Street station complex has ten platforms, the oldest of which are platforms 5 and 6 which serve the Circle & Hammersmith & City lines and which date from the opening of the world's first underground railway in January 1863 between Paddington (Bishop's Road) and Farringdon Street. Situated beneath a brick arch roof which dates back to the line's opening, they are in as near original condition as modern operating requirements will allow. Alongside to the north of these, platforms 1 to 4 are served by the Metropolitan Line and date from the opening of the Metropolitan & St John's Wood Railway to Swiss Cottage in 1868. Platforms 1 and 4 are dead end roads used by terminating trains from the north. Platforms 2 and 3 are through roads served by Metropolitan trains to and from Aldgate. Just beyond their south end and to the east of platforms 5 and 6, the Metropolitan, Circle and Hammersmith & City lines join together at Baker Street Junction.

Platforms 8 and 9 are served by the Bakerloo Line and the walls are decorated with silhouettes of the fictional character Sherlock Holmes, who supposedly lived at 221b Baker Street. Look closely at them and you will find that they are made up of lots of tiny Sherlock Holmes silhouettes.

On 20 November 1939, a new twin track tunnel section was opened between Finchley Road and a new junction with the Bakerloo Line at Baker Street, which allowed the Bakerloo to take over the Stanmore branch from the Metropolitan. Southbound trains from the Watford Junction and Stanmore branches each had their own separate platforms, but northbound trains to both branches had to share the current northbound Bakerloo platform, which created a bottleneck. A new line, to be known as the Jubilee Line, was constructed between Baker Street and Charing Cross and included a new northbound platform at Baker Street. This new line opened on 1 May 1979 and also included the transfer of the Bakerloo's Stanmore branch to the Jubilee. Today there is interchange between the lines for passengers, but the physical junction between them only sees occasional use, mostly by engineering trains between Ruislip Depot and the Bakerloo and also by empty Bakerloo Line 1972 MkII Tube Stock travelling to and from Acton Works for life extension work.

Balham ● Northern (zone 3)

Opened 6 December 1926.

Situated on the Morden extension, Balham boasts two station buildings, situated on opposite sides of Balham High Road. In common with the other stations on this extension, they were designed by Charles Holden and are clad in Portland Stone (see pictures on next page). This station was the scene of a tragic incident during World War II, when a bomb landed on the road above. A bus crashed into the crater and the platform tunnel partly collapsed and was also filled with water from a broken water main. 60 people lost their lives. A memorial plaque is located in the ticket hall.

Bank ○ Waterloo & City ● Northern ● Central ● District ○ Circle (zone 1)

Northern – Opened 25 February 1900.
Central – opened 30 July 1900.
Waterloo & City – Opened as City 8 August 1898.
Renamed Bank October 1940.
First served by the Underground 5 April 1994.
Interchange with the District and Circle lines at Monument opened 18 September 1933.

On 11 January 1941, Bank station suffered a direct hit from a German bomb. Fifty-six people lost their lives and a plaque remembering them is located in the circular subway. There are no station buildings above ground here, but sitting on top of a ventilation shaft on a plinth in front of the Royal Exchange is a statue of James Henry Greathead, the inventor of the Greathead Shield, a method by which early tube tunnels were bored through the ground. Below ground, located in a passageway that leads to the Waterloo & City Line, a section of a Greathead Shield can be found forming a part of the foot tunnel. This was in the former W&C siding tunnel and was re-discovered when the subway from the W&C to the Northern and DLR was being built.

This station is a large Underground complex which not only links the Waterloo & City, Northern and Central Lines, but also the Docklands Light Railway. The nearby Monument station is also connected below ground to the Bank complex, which provides interchange with the District and Circle lines as well. It is said that to walk through all of the foot tunnels within the complex would take well over an hour. There are currently construction works taking place to further increase the capacity of the Bank / Monument complex.

The Central Line platforms are on a sharp curve as they follow the roads above; the westbound platform (5) being a continuous curve, while the eastbound (6) has a short straight section at its east end. To the east of the station, the Central Line tracks also swerve to avoid the vaults of the Bank of England.

The Waterloo & City Line only has only two stations (Waterloo and Bank). The Bank end of the route consists of two terminal platforms (7 and 8), both of which see use, but at peak times just one is used to prevent Train Operators who are 'stepping back' from having to switch between platforms. As this line is used to ferry city workers between the mainline station at Waterloo and the City of London, it is usually closed on Sundays and Bank Holidays. The Waterloo & City Line did not become part of the London Underground until 1994.

The Northern Line platforms are numbered 3 and 4 and trains run on the right through here. Right hand running takes place from just south of Borough station, to just north of Bank station with the running tunnels rolling over each other at each location.

Platform numbers 1 and 2 are taken by the District and Circle lines at Monument. Platforms 9 and 10 form the Bank terminus of the Docklands Light Railway, platform 10 being set down only and platform 9 for boarding only (trains reverse in a siding beyond the platforms).

Barbican ○ Circle ● Hammersmith & City ● Metropolitan (zone 1)

Opened 23 December 1865 as Aldersgate Street. Renamed Aldersgate 1 November 1910, to Aldersgate & Barbican in 1923 and to Barbican 1 December 1968.

This station was opened as part of the Metropolitan Railway's extension from Farringdon Street to Moorgate Street on 23 December 1865. Alongside the two platforms used by the Underground are two abandoned platforms which used to serve the former 'Widened Lines' to Moorgate and which closed in December 2009. The station is just below street level and is flanked on either side by large retaining walls which used to support a glass and steel overall roof; close examination will reveal the brackets that held this roof in place are still attached to the walls. The overall roof was removed after being damaged in an air raid in December 1941. Until 2015, there was a (long-disused) signal cabin at the west end of the westbound platform, but it was removed as part of the Crossrail project.

Barking ● District ● Hammersmith & City (zone 4)

Opened by the London, Tilbury & Southend Railway 13 April 1854.
First served by District trains 2 June 1902 until 30 September 1905.
Then served again from 1 April 1908 onwards.

Barking has eight platforms, four of which are served by the Underground. There is interchange between the Underground and services on Network Rail operated by London Overground and C2C. All Hammersmith & City Line trains and selected District Line trains terminate here. H&C trains usually terminate via the sidings to the east of the station while, apart from one train, terminating District trains reverse in the bay platform. In order to avoid conflicting movements with Network Rail trains and to provide easy cross platform interchange between Underground and Network Rail trains, the westbound Underground line approaches from the east via an underpass and leaves to the west over a flyover. There is a physical link between Network Rail and the London Underground at the west end of platform 1a, which sees little use.

Barkingside ● Central (zone 4)

Opened 20 April 1903 by the Great Eastern Railway.
First served by the Underground 31 May 1948.

This station was opened by the Great Eastern Railway in 1903 as part of their Woodford to Ilford route and became a part of the Underground when the Central Line took over the line between Newbury Park and Woodford in May 1948. The station buildings are still in near original condition and are grade II listed. Things to look out for here are the letters GER which are cast into the platform canopy support brackets and the 'General Waiting Room' etched into the glass of the waiting room windows.

Barkingside station buildings were built by the Great Eastern Railway and are largely in original condition.

Barons Court ● District ● Piccadilly (zone 2)

Opened 9 October 1905.

The first railway through here was opened by the Metropolitan District Railway in September 1874, but the station was not built until 1905, to serve new developments in the area and to prepare for the coming of the Great Northern, Piccadilly & Brompton Railway which opened through here on 15 December 1906.

There is cross platform interchange here between the Piccadilly and the District. To the east of

Barons Court, the Piccadilly dives down into tube tunnel between the eastbound and westbound tracks of the District. Items to look out for here are the old style light box train describers (pictured) and the grade II listed station building designed by Harry Ford which still bears the name 'District Railway' above the entrance.

Bayswater ⬤ Circle ⬤ District
(zone 1)

Opened 1 October 1868 as
Bayswater. Renamed Bayswater (Queen's Road) & Westbourne Grove in 1923, to Bayswater (Queen's Road) in 1933 and to Bayswater (Queensway) 1 September 1946.
The suffix was later dropped to the leave the station with the name Bayswater.

This station retains its overall roof, although very little of it can be seen at platform level. Girders span the tracks just above train height; above this, the arch of the overall roof is used as a garage by a car hire firm. Just a short walk away from the station, in a street named Leinster Gardens, are a remarkable set of buildings. The line was built by the very disruptive 'cut and cover' method in the 1860s (opened in 1868). Being just below ground level, it cut through the terrace on Leinster Gardens and necessitated the destruction of part of the terrace. Rather than leave a gaping hole, the Metropolitan Railway built a pair of dummy houses (pictured below) to maintain the appearance of the terrace. The buildings are still there today and when viewed from the front do not appear to look out of place, however close examination will reveal that the doors and windows are painted on. Take a walk around the back into Porchester Terrace, and it can be clearly seen that the dummy houses are nothing more than a 5m thick wall.

Becontree ⬤ District (zone 5)

Opened in 1926 by the London, Tilbury & Southend Railway as Gale Street Halt.
First served by the Underground and renamed Becontree 12 September 1932.

Opened in 1926 with the name Gale Street Halt, the station was renamed Becontree and rebuilt in 1932 to include two new tracks which were installed by the LMS to serve the District. Alongside the two District Line platforms are two which are disused, originally for the former London, Tilbury & Southend Railway tracks that the District runs parallel to here. These were taken out of use in 1962 when the former LT&SR tracks (now part of Network Rail) were electrified.

Belsize Park ● Northern (zone 2)
Opened 22 June 1907.

With its fine Leslie Green designed red tiled building at street level, Belsize Park is situated on the Edgware branch of the Northern and was opened by the Charing Cross, Euston & Hampstead Railway. Immediately to the north of the platforms, the Edgware branch passes beneath the Network Rail Midland Main Line.

Bermondsey ● Jubilee (zone 2)
Opened 17 September 1999.

Bermondsey is on the Jubilee Line Extension and does not connect with any other railway lines. In common with all the other below ground JLE stations, Bermondsey is fitted with Platform Edge Doors (PEDs). Constructed as part tube and part cut and cover, there is even a small chink of daylight that reaches the east end of the eastbound platform.

Bethnal Green ● Central (zone 2)
Opened 4 December 1946.

Work on an extension to the Central Line east of Liverpool Street was started as part of the '1935-1940 New Works Programme', but was halted due to the outbreak of the Second World War. The partially completed Bethnal Green tube station was used as an air raid shelter and on 3 March 1943, a tragic event which resulted in a substantial loss of life occurred. It is believed that a new type of anti-aircraft rocket was launched from the nearby Victoria Park, the sound of which caused people to run to Bethnal Green station to take shelter. In the panic that followed, a woman carrying a small child tripped and fell on the stairs. As a crowd tried to push their way into the station, approximately 300 people became trapped in the small stairwell, of whom 173 lost their lives, mostly through suffocation. A small plaque above one of the station entrances marks this event, but a larger memorial (called the Stairway to Heaven) is now in place near one of the entrances in the adjacent Bethnal Green Gardens.

Blackfriars ● District ● Circle (zone 1)
Opened 30 May 1870.

Located on the south side of the 'inner circle', Blackfriars has two platforms on the Underground and is served by trains on both the District and Circle lines. Interchange is also available here with the Network Rail station served by Thameslink and Southeastern services. The station underwent a major refurbishment in 2012.

Blackfriars station, District and Circle lines.

Blackhorse Road ● Victoria (zone 3)

Opened 1 December 1968.

The penultimate stop before the northern terminus of the Victoria at Walthamstow Central, Blackhorse Road gives interchange with the London Overground Gospel Oak to Barking service. The seat recesses here are decorated with images of a long black horse which also resembles a road.

Bond Street ● Jubilee ● Central (zone 1)

Opened 24 September 1900 (Central Line) and 1 May 1979 (Jubilee Line).

Opened as part of the Central London Railway's Shepherd's Bush to Bank line in 1900, Bond Street was served only by the Central until the opening of the Jubilee Line in 1979. Since then it has provided interchange between the two lines, as well as serving the busy shopping area above. In the future there will also be interchange here with Crossrail. Bond Street is the nearest station to the Selfridges department store; Harry Selfridge attempted to change the station name to 'Selfridges' in 1909, but this was flatly refused by the CLR.

The main station entrance is through the West One shopping arcade on Oxford Street, which is located just west of the junction between Oxford Street and New Bond Street.

Borough ● Northern (zone 1)

Opened 18 December 1890.

Borough is the most northerly of the original City & South London Railway stations dating from 1890. The next station north of here would have been the original C&SLR terminus at King William Street, which closed on 24 February 1900, with the extension to Moorgate Street (which avoided King William Street) opening on 25 February 1900.

To the south of the station, the northbound and southbound tunnels roll over each other so that trains run on the right. The tunnels roll back over to give left hand running again to the north of Bank station.

Boston Manor ● Piccadilly (zone 4)

Opened 1 May 1883 as Boston Road.
Renamed Boston Manor on 11 December 1911.

Opened by the Metropolitan District Railway, this station still retains the old District Railway signal cabin (actually a Saxby & Farmer designed and built cabin) which was in use from the line's opening in 1883 until 1905 when automatic signalling was introduced. Although not used for its original purpose for over a century, the signal cabin is kept in very good condition. At platform level, the station retains its District Railway buildings and canopies. The street level entrance building and ticket hall dates from 1934; designed by Stanley Heaps, it includes an illuminated tower (pictured). The Piccadilly Line's Northfields depot can be viewed from the opposite side of the road to the station entrance, while the western entrance / exit and depot headshunt are behind the westbound platform.

Bounds Green ● Piccadilly (zones 3 and 4)
Opened 19 September 1932.

The station building here is of a style that is typical of the work of Charles Holden, but is in fact the only one on the Piccadilly Line Cockfosters extension not designed by him. It was the work of Holden's colleague C.H. James instead. Heading towards Cockfosters from Bounds Green, the line emerges into daylight between Bounds Green and Arnos Grove, the first time a train would see daylight since entering tube tunnel just east of Barons Court in west London.

At the east end of the westbound platform, a small plaque commemorates the sixteen Belgian refugees and three British citizens who died here on 13 October 1940 when houses above were hit and destroyed during an air raid, causing part of the platform tunnel to collapse.

Bow Road ● District ● Hammersmith & City (zone 2)
Opened 11 June 1902.

This is a very unusual station as the sub surface railway runs beneath Bow Road to the west, but emerges into daylight by curving away from the road in the station itself. This means that the west end is in cut and cover tunnel while the east end is in the open air. Interchange is available here with the Docklands Light Railway's Bow Church station, albeit with a 300 yard walk. Departing eastwards, trains face a climb of 1 in 32 up to Campbell Road Junction where the Underground's tracks come alongside the Network Rail lines in and out of Fenchurch Street (the former London, Tilbury & Southend Railway).

Brent Cross ● Northern (zone 3)
Opened 19 September 1923 as Brent.
Renamed Brent Cross 20 July 1976.

This station consists of an island platform on an elevated section of railway. The station building is at a lower level on the east side of the tracks and is a Stanley Heaps design fronted by a concrete roof which is supported by six sets of Doric columns. When opened, it was just called Brent; it was renamed when the nearby Brent Cross shopping centre opened in 1976. It will be noted that the

trackbed through the station is wide enough to accommodate two additional tracks, one on either side. In the mid 1920s, a passing loop was added in each direction to allow faster trains to overtake slower ones. The loops did not last long and were removed in the 1930s. Immediately to the north of the station, a viaduct carries the line over the A406 North Circular Road and the River Brent. This bridge is easily recognisable to passing motorists as it is adorned on both sides by large roundels pointing to Brent Cross station.

Brixton ● Victoria (zone 2)
Opened 23 July 1971.

The current southern terminus of the Victoria Line, Brixton opened as part of an extension from Victoria. The station entrance is a modern glass fronted building which bears a huge roundel, believed to be the largest on the Underground system. There is interchange here with Network Rail's Brixton station via a very short walk. Below ground is a two platform terminus with the running tunnels extending for a short distance beyond the south end of the platforms, where two trains stable outside of traffic hours. At the north end of the station is a scissors crossover which allows access to and from both platforms.

Bromley-by-Bow ● District ● Hammersmith & City (zones 2 and 3)
Opened by the London, Tilbury & Southend Railway 31 March 1858 as Bromley.
First served by the Underground 2 June 1902.
Renamed Bromley-by-Bow 18 May 1967.

There are four tracks through Bromley-by-Bow, with two tracks of the Underground running parallel to two of the former London, Tilbury & Southend Railway in and out of Fenchurch Street; these are now part of Network Rail and are served by trains operated by C2C. Opened as Bromley by the LT&SR in 1858, District Railway trains first called here in 1902 when they were still steam hauled. Electrification and separation of the District tracks followed in 1905. From 1962, the platforms on the tracks in and out of Fenchurch Street were closed and since then the station has only been served by the Underground. The platforms on the Network Rail tracks are still there, albeit disused and in poor condition. The station building dates from 1972 and replaced the previous 1894-built structure, which was destroyed by a fire in 1970.

Buckhurst Hill ● Central (zone 5)
Opened by the Eastern Counties Railway 22 August 1856.
First served by the Underground 21 November 1948.

This station became a part of the London Underground in November 1948 when the Central Line was extended eastwards over former LNER metals. The station building was built by the Great Eastern Railway and dates from 1892.

Burnt Oak ● Northern (zone 4)
Opened as Burnt Oak 27 August 1924.
Renamed Burnt Oak (Watling) circa 1928.
Suffix gradually dropped in the 1950s.

The first trains passed through here when the final section of the extension to Edgware was opened from Hendon Central on 18 August 1924, but the station was not ready in time and did not open until 27 October 1924. The station building, designed by Stanley Heaps, was not completed until 1925.

Caledonian Road ● Piccadilly (zone 2)
Opened 15 December 1906.

With a superb Leslie Green-designed grade II listed building, this station dates back to the opening of the Great Northern, Piccadilly & Brompton Railway. At platform level, it retains its unique tile colour scheme together with tiled station name and 'to Finsbury Park' and 'to Hammersmith' arrows on the platform tunnel walls. There are also 1908-style roundels at the end of each platform. Today, the next station on the westbound is King's Cross St Pancras, but when the line opened, the next station would have been York Road, which closed in 1932. It is visible from passing trains if you look carefully.

Camden Town ● Northern (zone 2)
Opened 22 June 1907.
This is a major Northern Line hub which today forms the junction of the Charing Cross and Bank branches to the south and the Edgware and High Barnet branches to the north. Opened by the Charing Cross, Euston & Hampstead Railway, it formed a junction where the Golders Green branch (since extended to Edgware) and the Highgate branch (since extended to High Barnet) split. On 20 April 1924, the City & South London Railway opened an extension from Euston which connected the C&SLR to the CCE&HR here. The entire junction is to the south of the platforms; trains from either of the two branches through the city (via Charing Cross or Bank) can reach both the Edgware and High Barnet branches and vice versa. Northbound trains serve platforms dedicated to whichever branch they are heading for, with platform 1 being for the Edgware branch and 3 for the High Barnet branch. Southbound trains from the Edgware branch arrive into platform 2, but can go forward either via Bank or Charing Cross, while southbound trains from the High Barnet branch arrive into platform 4 and again, can go forward via either of the branches through the city.

Canada Water ● Jubilee (zone 2)
Opened 17 September 1999.
Interchange is available here with London Overground (the former London Underground East London Line). At street level, the circular station building is a fine example of modern architecture, while at platform level, the station follows other below ground stations on the JLE in having platform edge doors.

Canary Wharf ● Jubilee (zone 2)
Opened 17 September 1999.
This station serves the busy Canary Wharf business district and has two glass domed entrances, one at each end. It has vast proportions below ground to accommodate a high volume of passengers. The island platform has platform edge doors on each face. A scissors crossover, located just beyond the west end of the platforms is used to reverse trains from either direction, normally only at times of service disruption. Interchange is available here with the Docklands Light Railway, either at the DLRs Canary Wharf station or the nearby Heron Quays station.

Canning Town ● Jubilee (zone 2)
Opened 14 May 1999.
The Jubilee Line Extension, having just emerged into daylight from the central London direction, arrives at Canning Town station where there is interchange with the Docklands Light Railway and numerous bus services which call at the adjacent bus station. Built on the location of the former Thames Iron Works, a concrete plaque pays homage to the site's previous incarnation. Above the plaque is a slab of iron from HMS Warrior, the world's first all-iron armour plated battleship, which still survives; it has been fully restored and is based in Portsmouth.

Cannon Street ● District ● Circle (zone 1)
Opened 6 October 1884.
Cannon Street sub-surface station is located immediately beneath the Cannon Street mainline terminus. Platform 1 serves the westbound District and outer rail Circle while platform 2 serves the eastbound District and inner rail Circle. Interchange is available here between the Underground and the mainline terminus above.

Canons Park ● Jubilee (zone 5)

Opened as Canons Park (Edgware) 10 December 1932.
Renamed Canons Park in 1933.

Originally a Metropolitan Railway station and opened with the MR's Stanmore branch in 1932, Canons Park is today served by the Jubilee Line. It stands atop an embankment, with entrances beneath the overbridge where the railway crosses over the B461 Whitchurch Lane. It is close to the entrance to 'The Hive' stadium, home of Barnet Football Club and the London Broncos Rugby League Club, which is clearly visible from passing Jubilee Line trains to the south of Canons Park station.

Chalfont & Latimer ● Metropolitan (zone 8)

Opened as Chalfont Road 8 July 1889.
Renamed Chalfont & Latimer 1 November 1915.

Located in Little Chalfont, this station opened as Chalfont Road when the Metropolitan Railway opened its extension beyond Rickmansworth to Chesham on 8 July 1889. It became a junction station when a further extension opened towards Aylesbury on 1 September 1892. Today it has three platforms, with 1 being northbound and 2 being southbound. Platform 3 is a bay which was used by Chesham services when the branch was worked as a shuttle between Chalfont & Latimer and Chesham. This ceased with the introduction of the S Stock, as these trains are too long to fit in the bay platform, the shuttle having been operated by a 4-car A Stock unit previously. The bay is now occasionally used to stable engineering vehicles, while services on the Chesham branch now operate to and from London. Of note here are the co-acting colour light signals at the start of the Chesham branch. As well as Metropolitan Line trains, Chalfont & Latimer is also served by Chiltern Railways' services between London Marylebone and Aylesbury.

Chalk Farm ● Northern (zone 2)

Opened 22 June 1907.

Chalk Farm is situated on the Edgware branch of the Northern Line. At street level it has a fine station building which fits into the wedge shape of the road intersection on which it sits. It has the longest frontage of all of the Leslie Green-designed station buildings. Those who fondly remember the 1980s may recognise the station entrance in Adelaide Road, as it was the backdrop to the photograph on the cover of the 1980 Madness album 'Absolutely' and also for their hit single 'Baggy Trousers'.

Chancery Lane ● Central (zone 1)

Opened as Chancery Lane 30 July 1900.
Renamed Chancery Lane (Grays Inn) 25 June 1934.
The suffix was gradually dropped.

Opened by the Central London Railway, Chancery Lane's eastbound tunnel was built directly above the westbound tunnel to avoid the railway having to pass beneath several surface buildings (for which compensation would have been payable). This arrangement means that the eastbound tunnel climbs steadily from Holborn. It is actually possible to see Holborn station from the west end of the eastbound platform at Chancery Lane; you can watch your train arrive and depart from Holborn and climb all the way up to you. The original station building was replaced by the current entrance and sub-surface ticket hall beneath the road junction of High Holborn and Grays Inn Road in 1934, at which time the station was renamed Chancery Lane (Gray's Inn), although the suffix did not last long. The original building designed by Harry Bell Measures still exists and can be found further along High Holborn carrying the name 'Chancery Station House'.

Charing Cross ● Northern ● Bakerloo (zone 1)

Bakerloo – Opened as Trafalgar Square 10 March 1906.
Renamed Charing Cross 1 May 1979.
Northern – Opened as Charing Cross 22 June 1907.
Renamed Charing Cross (Strand) 6 April 1914, Strand 9 May 1915 and Charing Cross 1 May 1979.
Jubilee – Opened 1 May 1979. Closed to passengers 19 November 1999.

Not only does this station serve the mainline terminus of the same name, but it is also the tube station for the National Gallery, The Strand and Trafalgar Square. The Baker Street & Waterloo Railway first opened a station here with the name 'Trafalgar Square' on 10 March 1906. Next, the Charing Cross, Euston & Hampstead Railway (now part of the Northern Line), opened a station called 'Charing Cross' nearby in June 1907. This was renamed 'Charing Cross (Strand)' in 1914 and then just 'Strand' in 1915. Strand station was closed in 1973 to allow construction of the new Jubilee Line Charing Cross terminus. When this opened in 1979, the three stations all became part of the same complex which took the name 'Charing Cross'. When the Jubilee Line extension opened in 1999, it bypassed the Charing Cross terminus, which closed on 20 November 1999. The Jubilee Line platforms are still there, disused and hidden behind closed doors. They can still be used to reverse trains (out of service) at times of disruption and are occasionally used to stable engineering trains. The Northern Line platform walls are decorated with murals by David Gentleman depicting the building of the original Charing Cross, while the Bakerloo Line platform walls are decorated with scenes from the National Gallery and National Portrait Gallery, which were designed by Richard Dragun and June Fraser.

Chesham ● Metropolitan (zone 9)

Opened 8 July 1889.

One of only two stations in zone 9 (the other being Amersham), Chesham is the furthest point west that passengers can travel to on the London Underground, although empty trains using the reversing sidings at nearby Amersham do travel slightly further west. Since the closure of the Central Line's Ongar branch in September 1994, Chesham has also been the most northerly point on the entire Underground. It is the only station on the single track branch which turns off from the Metropolitan Line's Amersham line at Chalfont & Latimer. The branch is just less than four miles long and runs through the rural Chess Valley. The station still has a signal box and steam age water tower, both disused but in fine condition.

Chigwell ● Central (zone 4)

Opened by the Great Eastern Railway 1 May 1903.
First served by the Underground 21 November 1948.

Chigwell station became a part of the London Underground when the Central Line took over between Newbury Park and Woodford and was first served by tube trains in November 1948. It still retains a fine example of a Great Eastern Railway station building.

Chiswick Park ● District (zone 4)

Opened as Acton Green 1 July 1879.
Renamed to Chiswick Park & Acton Green March 1887 and Chiswick Park 1 March 1910.

This station was opened by the Metropolitan District Railway as part of their line from Turnham Green to Ealing Broadway. It was rebuilt to a Charles Holden design in 1931/32 to accommodate the western extension of the Piccadilly Line from Hammersmith. Four tracks run through here (westbound local, westbound fast, eastbound fast and eastbound local) although there are only platforms on the local lines, which are served by District Line trains. The fast lines through the middle are used by Piccadilly Line trains which do not call here. That is the usual method of operation, but it is not unheard of for a Piccadilly Line train to run along the local lines from time to time.

Of particular note here are the heritage signs showing a list of destinations that trains go to from each platform. A small plaque states that the signs have been retained as part of the station's heritage and that Mark Lane is now called Tower Hill. Sadly, the heritage signs have since had Mark Lane crudely covered over with stickers stating Tower Hill.

Chiswick Park station can be seen in the distance as a Piccadilly Line train heads west. On the left of the picture, a District Line train passes the station front with a Richmond-bound service, having branched off the line towards Acton Town at Turnham Green. 2 April 2016.

Chorleywood ● Metropolitan (zone 7)
Opened as Chorley Wood 8 July 1889.
Renamed Chorley Wood & Chenies 1 November 1915, Chorley Wood circa 1934 and to Chorleywood circa 1964.
Chorleywood was opened by the Metropolitan Railway on 8 July 1889 as part of its extension from Rickmansworth to Chesham. At the south end of platform 1 is a disused Metropolitan Railway signal box, which had looked a little careworn until it was restored during late 2016. Behind platform 1 is the station car park, which had previously been a goods yard; a cable arch still carries the trackside cables up and over the disused yard entrance.

Clapham Common ● Northern (zone 2)
Opened 3 June 1900.
The entrance to Clapham Common station is located close to the junction of the A3 and A24 roads at the east end of the common. The western entrance has a very attractive dome and dates from when the station opened in June 1900. Until 1926, when the Morden extension opened, it was the terminus of the City & South London Railway after that railway had extended to Clapham Common from Stockwell. At platform level, it still has the original C&SLR style layout with both northbound and southbound tracks in the same tunnel, separated by a narrow island platform.

The central island platform at Clapham Common with two Northern Line trains of 1995 Tube Stock passing. A similar layout also exists at Clapham North.

Clapham North ● Northern (zone 2)
Opened as Clapham Road 3 June 1900.
Renamed Clapham North 13 September 1926.
Similar to Clapham Common, Clapham North also has a C&SLR style layout with both tracks inside one tunnel, separated by a narrow island platform. At street level, the original station building designed by TP Figgis was remodelled in the 1920s by Charles Holden.

Clapham South ● Northern (zones 2 and 3)
Opened 13 September 1926.
Located on the southern edge of Clapham Common, this is the first stop on the C&SLR's Morden extension. Like all stations on this stretch, its station building was designed by Charles Holden and finished in Portland Stone (pictured below). A deep level air raid shelter lies underneath; after the war it temporarily housed some of the UK's first Jamaican immigrants.

Cockfosters ● Piccadilly (zone 5)
Opened 31 July 1933.
The eastern terminus of the Piccadilly Line, Cockfosters station was the final part of the Piccadilly's extension from Finsbury Park. Designed by Charles Holden, the street level main entrance is a modest single storey brick building topped by a concrete roof with two large roundels mounted on short towers. The western entrance on the opposite side of the road is a simple concrete flat roofed affair with a large roundel mounted on top, adjacent to a small bus interchange; a subway beneath the main road links it to the station. The concourse and platform area is far more impressive with a concrete roof and a three track layout with two island platforms. There are four platform faces, the centre track having a platform face on each side.

Westbound trains actually depart from here in an easterly direction. On the south side of the line between Cockfosters and the next station at Oakwood is Cockfosters Depot. One of two main depots on the Piccadilly (the other being at Northfields), it can be accessed from either the Cockfosters end or the Oakwood end.

Colindale ● Northern (zone 4)
Opened 18 August 1924.

The original station building at Colindale was destroyed in a German air raid on 25 September 1940. The thirteen people killed are remembered by a plaque which was unveiled in the station in 2012. The current station building dates from 1962 and replaced a temporary structure placed there in 1940. A centre reversing siding to the north of the platforms allows trains from the south to turn back, but apart from when there is service disruption, this is only used to reverse one train per day (Monday to Saturday).

Colliers Wood ● Northern (zone 3)
Opened 13 September 1926.

Situated on the Morden extension, this station has a Charles Holden designed building which is angled around a street corner. On the opposite side of the road is a pub called 'The Charles Holden'.

Covent Garden ● Piccadilly (zone 1)
Opened 11 April 1907.

Although the Great Northern, Piccadilly & Brompton Railway opened their Finsbury Park to Hammersmith line through here on 15 December 1906, the station did not open until 11 April 1907. At street level there is a fine example of a Leslie Green designed station building with distinctive red tiling, which gives access to platform level either by lift or by using the stairs, of which there are 193! Decorated in a unique tile pattern of white and two shades of yellow, the platforms are typical of 37 Leslie Green stations, each of which had their own unique tiling to enable illiterate passengers to recognise each station. The original tiling was replaced on a 'like for like' basis during a refurbishment in 2010. From Covent Garden to the next station at Leicester Square is the shortest distance between two stations on the entire Underground at just 0.16 miles. If you travel between the two stations using a zone 1 cash single fare of £4.90 (as at the start of 2017), then you are paying over £30 per mile, surely one of the most expensive train journeys in the country! Of course few people would ever be likely to do so, as it is actually quicker to walk than enter and exit the stations and make the train journey. There are signs posted around both stations advising of their close proximity.

Covent Garden station is said to be haunted by the ghost of William Terriss, an actor who was murdered outside the stage door of the Adelphi Theatre on 16 December 1897.

Croxley ● Metropolitan (zone 7)
Opened as Croxley Green 2 November 1925. Renamed Croxley 23 May 1949.

This is the only intermediate station on the Watford branch of the Metropolitan and is located in Croxley Green.

Dagenham East ● District (zone 5)
Opened by the London, Tilbury & Southend Railway as Dagenham in 1885.
First served by District trains 2 June 1902 until 30 September 1905.
Served again from 12 September 1932 onwards. Renamed Dagenham East 1 May 1949.

Opened by the London, Tilbury & Southend Railway in 1885, the station was rebuilt by the London, Midland & Scottish Railway in 1932 with an extra pair of tracks to serve the District. These run parallel with two tracks of the former LT&SR main line, which are now part of Network Rail's Fenchurch Street to Southend route. Today there are only platforms serving the District tracks; those on the main line are still in situ but were closed when it was electrified in 1962. There is a bay platform where trains from the west can be turned back, which a handful of trains are timetabled to do. There is also a siding off the bay road.

Dagenham Heathway ● District (zone 5)
Opened as Heathway 12 September 1932. Renamed Dagenham Heathway 1 May 1949.
Unlike the next station at Dagenham East, Dagenham Heathway has never had any platforms on the adjacent main line, being opened in 1932 by the LMS when an extra pair of tracks were added for use by the District. The station building is on the A1240 'Heathway' which crosses over the line at this point, and the island platform is reached by a long sloping ramp from street level down to platform level.

Debden ● Central (zone 6)
Opened by the Great Eastern Railway as Chigwell Road 24 April 1865.
Renamed to Chigwell Lane December 1865 and to Debden 25 September 1949.
First served by the Underground 25 September 1949.
Opened by the Great Eastern Railway in 1865, the station was first served by the Underground when Central Line services took over from British Railways steam trains in September 1949. The rather bland station building dates from 1974, although the original stationmaster's house still survives alongside it. A centre reversing siding on the Epping side of the station can actually be used to turn back trains from either direction. A few peak hour services from the west are timetabled to terminate at Debden and head back west via this siding.

Dollis Hill ● Jubilee (zone 5)
Opened 1 October 1909.
Opened by the Metropolitan Railway in 1909, the Metropolitan ceased to call here after 7 December 1940. The station was served by Bakerloo Line trains from 20 November 1939 when the Bakerloo took over the Metropolitan's Stanmore service. From 1 May 1979, the Stanmore branch including Dollis Hill station became part of the Jubilee Line. The station consists of an island platform which only serves the Jubilee Line, with the northbound and southbound Metropolitan tracks passing by on the outside. The Network Rail lines in and out of Marylebone also run parallel with the Underground tracks on the northbound side of the station.

Ealing Broadway ● Central ● District (zone 3)
Opened 1 July 1879 (District Line) and 3 August 1920 (Central Line).
The first Underground line to reach Ealing Broadway was the Metropolitan District Railway on 1 July 1879. The Central Line arrived here much later with the GWR's Ealing & Shepherd's Bush Railway on 3 August 1920. The Central and District both serve this station, both interchanging with the Network Rail station on the parallel Great Western main line in and out of Paddington. Network Rail services which pass through or call here include First Great Western Railway, Heathrow Connect and Heathrow Express along with a fair amount of freight traffic. The Network Rail tracks pass through platforms 1 to 4 which are all through lines. The Central Line terminates in platforms 5 and 6 while the District Line terminates in 7, 8 and 9. Platform 7 is out in the open, but the west end of platforms 8 and 9 are covered by the original train shed. Look out for some 1908-style replica roundels on the District Line platforms. Until 2010 there was a physical connection between the District and Central lines here, branching off one of two sidings (numbered 24 and 25) at the east end of the District Line platforms. The two sidings were eventually removed during 2015, having seen very little use since the connection was removed.

Ealing Common ● Piccadilly ● District (zone 3)
Opened as Ealing Common 1 July 1879.
Renamed Ealing Common & West Acton in 1886 and Ealing Common 1 March 1910.
Served by both the Piccadilly and District lines, Ealing Common was opened by the Metropolitan District Railway with their line to Ealing Broadway on 1 July 1879. Rebuilt in 1930/31, it features a

An eastbound train of D Stock departs from platform 8 at Ealing Broadway. Note the replica 1908 roundels either side of the train.

heptagonal station building designed by Charles Holden and made from Portland Stone. At the east end of the station is the western entrance / exit to and from Ealing Common depot, where some District Line trains start and finish their journeys at the start and end of traffic. To the west of the station, the line crosses over the Great Western main line and the Central Line, while the District's branch to Ealing Broadway diverges to the left at Hanger Lane Junction, leaving the Piccadilly to continue towards South Harrow, Rayners Lane and Uxbridge.

Earl's Court ● Piccadilly ● District (zones 1 and 2)

District - Original station opened 30 October 1871 and closed 31 January 1878.
Current station opened 1 February 1878.
Piccadilly – Opened 15 December 1906.

The Metropolitan District Railway opened a branch through here from South Kensington to West Brompton on 12 April 1869, but there was no station here until 1871. Located in the cutting to the east of the current station, the original station building was damaged by fire in 1875 and a larger replacement was built on the opposite side of Earl's Court Road, opening on 1 February 1878. Earl's Court is the hub of the District Line, with all branches converging here. The District Line section is situated in a cutting under a fine overall glass and steel roof, with four platforms. 3 and 4 are westbound and trains can go towards either Wimbledon or Hammersmith/Olympia from either. Trains arriving from the Gloucester Road direction can reach both platforms 3 and 4, but those approaching from the High Street Kensington direction can only access platform 4. In the eastbound direction, platforms 1 and 2 are used. Over the Christmas period 2016 a new scissors crossover was installed at the west end of platforms 1 and 2, allowing trains from the Hammersmith / Olympia direction and the Wimbledon branch to access both. Previously, trains from the Wimbledon branch could only reach 2. Upon departure, eastbound trains can travel towards either Gloucester Road or High Street Kensington from either platform.

The new scissors crossover at the west end of Earl's Court District Line platforms, as viewed from the end of platform 1. The train of S Stock in the background is on a Wimbledon bound service and is about to branch left towards West Brompton.

Of note on the District Line platforms are the old style train describers with illuminated arrows which point to the destination of the next train, still performing this function today. Several modern dot matrix indicators positioned along each platform give more detail, but these - while very visible - are quite discreet and do not detract from the overall heritage feel of the station.

The Piccadilly Line also calls at Earl's Court, using platforms 5 (eastbound) and 6 (westbound), both of which are directly beneath the District Line platforms, albeit in tube tunnel. The Piccadilly platforms opened here when the Great Northern, Piccadilly & Brompton Railway opened its tube line from Finsbury Park to Hammersmith on 15 December 1906.

East Acton ● Central (zone 2)
Opened 3 August 1920.

This station is notable for having a replica Great Western Railway waiting shelter on each platform (dating from 1976), which reflects the fact that the section of line from Wood Lane to Ealing Broadway was built by the Great Western Railway, and that initially the Central London Railway only had running powers over it. The CLR shared tracks with GWR freight traffic until an extra pair of tracks was added in 1938, onto which the freight traffic was diverted. These were closed and lifted in 1964; the space they used to occupy behind the eastbound platform is now very overgrown.

Eastcote ● Metropolitan ● Piccadilly (zone 5)
Opened 26 May 1906.

Although the Metropolitan Railway opened its line through here between Harrow-on-the-Hill and Uxbridge on 4 July 1904, there was initially only one intermediate stop (at Ruislip). Eastcote station eventually opened nearly two years later. The main station building which fronts on to Field End Road, dates from a rebuild in 1939 and was designed by Charles Holden.

East Finchley ● Northern (zone 3)
Opened by the Great Northern Railway as East End Finchley 22 August 1867.
Renamed East Finchley in 1886.
First served by the Underground 3 July 1939.

This station was originally on the GNR's line between Finsbury Park and Edgware (via Highgate). Following the '1921 Railways Act' this line and the rest of the GNR became part of the London, North Eastern Railway (LNER). On 3 July 1939, the station became the temporary terminus of the Northern Line's extension from Highgate, followed by further extension over LNER tracks beyond East Finchley to High Barnet from 14 April 1940. The station was rebuilt to coincide with the arrival of the Northern and also to accommodate its proposed extension over the former GNR line to Finsbury Park (then over the former GN&CR to Moorgate). This development did not happen, but a short section of the route still exists as far as Highgate Sidings where a number of Northern Line trains stable. Of East Finchley's four platforms, the two in the centre (2 and 3) allow access to and from Highgate Sidings. Platform 2 sees use by trains leaving Highgate as they enter service, while 3 is used by trains stabling at Highgate as they leave service. All other trains use platform 4 (southbound) and platform 1 (northbound).

To the north of the station is a disused and boarded up former Great Northern Railway signal box (pictured right) which is visible from the car park and the platform ends.

Standing above platform 4 is a statue designed by Eric Aumonier, called 'The Archer', of a kneeling archer firing his arrow towards Central London.

East Ham ● District ● Hammersmith & City (zones 3 and 4)
Opened by the London, Tilbury & Southend Railway in 1858.
First served by the Underground 2 June 1902.

Originally opened by the London, Tilbury & Southend Railway, the current buildings and platforms served by the District were a later addition which date back to when the District tracks were electrified in 1905. East Ham served as the eastern terminus of the District from 1905 until 1908 when the electrified tracks were extended through to Barking. Parallel to the Underground tracks here are the Network Rail lines in and out of Fenchurch Street. Up until 1962, trains on this line used to call at East Ham and the remains of the main line platforms can still be seen from passing trains. There is also an abandoned bay platform adjacent to the eastbound Underground platform which was served by trains to and from the Gospel Oak to Barking line via an abandoned curve known as the East Ham Loop; this joined the Gospel Oak to Barking line at East Ham Loop North Junction. This line closed in 1958. Several items at East Ham are worth looking out for. The platform canopies are held up by brackets with the letters LTSR cast into them, a painted sign advertises tea at 2d (two old pence) per cup and to the west of the platforms, adjacent to the westbound track, is a water tower which was installed to top up the water tanks of steam locomotives. Having not been required for this job for many, many years, this is a truly remarkable survivor, although not as old as some may think, as it was installed on behalf of London Transport by British Railways in 1959 as part of the resignalling and track segregation. It is believed its purpose was to quench the thirst of any steam loco that may have strayed that far east (London Transport were still using steam locomotives on engineering trains up until 1971).

East Putney ● District (zones 2 and 3)
Opened 3 June 1889.

Located about half a mile to the south of Fulham Rail Bridge, East Putney is situated on the Wimbledon branch of the District. Immediately to the south of the station is East Putney Junction where a chord diverges between the District and Network Rail's Point Pleasant Junction on the Clapham Junction to Barnes line. This is used by empty stock trains travelling to and from Wimbledon depot, reflecting the fact that this section of line was built by the London & South Western Railway (LSWR) while the District only had running powers over it. The line passed over to the Southern Railway and then British Railways before it was sold to London Underground in 1994 with main line trains keeping their access to the route for empty stock movements only. The Southern Railway ceased operating passenger trains over the route in 1941. The station has three platforms, with 1 and 2 serving the District, and the disused platform 3 (the opposite face of platform 2) adjacent to the East Putney Junction to Point Pleasant Junction track. There are also the abandoned remains of the fourth platform in the undergrowth adjacent to the track from Point Pleasant Junction to east Putney Junction.

Edgware ● Northern (zone 5)
Opened 18 August 1924.

Edgware is the terminus of the former Charing Cross, Euston & Hampstead Railway's extension from Golders Green. The station consists of three platforms, with platform 1 out in the open and 2 and 3 situated beneath a train shed. A fan of sidings alongside provides stabling for trains outside traffic hours. There are also three sidings which serve Edgware Track Depot.

Designed by Stanley Heaps, Edgware's station building fronts onto the A5100 Station Road. It is possible to interchange here between the Underground and local bus services via Edgware bus station which is located alongside.

Edgware Road ● Bakerloo (zone 1)

Opened 15 June 1907.

Originally opened as a terminus, Edgware Road became a through station from 1 December 1913 when the Baker Street & Waterloo Railway extended to Paddington. At street level, the station still retains its original red tiled building designed by Leslie Green. This is of course one of two Underground stations at Edgware Road, with this one serving the Bakerloo Line and, just a short walk away, the sub-surface station for the Hammersmith & City, Circle and District lines. The Underground map does not show an interchange between the two lines and there is no direct link between the two.

Edgware Road ● District ● Hammersmith & City ● Circle (zone 1)

Opened 10 January 1863.

Located in a cutting alongside the A40 Marylebone Road, close to its junction with the A5 Edgware Road, this is used as both a through station and a terminus. Under normal operating conditions, platform 1 is a through road for Circle and Hammersmith & City trains coming from the Hammersmith branch and travelling on the outer rail of the inner circle towards King's Cross St Pancras. Platform 2 is used to terminate Circle Line trains which have travelled around the inner circle on the outer rail and are about to return via the inner rail. Platform 3 is used to terminate District Line trains on the Wimbledon to Edgware Road route, while platform 4 is served by Hammersmith & City and Circle line trains on the inner rail heading for Hammersmith. Opposite platform 4 is number 26 siding which is used to stable one train outside traffic hours.

Originally opened as part of the Metropolitan Railway's first line in 1863, Edgware Road was home to the MR's engine sheds, but these were moved to Neasden due to a lack of space. The station today bears little resemblance to that which first opened to the public on 10 January 1863.

Approaching Edgware Road from the east, a terminating Circle Line train can be seen in platform 2, while number 26 siding hosts a stabled train of S Stock.

Elephant & Castle ● Northern ● Bakerloo (zones 1 and 2)
Opened 18 December 1890 (Northern Line) and 5 August 1906 (Bakerloo Line).

There is interchange between the Northern and Bakerloo lines here and it is also possible, via a short walk, to interchange with the nearby Network Rail station.

The Northern Line platforms (numbered 1 and 2) were the first to be built and were opened by the City & South London Railway as part of the world's first deep level tube railway which ran between King William Street and Stockwell. The Bakerloo platforms (numbered 3 and 4) were opened by the Baker Street & Waterloo Railway on 5 August 1906; although the two sets of platforms belonged to separate companies, they were connected by foot tunnels below ground from 10 August 1906. Look out for the original City & South London Railway tiles, which are located in the emergency stairs from the Northern Line platforms to street level.

At street level, there are two station buildings separated by a large roundabout. The most northerly is the original Leslie Green designed building, constructed for the opening of the BS&WR in 1906. The Bakerloo Line platforms form the southern terminus of the Bakerloo. The line continues for a short distance to the south of the platforms where up to two trains can be stabled in the northbound and southbound sidings. At the north end of the station is a scissors crossover allowing trains to arrive and depart from either platform.

Elm Park ● District (zone 6)
Opened 13 May 1935.

This is the newest station on the section of the District Line between Barking and Upminster, opened by the LMS in 1935. Elm Park has only ever had platforms serving the District tracks, and has never had any serving the adjacent Network Rail tracks. It consists of an island platform, reached by a sloping walkway from the station building located on The Broadway which crosses over the railway here.

Embankment ● District ● Circle ● Northern ● Bakerloo (zone 1)
District and Circle – Opened as Charing Cross 30 May 1870.
Renamed Charing Cross Embankment 4 August 1974 and Embankment 12 September 1976.
Bakerloo – Opened as Embankment 10 March 1906.
Renamed Charing Cross (Embankment) 6 April 1914, Charing Cross 9 May 1915, Charing Cross Embankment 4 August 1974 and Embankment 12 September 1976.
Northern – Opened as Charing Cross (Embankment) 6 April 1914.
Renamed Charing Cross 9 May 1915, Charing Cross Embankment 4 August 1974 and Embankment 12 September 1976.

This station has a rather complex history. It is situated on the north bank of the River Thames, beneath the platform ends of Charing Cross main line station and first opened as Charing Cross on 30 May 1870 when the Metropolitan District Railway extended its line from Westminster Bridge to Blackfriars. This is the sub-surface part of the station, which is today served by trains on the Circle and District lines. Next came the Bakerloo Line station, opened by the Baker Street & Waterloo Railway as Embankment on 10 March 1906, with an interchange provided between the two railways. The Northern Line station was opened as a terminus by the Charing Cross, Euston & Hampstead Railway on 6 April 1914, consisting of a single through platform located on a balloon shaped loop. This new CCE&HR station was opened as Charing Cross (Embankment) and the BS&WR station changed its name to match, while the sub-surface station retained the name Charing Cross. In 1915, the Embankment in brackets was dropped from the names of the deep level lines so that the deep level station and the sub-surface station had the same name.

In preparation for a further extension of the CCE&HR south of here (to join up with the City & South London Railway at Kennington), the original CCE&HR platform became the northbound platform and a new southbound platform was opened in 1926. The southbound platform is on a straight alignment, but the northbound platform, being on what used to be part of the balloon shaped loop, is curved, and the old 'Mind the Gap' announcement recorded by Oswald Laurence can still be heard when trains arrive. This could at one time be heard at several stations across the Underground, but has been phased out. The recording at Embankment was restored to use at the request of Mr Laurence's widow so that she could hear his voice whenever she passes through the station.

In 1974 the whole station was renamed yet again to Charing Cross (Embankment), then renamed to just Embankment in 1976. This latter name change was to facilitate the renaming of the Bakerloo's Trafalgar Square station and the Northern's Strand station to Charing Cross, when they were merged together, to form a complex with the then under construction terminus of the new Jubilee Line.

To the south of this station, the Bakerloo and Northern lines pass beneath the River Thames and at some points the Bakerloo Line tunnels are just a few feet below the bottom of the river bed. Due to a fear that German bombing during the war could penetrate the tunnels, floodgates were installed on both lines here and at Waterloo in 1939. These are still in situ on both lines at Embankment.

Epping ● Central (zone 6)
Opened by the Great Eastern Railway 24 April 1865.
First served by the Underground 25 September 1949.

Epping station opened as part of the Great Eastern Railway's extension from Loughton to Ongar. The line was transferred to the Underground's Central Line on 25 September 1949, although electrification did not go beyond Epping to Ongar until 1957. Until then, hired-in British Railways steam locos and coaching stock were used between Epping & Ongar, with passengers having to change trains at Epping. Closure of the Ongar branch came on 30 September 1994 and Epping became the eastern terminus of the Central Line from that date. Looking towards Ongar from the platforms at Epping, it will be noted that the tracks run beyond the red stop lights, with the track through platform 2 continuing into the now disused east siding, and the track through platform 1 reaching Ongar. The Ongar branch is now a privately owned railway operated by preserved diesel and steam traction (see eorrailway.co.uk). Trains on the Epping & Ongar Railway do not run into Epping station, but when the railway is operating, visitors can reach the EOR from Epping station by using the vintage bus service which operates between there and North Weald station. After closure in 1994, no trains ran through to the Ongar branch, although the track was left in place. During the early hours of 25 September 2014, the stop lights at the end of platform 1 were lowered and a special train worked through. Hauled by two Schöma diesel locomotives, it conveyed a preserved 3-car Cravens 1960 Tube Stock train (with 1938 Tube Stock trailer) to the railway to participate in an event to celebrate 20 years since the closure of the line by London Underground. Since then, the connection between the two railways has seen further limited use by engineering trains.

At the west end of the station is Epping signal cabin, which is no longer used by the Underground and is now in the hands of Cravens Heritage Trains, being converted into a museum. Standing on a plinth between the signal cabin and the running lines is loco L11 which is being restored as a static exhibit. This is an electric shunting locomotive which was made from two redundant Standard Stock driving motors to make one vehicle with a cab at each end. In this guise, it saw use as a shunter at Acton Works. (More information can be found at www.l11.org.uk)

Epping station is the only one served by tube trains outside the M25 London Orbital motorway. The railway passes beneath the M25 about ¾ mile west of Epping.

Euston ● Northern ● Victoria (zone 1)
Northern (Bank Branch) – Opened 12 May 1907.
Northern (Charing Cross Branch) – Opened 22 June 1907.
Victoria – Opened 1 December 1968.

Euston has six platforms on the Underground: 1 and 2 serve the Northern Line's Charing Cross branch, platforms 3 and 6 are used by the Northern Line's Bank branch while 4 and 5 are for the Victoria Line.

The first tube line to serve Euston was the City & South London Railway which reached here in May 1907 when an extension from Angel to Euston was opened. This was a typical C&SLR station with two tracks inside one tunnel, separated by an island platform. When the line was further extended to join up with the CCE&HR on 20 April 1924, it changed from a terminus to a through station. The island platform remained in place until the 1960s when the station was rebuilt to accommodate the new Victoria Line. While the southbound line still uses the original station tunnel (platform 6), the northbound line was diverted into a newly built tunnel on the opposite side of the new Victoria Line platforms, resulting in platform 6 being very wide where the position of the former northbound track has been filled in. The original northbound track is still in place to the south side of the station and forms the Euston loop, which can be used by engineering trains travelling between the southbound Northern and the Piccadilly Line (via the King's Cross loop).

The second tube line to serve Euston was the CCE&HR which opened its line between Charing Cross and Golders Green and Highgate on 22 June 1907. Although the station complex is now reached via entrances in Euston mainline station, the original Leslie Green designed CCE&HR station building is still in situ on the corner of Melton Street and Drummond Street.

The Victoria Line opened through Euston on 1 December 1968. Victoria Line trains run on the right through Euston to give cross platform interchange between the southbound Victoria and southbound Northern (Bank branch), and between the northbound Victoria and northbound Northern (Bank branch). The Victoria Line tunnels revert to left hand running to the north of King's Cross St Pancras and to the south of Warren Street. Although the Northern (Bank branch) and the Victoria are both north to south railways, both lines actually pass through Euston in opposite directions on an east to west axis.

The view from the cab of a southbound Northern Line train as it waits to depart from Euston platform 6 (Bank branch). The left hand track is the southbound Northern Line towards Bank. The track on the right used to be the northbound Northern Line from Bank, but now forms the Euston loop, the northbound line from Bank having been diverted into a new tunnel to accommodate the Victoria Line in the 1960s. The non-electrified track running to the bottom right hand corner of the picture used to run into the platform tunnel and serve the original central island platform, but now ends just out of shot. Engineering trains travelling to the Bank branch from Ruislip Depot will reverse at King's Cross St Pancras platform 6 (Piccadilly Line), and run via the King's Cross loop on to the northbound Northern Line (Bank branch), and then cross into the Euston loop and then arrive at Euston via the crossover in the picture above.

Euston Square ● Metropolitan ● Hammersmith & City ● Circle (zone 1)

Opened as Gower Street 10 January 1863. Renamed Euston Square 1 November 1909.

Many original features are still in place at this station, but they are hidden beneath modern-looking tiling which gives the station a rather Spartan appearance at platform level. There are no station buildings at street level, just subway entrances on the north side of Euston Road and in the bottom of the Wellcome Trust building on Gower Street. There is no direct link between Euston Square and Euston station, but it is only a short walk between the two and a similar distance to the Northern Line (Charing Cross Branch) and the Victoria Line at Warren Street.

Fairlop ● Central (zone 4)

Opened by the Great Eastern Railway 1 May 1903.
First served by the Underground 31 May 1948.

This station was opened by the Great Eastern Railway as part of its Woodford to Ilford route. Steam trains ceased running through here in November 1947, with Central Line trains operating in passenger service from 31 May 1948, although these had been running empty through here to reach Hainault depot from December 1947. The station still retains many original features, including the letters GER cast into the platform canopy support brackets.

It could all have been so different though, as a proposal prior to the Second World War would have seen Fairlop become the location of a passenger airport. Instead it became an RAF fighter station during the war. By the time hostilities had ceased, the site was no longer considered suitable for a major airport and Heathrow was chosen instead. The RAF station closed in 1946; the site is now occupied by the Fairlop Waters country park and golf course, located immediately to the east of the station.

Farringdon ● Metropolitan ● Hammersmith & City ● Circle (zone 1)

Original station opened as Farringdon Street 10 January 1863, closed 22 December 1865.
Current station opened as Farringdon Street 23 December 1865.
Renamed Farringdon & High Holborn 26 January 1922 and Farringdon 21 April 1936.

The first station to open here was called Farringdon Street and it was the eastern terminus of the Metropolitan Railway's line from Paddington Bishop's Road. This was the world's first underground railway which opened to the public on 10 January 1863. The original station was in a slightly different position to the current one; the change in location took place when the MR opened their extension to Aldersgate Street in December 1865.

It was renamed Farringdon & High Holborn in 1926, a name which can still be seen adorning the station building in Cowcross Street, along with a sign for 'Parcels Office' on the side of the building. As well as the Metropolitan, Hammersmith & City and Circle lines, Farringdon is also served by Thameslink on what used to be known as the 'City Widened Lines' and there is interchange between the Underground and Thameslink. The 'City Widened Lines' got their name when the Metropolitan Railway increased the width of the cutting to accommodate two extra tracks. Used by other railways as well as the Metropolitan, these linked both the Great Northern Railway and the Midland Railway with the London, Chatham & Dover Railway. Today they are used by Thameslink services and the link with the former GNR no longer exists. To the west of Farringdon, the Thameslink line, which has been on the north side of the Underground lines from King's Cross, dives down beneath the Underground lines to emerge on the south side on the approach to Farringdon station. Where they pass beneath the Underground lines has been known as the 'Ray Street Gridiron', which when built was the world's first triple deck cast iron bridge, although the structure today is mostly made of concrete. Beneath both railways here is the River Fleet, an underground sewer which runs from Hampstead Heath to the River Thames at Blackfriars Bridge.

The 'Widened Lines' used to run to Moorgate with a junction at the west end of the station where the line towards Blackfriars split away from the Moorgate line. Today only the line towards Blackfriars remains, as the junction was removed to allow the Thameslink platforms to be extended to accommodate longer trains. The Farringdon to Moorgate section closed in March 2009. Also to the west of the station is the site of the former Farringdon Sidings, which were used to stable C Stock trains. As they were not long enough to stable the longer S Stock trains which replaced them, they fell out of use and were removed during 2016. At the time of writing, work was taking place to provide a connection between the Underground lines and the abandoned former Thameslink tracks to Moorgate to create some additional train stabling. Eventually, both the Underground and Thameslink lines will be able to interchange at Farringdon with the currently-under-construction Crossrail route (Elizabeth Line).

Finchley Central ⬤ Northern (zone 4)
Opened by the Great Northern Railway 22 August 1867.
First served by the Underground 14 April 1940.
This station boasts a fine set of former Great Northern Railway-style station buildings, having been opened by the GNR-sponsored Edgware, Highgate & London Railway as part of its line to Edgware. Today it is the junction for the Mill Hill East branch (all that remains of the former route to Edgware) and the High Barnet branch (which was opened by the GNR on 1 April 1872). The line through here became part of the Underground in 1940.

There are three platforms, with platform 1 normally only used by trains serving the Mill Hill East branch. There are two reversing sidings, one at each end of the station.

Finchley Road ⬤ Metropolitan ⬤ Jubilee (zone 2)
Opened as Finchley Road 30 June 1879.
Renamed Finchley Road (South Hampstead) 11 September 1885 and Finchley Road circa 1914.
At this four platform station served by both the Jubilee and Metropolitan lines, the two Jubilee platforms (2 and 3) sit between the two Metropolitan platforms (1 and 4). To the south of the station, the Jubilee Line dives down in to tube tunnel while the Metropolitan carries on to Baker Street in sub surface tunnel (with some short open air stretches). To the north, the tracks of the Jubilee Line are between the northbound and southbound Metropolitan tracks until just north of Wembley Park. Alongside Finchley Road station, the two track Network Rail line in and out of Marylebone comes alongside to make a six track wide formation. A gantry at the north end of the southbound

island platform used to have three glass hoops suspended from it to prevent full sized Metropolitan Line trains from reaching the tube tunnel at the south end of the station (smashing them would break a circuit, turn signals to red and raise train stops). They were removed concurrent with the removal of the crossover between the two lines here and the conversion of the Jubilee to automatic operation using the TBTC 'moving block' system. Protection is now provided by fixed train stops at Neasden.

A southbound Jubilee Line train of 1996 Stock descends into tube tunnel as it departs from Finchley Road.

Finsbury Park ⬤ Piccadilly ⬤ Victoria (zone 2)
Opened 15 December 1906 (Piccadilly Line) and 1 September 1968 (Victoria Line).
A physical link here between the Piccadilly and Victoria lines is used by engineering trains to access the Victoria Line. There is passenger interchange between the two lines and also with the Network

Rail station. The Piccadilly was altered here in the 1960s to accommodate the Victoria Line. The former Great Northern & City Railway tunnels, which were built to accommodate full height trains (as opposed to tube sized trains), were taken over by the westbound Piccadilly and the southbound Victoria. The old Piccadilly westbound platform became the northbound Victoria and the eastbound Piccadilly remained the same. Evidence of the former Great Northern & City Railway is apparent in the size of the overall bore of the westbound Piccadilly and southbound Victoria, which are both much larger than the trains that use them. Mosaics of hot air balloons line the walls of the Piccadilly Line platforms to mark the fact that Finsbury Park was the location of one of the first hot air balloon flights.

A train of 1973 Tube Stock arrives in the Piccadilly Line westbound platform at Finsbury Park. Note the large tunnel bore, built to accommodate the full height trains of the GN&CR. Also note the hot air balloon mosaic.

Fulham Broadway ● District (zone 2)
Opened as Walham Green 1 March 1880. Renamed Fulham Broadway 2 March 1952.
Situated on the District Line's Wimbledon branch, Fulham Broadway is the station to use to reach Chelsea's Stamford Bridge football ground. It was rebuilt in 1905 to cope better with match day crowds. In more recent times, the Fulham Broadway shopping complex has been built over part of the station, giving the Earl's Court end a very bland and modern appearance. However the Wimbledon end is in a time warp and still retains many of the features from the 1905 rebuild, such as the overall roof and side walls.

Gants Hill ● Central (zone 4)
Opened 14 December 1947.
The section of tube tunnel between Leytonstone and Newbury Park was under construction when war broke out and work was halted. The tunnels were complete but not fitted out and were used during the war as a secret underground bomb-proof aircraft components factory. Gants Hill was eventually opened to traffic on 14 December 1947. The circulating area between the platforms has been finished to a design by Charles Holden that is based on the style of a Moscow Metro station.

Gloucester Road ● Circle ● District ● Piccadilly (zone 1)

Circle and District – Opened as Brompton (Gloucester Road) 1 October 1868.
Renamed Gloucester Road in 1907.
Piccadilly – Opened as Gloucester Road 15 December 1906.

This sub-surface station was opened by the Metropolitan Railway on 1 October 1868 as a part of its extension from Praed Street Junction to South Kensington. The station was also served by Metropolitan District Railway trains when it opened an extension westwards from South Kensington to West Brompton on 12 April 1869. On 15 December 1906, the Great Northern, Piccadilly & Brompton Railway opened its tube line from Finsbury Park to Hammersmith, which included a station at Gloucester Road. The two railways had separate entrances at street level, which can still be evidenced today, although the former GNP&BR station is now used as retail outlets, with public access to and from both the sub-surface and tube platforms being through the former Metropolitan & District Railway station building. Today it is served by the Piccadilly at tube level and by the District and Circle lines at sub-surface level. The west end of the station is where the Circle and District diverge away from each other, with the District heading to and from Earl's Court and the Circle heading to and from High Street Kensington. The sub-surface platforms were rafted over and apartments and a shopping mall built over the top in the 1990's, but there are still some historic features remaining at platform level, including the original retaining walls and old-style train describers on platform 1.

Golders Green ● Northern (zone 3)

Opened 22 June 1907.

Opened as the northern terminus of the Charing Cross, Euston & Hampstead Railway, Golders Green became a through station when the line was extended towards Edgware, initially to Hendon on 19 November 1923. Alongside the station is Golders Green depot, one of two main depots on the Northern Line. To the south of the station, the Northern enters tube tunnel; of the three tunnel mouths, the most easterly is the Golders Green depot headshunt and is only long enough to accommodate about one car.

Goldhawk Road ● Hammersmith & City ● Circle (zone 2)

Opened 1 April 1914.

The first stop on the Hammersmith branch after departing from Hammersmith, Goldhawk Road opened in 1914. It replaced the original Shepherd's Bush station which was situated roughly halfway between Goldhawk Road and the current Shepherd's Bush Market station (which opened on the same day as Goldhawk Road). This is the closest station to Queen's Park Rangers' Loftus Road football ground.

Goodge Street ● Northern (zone 1)

Opened as Tottenham Court Road 22 June 1907. Renamed Goodge Street 9 March 1908.

Opened by the Charing Cross, Euston & Hampstead Railway as Tottenham Court Road, the station was renamed Goodge Street on the same day that the current Tottenham Court Road had its name changed from Oxford Street. Goodge Street retains its Leslie Green station building at street level.

Grange Hill ● Central (zone 4)

Opened by the Great Eastern Railway 1 May 1903.
First served by the Underground 21 November 1948.

Situated on the Hainault loop at the Woodford end of Hainault Depot, some trains enter or leave service here as they come off or go onto Hainault Depot at the start and end of traffic. Grange Hill station was opened by the Great Eastern Railway in 1903 and was first served by Central Line trains from 21 November 1948. At platform level, it retains many GER features, but the station building is a more modern affair dating from 1949, the original GER building having been flattened by a German V1 flying bomb during the war.

Great Portland Street ● Metropolitan ● Hammersmith & City ● Circle (zone 1)

Opened as Portland Road 10 January 1863.
Renamed Great Portland Street 1 March 1917, Great Portland Street & Regent's Park in 1923 and Great Portland Street in 1933.

Opened as part of the world's first Underground railway, this station retains many 1863 features at platform level, however, the actual building is a much later addition which dates from 1930.

The station building at Great Portland Street, designed by C.W. Clark and grade II listed.

Greenford ● Central (zone 4)

Opened 30 June 1947.

The Great Western Railway opened a station here as long ago as 1 October 1904, but this was at a lower level than the current station and served the adjacent main line tracks. The Central Line station opened as the temporary terminus of the Central Line extension in June 1947, becoming a through station when the extension was completed through to West Ruislip on 21 November 1948. A chord was built from the line from West Ealing into a bay platform between the eastbound and westbound Central Line platforms to allow interchange between mainline trains and the Underground. This bay platform still has a regular passenger service today. The lower level main line platforms adjacent to the current station fell out of use and were closed in 1963. Greenford was until 2014 the home of the last wooden escalator on the Underground, but this has now been replaced and there is now also an inclined lift.

Green Park ● Piccadilly ● Victoria ● Jubilee (zone 1)

Opened as Dover Street 15 December 1906. Renamed Green Park 18 September 1933.

Until 1969, Green Park was only served by the Piccadilly Line, but on 7 March 1969 the Victoria Line opened through here. A third line was added from 1 May 1979 when the Jubilee Line opened to Charing Cross. Now the last station on the original Jubilee before the Jubilee Line Extension (JLE) is reached, this station is today a very important interchange between the Piccadilly, Victoria and Jubilee lines.

Gunnersbury ● District (zone 3)

Opened by the London & South Western Railway as Brentford Road 1 January 1869.
Renamed Gunnersbury in 1871. First served by the Underground 1 June 1877.

Opened by the London & South Western Railway, today Gunnersbury is served by both the District Line and London Overground services, with these trains parting company at Gunnersbury Junction at the east end of the platforms.

Hainault ● Central (zone 4)

Opened by the Great Eastern Railway 1 May 1903.
First served by the Underground 31 May 1948.

Hainault is a three platform station which still retains a lot of Great Eastern Railway features on platform 1. Most trains from the west terminate here, with a roughly 20 minute interval service continuing via Chigwell to Woodford. To the north of the platforms is the large Hainault Depot, one of two main depots serving the Central Line.

Hammersmith ● Hammersmith & City ● Circle (zone 2)

Original station opened 13 June 1864, closed 30 November 1868.
Current station opened 1 December 1868.

When the Hammersmith branch opened in 1864, the original terminus was sited slightly further to the north, with the station being relocated to the present site in 1868. The current station dates from a rebuild by the GWR in 1907 and bench seats with the letters GWR on them can still be found on the platforms to this day. Some of these have the later style of lettering not associated with the GWR until the 1930s, by which time the GWR had no involvement with the Hammersmith branch, so they must be replicas.

Hammersmith is a three platform terminus station located on the opposite side of Hammersmith Broadway to the Hammersmith station which serves the District and Piccadilly lines. It is a very short walk between the two stations, although there is no physical connection. To accommodate the new S Stock trains which are longer than the C Stock trains that they replaced, the buffer stops were moved further towards the Broadway. At the north end of the station is a footbridge which is very lightly used as passengers enter the station at the buffer stop end and go straight to the next departing train. This footbridge used to extend westwards to link the station with the Grove Road platforms on the L&SWR's Addison Road to Richmond line. Beyond the north end of the station is Hammersmith Depot, which has been reduced to stabling point status.

Hammersmith ● District ● Piccadilly (zone 2)

Opened 9 September 1874.

Opened by the Metropolitan District Railway as a terminus in 1874, this became a through station when the MDR was extended to join up with the L&SWR at Studland Road Junction from 1 June 1877. On 15 December 1906, it became the western terminus of the Great Northern, Piccadilly & Brompton Railway (Piccadilly Line), which too was projected west from 4 July 1932. In the 1990s, the station buildings were demolished to make way for the Hammersmith Broadway shopping complex and bus station. Part of the façade of the H.W.Ford-designed building dating back to 1906 that was demolished has been incorporated into one of the walls close to the exit.

Located within the Hammersmith Broadway shopping complex this is a modern four platform through station with cross platform interchange between the District and Piccadilly lines. Travelling west from here, the Piccadilly runs non-stop to Acton Town, with the District calling at all stations. Interchange with the Circle and Hammersmith & City lines is also possible via a short walk across Hammersmith Broadway. It is also easy to interchange with local bus services at the adjacent Hammersmith bus station. Look out for the station clocks which have the colours of the two lines that serve the station and the colour-coded platform lighting surrounds (blue along the Piccadilly Line and green along the District Line).

Hampstead ● Northern (zones 2 and 3)
Opened 22 June 1907.

This is the deepest station on the entire London Underground at 58.5 metres below the surface. If you fancy some exercise, take the stairs instead of the lift - there are only 320 of them! The depth of this station is more to do with the ground going up than the railway going down, as by the next station at Golders Green, the line emerges into daylight. Between Hampstead and Golders Green is a station which never opened called North End (often referred to as Bull & Bush), although it was excavated at track level. Had it opened, it would have taken the title for deepest station away from Hampstead as it is 67 metres below the ground.

Hampstead station was to have been called Heath Street. This proposed name is shown in tiles on the platform walls (pictured right) which have been restored in recent years. On the surface, this station boasts a fine example of a Leslie Green station building.

Hanger Lane ● Central (zone 3)
Opened 30 June 1947.

Located beneath the Hanger Lane gyratory where the A40 Western Avenue meets the A406 North Circular Road, the station building is in the centre of the gyratory and is reached by several passenger subways.

Harlesden ● Bakerloo (zone 3)
Opened 15 June 1912. First served by the Underground 16 April 1917.

Located on the Watford DC Line to the north of Willesden Junction, Harlesden station was opened by the London & North Western Railway and retains many LNWR features. It was not served by Bakerloo trains until 1917; today the station is served by both the Bakerloo Line and London Overground.

Harrow & Wealdstone ● Bakerloo (zone 5)
Opened 8 July 1837.
First served by the Underground 16 April 1917 until 24 September 1982.
Re-served from 4 June 1984 onwards.

The first station here was opened by the London & Birmingham Railway in 1837. It was expanded and remodelled for the introduction of DC electric services to Watford Junction from London Euston in 1912 (known as the Watford DC lines). The DC lines were routed through platforms 1 and 2, which had previously been the northbound and southbound main lines of the London & Birmingham Railway. Bakerloo Line services were introduced over the Watford DC lines from 16 April 1917, with the Bakerloo running through to Watford Junction. This arrangement lasted until 24 September 1982 when Bakerloo Line services were cut back to Stonebridge Park. They were re-introduced from 4 June 1984, but only as far as Harrow & Wealdstone, which is now the northern terminus of the Bakerloo. London Overground services from London Euston continue beyond here to Watford Junction, while Bakerloo Line trains go into a centre reversing siding to the north of the station where the driver changes ends ready to form the next southbound working. Interchange is available here with the Overground and also with various local electric services which call at the adjacent Network Rail platforms. The Bakerloo and Overground serve platforms 1 and 2, with Network Rail services using platforms 3 to 6.

Harrow & Wealdstone will forever be remembered for the terrible crash that happened here on the morning of 8 October 1952 when a Perth to Euston express crashed into the rear of a stationary local train. The wreckage was then run into by a Euston to Manchester and Liverpool express. In total, 112 people lost their lives that day and more than 300 people were seriously injured. A memorial plaque is located on the station building.

Harrow-on-the-Hill ● Metropolitan (zone 5)

Opened as Harrow 2 August 1880.
Renamed Harrow-on-the-Hill 1 June 1894.

Harrow-on-the-Hill has six platforms and is served by Chiltern Railways services as well as Metropolitan Line trains, with interchange possible between the two. Platform 1 is used by northbound Chiltern Railways services and also by northbound Metropolitan Line trains that are going to run fast north of Harrow-on-the-Hill. Platform 2 is served by southbound Chiltern Railways services, and can also be used by Metropolitan Line trains, but only by those from the north which are terminating at Harrow-on-the-Hill as the conductor rails end at the south end of the platform. Platforms 3 and 4 are normally used by northbound Metropolitan trains with southbound Metropolitan trains serving platforms 5 and 6. A reversing siding is located between platforms 4 and 5 at the north end of the station. The light box train describers on the platforms here were removed during 2016 and replaced by new digital dot matrix indicators.

North of the station is the junction where the Uxbridge branch diverges from the main route to Watford, Chesham, Amersham and Aylesbury.

Hatton Cross ● Piccadilly (zones 5 and 6)

Opened 19 July 1975.

This was the first station on the Heathrow extension to open and formed the terminus of the line until the opening of Heathrow Central on 16 December 1977. Further development took place with the opening of Heathrow Terminal 4 on 12 April 1986, the junction for the Terminal 4 loop being just west of Hatton Cross. Look out for the former 'Speedbird' emblem of Imperial Airways, British Overseas Airways Corporation (BOAC) and British Airways in the tiling.

Heathrow Terminals 2 & 3 ● Piccadilly (zone 6)

Opened 16 December 1977 as Heathrow Central.
Renamed Heathrow Central Terminals 1, 2 & 3 3 September 1983, Heathrow Terminals 1, 2 & 3 12 April 1986 and Heathrow Terminals 2 & 3 in 2016 (on maps only).

Shown on the Underground map from 2016 as Heathrow Terminals 2 & 3, signage on the platforms still states Heathrow Terminals 1, 2 & 3, as do train destination displays. The renaming on maps is due to the fact that Terminal 1 of the airport closed in June 2015 and has been demolished to make way for a larger Terminal 2. Originally a terminus, this became a through station with the opening of the Heathrow Terminal 4 loop in 1986. A scissors crossover to the east of the station allows trains to reverse here. Few are timetabled to do so, as the station is served by eastbound trains coming from either Heathrow Terminal 4 or Heathrow Terminal 5 and by westbound trains going to Heathrow Terminal 5.

Heathrow Terminal 4 ● Piccadilly (zone 6)

Opened 12 April 1986.

Terminal 4 is located on a single track clockwise loop which branches off the main line to the west of Hatton Cross. Trains arriving here immediately form one back towards Central London via Terminals 2 & 3.

Heathrow Terminal 5 ● Piccadilly (zone 6)
Opened 27 March 2008.
The Terminal 5 branch is the newest section of the Underground. Platform 5 is set down only and platform 6 is pick up only. Trains reverse in a pair of sidings to the west of the station.

Hendon Central ● Northern (zones 3 and 4)
Opened 19 November 1923.
This was the temporary terminus of the Northern's Edgware branch from 19 November 1923 until 18 August 1924. To the north of the platforms, the line goes back into tube tunnel. Originally known as Burroughs Tunnel and subsequently as Hendon Tunnel, it takes the Northern Line beneath the Midland Main Line and the M1 motorway.

High Barnet ● Northern (zone 5)
Opened by the Great Northern Railway 1 April 1872.
First served by the Underground 14 April 1940.
Terminus of the Northern Line, High Barnet was opened by the Great Northern Railway in 1872 and became part of the Underground in 1940. The station has three platforms, alongside which is a fan of sidings where trains stable outside traffic hours. The buildings here are of GNR origin and include a disused signal box at the south end of platform 1, which is in good condition.

High Street Kensington ● Circle ● District (zone 1)
Opened as Kensington (High Street) 1 October 1868.
Renamed High Street Kensington by 1880.
First opened by the Metropolitan Railway in 1868, High Street Kensington today consists of four platforms. 1 and 2 are through platforms which are served by Circle Line and District Line trains operating between Edgware Road and Wimbledon. Platforms 3 and 4 are bays served by terminating District Line services. To the south of the station is the junction where District Line trains go to and from Earl's Court and Circle Line trains go to and from Gloucester Road.

Entrance to the station from the High Street is via a shopping arcade which features an octagonal circulating area ringed with shops, which was part of a station rebuild dating from 1907, designed by George Sherrin. The letters MR (Metropolitan Railway) and DR (District Railway) can be found on the walls of the octagon above the main station entrance.

Highbury & Islington ● Victoria (zone 2)
Opened 1 September 1968.
The first station here dates from 1850 and was opened by the North London Railway. The Great Northern & City Railway opened a deep level station in 1904 as part of its line between Moorgate and Finsbury Park. The Victoria Line was opened through here in 1968 and today interchanges with the former Great Northern & City Line (now served by Great Northern class 313 EMUs) and London Overground services on the East London and North London lines. The original GN&CR station building still survives (disused) on the opposite side of the road to the current station entrance. A re-arrangement of platforms here to accommodate the Victoria Line saw a new platform constructed for the northbound former GN&CR line from Moorgate, while the southbound Victoria Line uses what used to be the northbound GN&CR platform.

The Victoria Line seat recesses show a castle on a hill. The term 'bury' is an old English word meaning castle or manor. In 1271, a manor was built on a hill nearby (destroyed in 1381), giving the name of Highbury to the area.

Highgate ● Northern (zone 3)

Opened 19 January 1941.

Highgate has a low level station (in deep level tube) and an abandoned high level station. Interchange between the two was available from 19 January 1941 until British Railways closed the high level station on 3 July 1954. The high level was to have become part of the Northern Line's Finsbury Park to Edgware, High Barnet and Alexandra Palace 'Northern Heights' project, but this was shelved. The abandoned station above ground is still in situ. The low level platforms are served by Northern Line trains on the High Barnet branch and are unusual in having platforms much longer than the trains that serve them. This came about due to a plan to ease overcrowding through the use of 9-car trains (the normal length being 7 cars at the time). The platforms here were built to accommodate 9 cars. The intention was that passengers travelling to Tottenham Court Road would board the rear two cars, which would remain in the tunnels at each station, but the train would draw forward to allow passengers to alight at Tottenham Court Road. This method of operation was introduced on the Edgware branch before the war, but ceased during it. Highgate tube station wasn't opened until nearly two years into the war. 9-car train operation was not resumed after hostilities ended, so Highgate was never used by 9-car trains despite being built to accommodate them.

Hillingdon ● Metropolitan ● Piccadilly (zone 6)

Original station opened as Hillingdon 10 December 1923.
Renamed Hillingdon (Swakeleys) April 1934. Suffix gradually dropped.
Station closed 5 December 1992.
Current station opened 6 December 1992.

Hillingdon was the last station to open on the Uxbridge branch on 10 December 1923 as Hillingdon (Swakeleys). The current station, which opened in 1992, is slightly closer to Uxbridge than the original, which was closed to make way for the A40 Western Avenue diversion. Although shown on the Underground map as just Hillingdon, the roundels on the station still state Hillingdon (Swakeleys).

An autumnal scene as an Uxbridge bound Metropolitan Line train led by 21100 approaches Hillingdon on 6 November 2016.

Holborn ● Central ● Piccadilly (zone 1)

Piccadilly – Opened as Holborn 15 December 1906.
Renamed Holborn (Kingsway) 22 May 1933, the suffix was gradually dropped.
Central – Opened as Holborn (Kingsway) 25 September 1933. The suffix was gradually dropped.

The Piccadilly Line platforms were opened by the Great Northern, Piccadilly & Brompton Railway on 15 December 1906. The Central Line station however, which provided a much needed interchange with the Piccadilly Line, did not open until 25 September 1933 and resulted in the closure of the nearby British Museum station. Until 2016, British Museum retained a reversing siding, but it was disconnected in 2016.

On the Piccadilly Line is a junction with the Aldwych branch which was served by a 3-car shuttle train at peak times until its closure on 30 September 1994. The branch is still intact and is used for training and filming purposes. The Central Line platforms are numbered 1 (westbound) and 2 (eastbound), the Piccadilly platforms are numbered 3 (eastbound) and 4 (westbound) while the disused Aldwych branch platform is numbered 5.

Holland Park ● Central (zone 2)

Opened 30 July 1900.

This station spent the first half of 2016 closed while the lifts were replaced and a facelift at ticket hall and platform level was performed. It had a 1960's look prior to this refurbishment but now has a much brighter appearance with new white tiling and freshly painted white walls. The old enamel station name boards have gone, but their modern equivalents have a

retro look. Dot matrix indicators have been installed as well as tactile paving close to the platform edges. Several heritage features have however been retained such as the line map on the westbound platform, the clocks and the 'Way Out' light boxes on both platforms.

The westbound platform at Holland Park showing the tactile paving, new white tiling, dot matrix indicator and station name boards. The line map, believed to date from the 1940s has been retained on the westbound - but not on the eastbound where an updated modern version has been fitted.

Holloway Road ● Piccadilly (zone 2)

Opened 15 December 1906.

This station still retains its Leslie Green designed building. Since Arsenal Football Club moved to the Emirates Stadium, this station is better placed for match day traffic than Arsenal station is, but it struggles to cope with the crowds, becoming exit only close to match time, because platform access is by lift and stairs only. A second lift shaft here was once home to an unsuccessful experimental spiral escalator, which was never used by the public. Some remains of this escalator are preserved in the London Transport Museum's Acton Depot.

Hornchurch ● District (zone 6)
Opened by the London, Tilbury & Southend Railway 1 May 1885.
First served by the Underground 2 June 1902 to 30 September 1905 and from 12 September 1932 onwards.
First opened by the London, Tilbury & Southend Railway in May 1885, Hornchurch was rebuilt in 1932 with two new platforms serving the District only. The platforms against the former LT&SR tracks became disused after 1962, but are still in place. There used to be a crossover to the west of the station that could be used to reverse trains at times of service disruption, but it was removed in January 2016.

Hounslow Central ● Piccadilly (zone 4)
Opened as Heston-Hounslow 1 April 1886.
Renamed Hounslow Central 1 December 1925.
The station building here is at street level, with the railway on an embankment above. The station building dates from 1912.

Hounslow East ● Piccadilly (zone 4)
Opened as Hounslow Town 2 May 1909.
Renamed Hounslow East 1 December 1925.
This station was opened by the Metropolitan District Railway as Hounslow Town in 1909 to replace the terminus of the same name and remove the need for reversing (see District Line history on page 73). It was renamed Hounslow Central on 1 December 1925. The station building dates from a rebuild in 2002.

Hounslow West ● Piccadilly (zone 5)
Opened as Hounslow Barracks 21 July 1884.
Renamed Hounslow West 1 December 1925.
This station was the original terminus of the Metropolitan District Railway, and remained as a terminus until the Heathrow extension was built in the 1970s. To accommodate the extension, new platforms had to be built and track slewed onto a new alignment, with the terminus platforms closing and replacements opening on 14 July 1975. The station building was designed by Stanley Heaps in conjunction with Charles Holden, in a style similar to those the on Northern Line's Morden extension. It was built in 1931 and features a heptagonal ticket hall clad in Portland Stone. The station building and car park are on the site of the old terminus with a covered walkway linking it to the current building.

Hyde Park Corner ● Piccadilly (zone 1)
Opened 15 December 1906.
Access to this station is by subway only, however the original station building still survives and now forms part of a hotel. It is located on the opposite side of the road to Hyde Park itself and is easily identifiable by its Leslie Green red tiled façade.

Ickenham ● Metropolitan ● Piccadilly (zone 6)
Opened 25 September 1905.
The Metropolitan Railway opened its line to Uxbridge through here on 4 July 1904, at which time there was only one intermediate stop at Ruislip. Following pressure from Ickenham Parish Council, the MR - reluctant to build a station here - opened a small halt with short platforms, which were eventually extended to accommodate full length trains in 1922. The station was rebuilt in 1970/71.

Kennington ● Northern (zone 2)

Opened 18 December 1926.

At street level, Kennington is the only former City & South London Railway station to retain its station building, complete with the dome, which houses the winding gear for the lifts. Kennington is also the junction on the Northern Line where the two branches through central London (Charing Cross branch and Bank branch) meet. During normal daytime operation, only a few trains run through to Morden via the Charing Cross branch, with most terminating in platform 2 then proceeding round the Kennington loop to platform 1 to form a northbound train via Charing Cross. During 'Night Tube', all trains on the Charing Cross branch are booked to run to and from Morden. Trains via the Bank branch use platform 3 (northbound) and platform 4 (southbound). There is interchange between platforms 1 and 3 and platforms 2 and 4, making it easy for passengers arriving on a southbound train from the Charing Cross branch to change onto one heading towards Morden, or for those on a train heading for the Bank branch to change onto one via Charing Cross. There is also a central reversing siding to the south of the station which can be reached by southbound trains from either branch; any train leaving the siding can depart via Bank or via Charing Cross. Of note is platform 3, which is used by northbound trains via Bank. When built, it was on the right of trains as they entered the station. To accommodate the Charing Cross branch when it was extended to here in 1926, platform 3 was altered so that it is on the left as trains enter the station. The outline of some of the entrances onto the old platform can just be made out in the wall opposite platform 3 if you look carefully.

Kensal Green ● Bakerloo (zone 2)

Opened 1 October 1916.

The station is located at the London end of the 317 yard long Kensal Green tunnel. Opened in 1916, the platform buildings are of LNWR origin, but the station building at street level is a much more modern affair dating from 1980. Kensal Green is served by Bakerloo Line trains and also the London Overground's London Euston to Watford Junction service.

Kensington (Olympia) ● District (zone 2)

Opened by the West London Railway as Addison Road 2 June 1862.
First served by the Underground 1 July 1864.
Renamed Kensington Addison Road in 1868 and Kensington (Olympia) in 1946.

The first Underground trains to reach here were Metropolitan Railway trains which turned off the Hammersmith branch at Latimer Road. This line closed on 19 October 1940 after suffering bomb damage. The Metropolitan District Railway had built a connection between Earl's Court and Kensington Addison Road which opened on 1 February 1872. This link allowed the London & North Western Railway to operate a service between Broad Street and Mansion House via Willesden Junction and Earl's Court, the Great Western Railway to operate a service from Moorgate Street to Mansion House via Paddington and Earl's Court and District trains to reach Lillie Bridge depot. The District first served Kensington (Olympia), mostly during exhibitions, from 20 December 1946 and regularly from 7 April 1986. The current single track bay platform dates from 1958. The physical track connection between the District and the main line here was removed in 1992.

Today the Olympia branch usually works as a shuttle to and from High Street Kensington at weekends, Bank Holidays and when there is an exhibition taking place at Olympia. District trains use platform 1, while Network Rail trains use platforms 2 and 3. The Olympia end of the District's branch is single track, becoming double at Earl's Court Junction and then joining the District's Ealing Broadway and Richmond branch between West Kensington and Earl's Court.

Kentish Town ● Northern (zone 2)
Opened 22 June 1907.
Kentish Town still has its original Leslie Green designed station building at street level. Interchange is available here with Network Rail Thameslink services.

Kenton ● Bakerloo (zone 2)
Opened 15 June 1912. First served by the Underground 16 April 1917.
Opened by the L&NWR, Kenton still retains its original station building, platform buildings and canopies. There are no platforms here to serve the adjacent West Coast Main Line and never have been as the station was built to serve the Watford DC tracks only. The footbridge is currently being replaced here, so a temporary footbridge has been installed at the London end of the station.

Kew Gardens ● District (zones 3 and 4)
Opened by the London & South Western Railway 1 January 1869.
First served by the Underground 1 June 1877.
This station is served by both District Line and London Overground trains. Of note is the grade II listed footbridge to the south of the station which dates from 1912 and still has high sides and smoke deflectors to protect those walking across it from soot and smoke from passing steam trains. To the north of the station, the railway crosses the River Thames on Kew Bridge, one of only two locations where the Underground passes over the Thames (the other being Fulham Rail Bridge).

Kilburn ● Jubilee (zone 2)
Opened as Kilburn & Brondesbury 24 November 1879.
Renamed Kilburn 25 September 1950.
The island platform which serves the Jubilee Line today was part of a station rebuild to coincide with the taking over of the route between Finchley Road and Stanmore by the Bakerloo Line from 20 November 1939 (later to be taken over by the Jubilee Line). The Metropolitan had called here from the station's opening in 1879 until 7 December 1940. Since then, Metropolitan trains have passed straight through, there no longer being any platforms against the Metropolitan tracks, which are on the outside of the Jubilee Line tracks. The Network Rail lines in and out of Marylebone also run parallel through here. To the south of the station, the southbound Jubilee and southbound Metropolitan pass over Kilburn High Road on an impressive steel bridge which has the words 'Metropolitan Railway' in raised letters.

Kilburn Park ● Bakerloo (zone 2)
Opened 31 January 1915.
This station boasts a very fine grade II listed station building finished in red glazed tiles to a design by Stanley Heaps. When opened in 1915, it was the temporary terminus of the Bakerloo until the next section through to Queen's Park opened on 11 February.

King's Cross St Pancras ● Metropolitan ● Hammersmith & City ● Circle ● Northern
● Piccadilly ● Victoria (zone 1)
Metropolitan, Hammersmith & City and Circle – Original station opened as King's Cross 10 January 1863.
Renamed King's Cross & St Pancras in 1925 and King's Cross St Pancras in 1933. Closed 9 March 1941.
Current station opened 14 March 1941.
Northern – Opened as King's Cross for St Pancras 12 May 1907. Renamed King's Cross St Pancras in 1933.
Piccadilly – Opened as King's Cross 15 December 1906.
Renamed King's Cross for St Pancras in 1927 and King's Cross St Pancras in 1933.
Victoria – Opened 1 December 1968.

Not only is this station a very important interchange between all the lines noted above, but it serves the main line termini of King's Cross and St Pancras International and also the Thameslink station at St Pancras. This station will of course always be remembered for the terrible fire of 18 November 1987 which claimed 31 lives. A memorial plaque and clock in the main ticket hall remembers them.

Look out for the multi-coloured passageway to Granary Square and the large passageway that runs between - and parallel to - the Metropolitan / Hammersmith & City / Circle platforms. Prior to the re-siting of the station in 1941, this used to be part of the railway tunnel. The old 'Met' platforms can be seen from trains as they depart or arrive at the east end of the current station. A new scissors crossover was installed at the west end to give greater operational flexibility at times of disruption. One train is booked to reverse here via this crossover at the end of service on weekdays.

Kingsbury Jubilee (zone 4)
Opened 10 December 1932.

Opened by the Metropolitan Railway in 1932, the station is today served by Jubilee Line trains on the Stanmore branch. It is actually on the eastern fringes of Kenton; Kingsbury itself is closer to Neasden.

Knightsbridge Piccadilly (zone 1)
Opened 15 December 1906.

The closest station to the famous Harrods Store and the surrounding fashionable shopping district, Knightsbridge has always been a busy station, which is more than can be said for the nearby Brompton Road station which closed on 29 July 1934 due to low passenger numbers.

Ladbroke Grove Hammersmith & City Circle (zone 2)
Opened as Notting Hill 13 June 1864.
Renamed Notting Hill & Ladbroke Grove in 1880, Ladbroke Grove (North Kensington) 1 June 1919 and Ladbroke Grove in 1938.

Located on the Hammersmith branch, this station serves the famous Portobello Road market and is where the elevated A40 'Westway' comes alongside. The A40 parallels the Hammersmith branch from here to Westbourne Park.

Lambeth North Bakerloo (zone 1)
Opened as Kennington Road 10 March 1906.
Renamed Westminster Bridge Road 5 August 1906, Lambeth (North) 15 April 1917 and Lambeth North circa 1928.

When opened, this station acted as the southern terminus of the Baker Street & Waterloo Railway for a short while until the rest of the line opened to Elephant & Castle on 5 August of the same year. At street level, it still retains its Leslie Green designed station building, while at platform level it can be forgiven for looking a little unkempt. The platform tunnels suffer more than their fair share of damp and water ingress which makes them look a little tatty. To the north of the station is a scissors crossover and a spur which leads to the Bakerloo Line's London Road Depot. Eleven trains stable here outside traffic hours, but the depot is often empty during the day, except for a train of 1967 Tube Stock which lives here and is used for training purposes. Lambeth North is the station to alight at for the Imperial War Museum, which also just happens to be alongside London Road Depot, which can be viewed from the corner of Lambeth Road and St George's Road (the wall is a little high though…).

Lancaster Gate ● Central (zone 1)
Opened 30 July 1900.
This station was closed from 4 January 2017 to allow the two lifts to be replaced. It is expected to re-open in July 2017.

Although not shown on the Underground map, Lancaster Gate is located within easy walking distance of Paddington mainline station. If you are travelling along the Central Line with the aim of getting to Paddington, it is quicker to alight here and walk than to change at Notting Hill Gate onto the Circle and District Lines.... or at least it will be after it re-opens!

Latimer Road ● Hammersmith & City ● Circle (zone 2)
Opened 16 December 1868.
This station was not opened until just over four years after the Hammersmith branch opened. Despite the name, Latimer Road is actually nearly half a mile from the station, which is located on the opposite side of the A40 'Westway'. At the Hammersmith end of the station, the stub of the former Latimer Road Junction can still be seen. This is where a line branched off to Addison Road (Kensington Olympia); it was damaged by a bomb in October 1940 and never re-opened.

Leicester Square ● Northern ● Piccadilly (zone 1)
Piccadilly – Opened 15 December 1906.
Northern – Opened 22 June 1907.
The bustling west end station of Leicester Square has two buildings at street level, one designed by Leslie Green and the other by Charles Holden. It offers an interchange between the Charing Cross branch of the Northern Line and the Piccadilly Line as well as serving the many pubs, clubs, restaurants, cinemas and theatres. A recent attraction close to here that may be of interest to London Underground fans is the new Lego Store on the west side of Leicester Square itself. Within the store are many items made of Lego, including an S Stock carriage and an Underground subway entrance (pictured). It is well worth a visit, though there is often a queue to get in.

Leyton ● Central (zone 3)
Opened as Low Leyton by the Eastern Counties Railway 22 August 1856.
Renamed Leyton 1868. First served by the Underground 5 May 1947.
This station pre-dates the whole Underground and was opened by the Eastern Counties Railway in 1856. The station and the line through here became a part of the Central Line from 5 May 1947. The current station buildings date from 1879.

Leytonstone ⬤ Central (zone 3)

***Opened by the Eastern Counties Railway 22
August 1856.***
First served by the Underground 5 May 1947.

The three platforms at Leytonstone are
reached by a subway beneath the line, which
also acts as a public footpath from one side
to the other. The subway is decorated with
murals celebrating the life of film maker
Alfred Hitchcock who was born in
Leytonstone. Also of note are two old
advertisements that have been preserved.

At the east end of the station, the line splits
with the Newbury Park line diving down into
tube tunnel while the Epping-bound line
continues straight and passes through
Whipps Cross Tunnel.

*One of the murals at Leytonstone depicting scenes
from Alfred Hitchcock films. This one depicts a scene
from the 1959 film 'North by Northwest'.*

Liverpool Street ⬤ Central ⬤ Metropolitan ⬤ Hammersmith & City ⬤ Circle (zone 1)

Metropolitan, Hammersmith & City and Circle - Opened as Bishopsgate 12 July 1875.
Renamed Liverpool Street 1 November 1909.
Central – Opened 28 July 1912.

Sitting proud at the west end of the eastbound sub-surface platform is a disused (and listed)
Metropolitan Railway signal box. As well as the current two sub-surface platforms, there
also used to be a third (bay) platform for turning back eastbound trains. This has now been
partially built on and covered up and it is difficult to see where this once was.

The disused Metropolitan Railway signal box at Liverpool Street.

Heading west on a train from here, look behind the signal box as you depart and you can just see the top of the tunnel mouth that once led to the Liverpool Street mainline terminus. It was used by Metropolitan Line trains from 1 February 1875 until 11 July 1875 when the current station (then called Bishopsgate) was opened. At the east end of the station, during the daytime, look down the tunnel towards Aldgate and look for a shaft of light onto the track (pictured), a ventilation shaft that acts as a reminder that this railway was once steam worked.

The Central Line station was the eastern terminus of the Central from 28 July 1912 until 4 December 1946. There is a pair of reversing sidings in tunnel at the east end of the station, which only tend to be used at times of disruption these days.

London Bridge ● Northern ● Jubilee (zone 1)
Northern – Opened 25 February 1900.
Jubilee – Opened 7 October 1999.
The Northern Line platforms here underwent a major alteration in the 1980s when the southbound track was diverted into new tunnel and the former southbound tunnel was used to create additional space for escalators and a large circulating area to improve passenger flow. The Jubilee Line platforms here are part of the Jubilee Line Extension (JLE) and are fitted with platform edge doors. Interchange is available here between the Jubilee and Northern lines and also with the mainline railway station above ground.

Loughton ● Central (zone 6)
Opened by the Great Eastern Railway 24 April 1865.
First served by the Underground 21 November 1948.
The first station on the current site was opened by the GER in 1865, replacing the nearby terminus station opened by the Eastern Counties Railway in 1856. The current buildings, which date from 1940, were designed by John Murray Easton and are grade II listed. The platforms have reinforced concrete canopies and wooden benches with roundel nameboards as seat backs. Some trains from central London reverse here, usually in the centre platform. Loughton is currently the easternmost extremity of Central Line Night Tube operations.
On the Woodford side of the station is a fan of sidings where ten trains stable outside traffic hours.

Maida Vale ● Bakerloo (zone 2)
Opened 6 June 1915.
This station has a grade II listed building finished in red glazed tiles and designed by Stanley Heaps. Inside the entrance, look up as you descend the stairs to the ticket hall and you will see two superbly restored Underground roundel mosaics. When the Bakerloo was extended through to Kilburn Park and Queen's Park on 31 January 1915, Maida Vale station was not ready and trains ran non-stop through here until 6 June 1915.

Manor House ● Piccadilly (zones 2 and 3)
Opened 19 September 1932.
Located on the Piccadilly's Cockfosters extension, Manor House has the plainest buildings of all the stations on this section of line and as such they are the only ones that are not grade II listed.

Mansion House ● District ● Circle (zone 1)
Opened 3 July 1871.
One of only two station names on the entire Underground that contains all of the vowels (the other being South Ealing). Mansion House was opened by the Metropolitan District Railway in 1871 and was the eastern terminus of the MDR's line until a further extension, opened on 6 October 1884, took it to Mark Lane (completing the 'inner circle') and on to Whitechapel. The three track layout here was reduced to two in 2016 with the removal of the track in platform 2 during the weekend of 8/9 October. The crossover at the west end of the station was also removed, so eastbound trains can no longer be reversed and sent back west. The hydraulic buffer stop at the east end of platform 2 is still in situ, but with the hydraulic ram pushed in.

The view from platform 3 at Mansion House showing platform 2 which is now devoid of track. An eastbound District Line service led by 21557 is entering the station. 22 October 2016.

Marble Arch ● Central (zone 1)
Opened 30 July 1900.
Located at the west end of Oxford Street, this station takes its name from the white marble triumphal arch which stands opposite and which used to stand in front of Buckingham Palace. A reversing siding to the west of the station can be used to turn back westbound trains, but is only used at times of service disruption. The station is decorated by 17 different murals created by Annabel Grey as part of a renovation in the early 1980s.

Marylebone ● Bakerloo (zone 1)
Opened as Great Central 27 March 1907.
Renamed Marylebone 15 April 1917.
Opened with the name Great Central (the name of the railway company that served the mainline terminus above) in 1907, the station had its name changed to Marylebone in April 1917. At the north end of the northbound platform, the name Great Central can still be seen in the tiles on the wall (as pictured right).

Mile End ● District ● Hammersmith & City ● Central (zone 2)
District and Hammersmith & City – Opened 2 June 1902.
Central – Opened 4 December 1946.
Mile End has four platforms: the centre two are used by the sub-surface District and Hammersmith & City lines, while the outer two are used by the tube sized Central Line. This is the only place on the entire Underground network where cross platform interchange between sub-surface and tube takes place beneath the ground. The station was first opened on 2 June 1902 by the Metropolitan District Railway. The Central Line reached here on 4 December 1946, when that line was extended from Liverpool Street to Stratford. The name Mile End comes from a milestone nearby which marks a distance of one mile from the boundary of the City of London. The station took its name from the road on which it is located, although the milestone itself is actually closer to Stepney Green station. Note the roundel above the entrance which still says 'London Transport'.

Mill Hill East ● Northern (zone 4)
Opened as Mill Hill by the Great Northern Railway 22 August 1867.
Renamed Mill Hill East for Mill Hill Barracks 1 March 1928 and Mill Hill East 18 May 1941.
First served by the Underground 18 May 1941.
Served by a single track branch from Finchley Central, Mill Hill East is located on what used to be a through route to Edgware. Passenger services were operated by the LNER until September 1939 and the Northern Line took over from 18 May 1941. It was proposed that Northern Line trains would be projected through to Edgware, but this never happened and the line was only ever electrified as far as Mill Hill East. Freight trains continued to use the line to Edgware until 1964, after which the line beyond Mill Hill East was lifted. Despite being only a very short single track branch, it can claim an Underground record, as it features the impressive Dollis Brook viaduct that stands 60 feet above the ground, the highest point above the ground on the entire Underground.

Monument ● District ● Circle (zone 1)
Opened as Eastcheap 6 October 1884.
Renamed The Monument 1 November 1884. The prefix was gradually dropped.
This station is linked to the large Bank complex and therefore offers interchange with the Docklands Light Railway and the Central, Northern and Waterloo & City lines. It is named after the large stone Doric column which marks the spot where the Great Fire of London started in September 1666.

Moorgate ● Metropolitan ● Hammersmith & City ● Circle ● Northern (zone 1)
Metropolitan, Hammersmith & City and Circle – Opened as Moorgate Street 23 December 1865.
Renamed Moorgate 24 October 1924.
Northern – Opened as Moorgate Street 25 February 1900. Renamed Moorgate 20 April 1924.
In the sub-surface part of the station, the abandoned platforms of the former City Widened Lines are still in situ, although now without track. The two bay platforms here (3 and 4) are used to turn back trains from the west. The area around Moorgate was badly damaged during the war; the 1960s redevelopment involved rebuilding the station and covering it over with buildings. At a deeper level, Moorgate is served by the Bank branch of the Northern Line and the former Great Northern & City Railway platforms are now served by Great Northern class 313 EMUs running to and from Welwyn Garden City and Stevenage.

Moor Park ● Metropolitan (zones 6 and 7)
Opened as Sandy Lodge 9 May 1910.
Renamed Moor Park & Sandy Lodge 18 October 1923 and Moor Park 25 September 1950.
Platforms 1 and 2 here are only used when the Metropolitan Line is operating fast services; all other trains use platforms 3 and 4. Chiltern Railways trains do not call here. To the north of the station is Watford South Junction where the Watford route diverges from the Amersham and Chesham route.

Morden ● Northern (zone 4)
Opened 13 September 1926.

The station building here is a Charles Holden design in Portland Stone. With the development of surrounding buildings, only the front is now visible. There are three tracks through the station, but with platform faces on both sides of two of the tracks, there are five platforms. This is the most southerly station on the entire Underground, but the railway continues south of here to Morden Depot, making that the most southerly point reached by the entire Underground. To the north, just a short distance from the platform ends, the line enters tunnel. The first part of this tunnel is cut and cover, changing to tube tunnel at the north end of Kenley Road. If a train travels from Morden to High Barnet via Bank, it will be in tunnel for 17.25 miles until it emerges into the open at East Finchley, the longest continuous tunnel on the Underground.

Mornington Crescent ● Northern (zone 2)
Opened 22 June 1907.

The Underground map tells a little lie here, as it shows the Charing Cross branch through Mornington Crescent to the west of the Bank branch, when it is in fact to its east. The two branches cross over each other close to Euston. Mornington Crescent still has its original Leslie Green station building. When opened, passengers entered the lifts down to the platforms directly from the street, and exiting passengers were deposited directly onto the street from the exit lifts. Today, the position of the entrance lifts forms the main entrance to the station where ticket machines and the gateline are located. The current lifts are located in the position of the original exit lifts, although passengers now access them from inside the station building. The decorative grilles above where passengers used to exit the lifts onto the street are still in situ and marked as '1' and '2' as seen in the accompanying photograph. The station was closed from October 1992 until April 1998 for lift replacement work; at one time it was feared that it might remain closed; but thankfully this did not happen. A memorial plaque to the late Willie Rushton is located in the ticket hall. Willie Rushton was one of the panellists on the BBC Radio 4 panel game 'I'm Sorry I Haven't A Clue' which features a game called 'Mornington Crescent'.

Neasden ● Jubilee (zone 3)
Opened as Kingsbury & Neasden 2 August 1880.
Renamed to Neasden & Kingsbury 1 January 1910 and to Neasden 1 January 1932.

Originally served by the Metropolitan, 'Met' trains ceased to call here regularly after 7 December 1940. From 20 November 1939, Bakerloo Line trains called here as that line took over Stanmore services from the Metropolitan. In 1979, the Stanmore services were taken over by the Jubilee Line and Neasden has been served by the Jubilee ever since. Metropolitan Line trains can still call here at times of service disruption and S Stock marker boards are fitted at the platform ends. Look out for several fixed train stops on the Jubilee Line tracks. These are to prevent a wrongly routed Metropolitan Line train from proceeding along the Jubilee Line tracks towards the tube tunnel at Finchley Road, Neasden being the last location where a Metropolitan train could be wrongly routed.

Newbury Park ⬤ Central (zone 4)
Opened by the Great Eastern Railway 1 May 1903.
First served by the Underground 14 December 1947.
Newbury Park was opened in 1903 by the Great Eastern Railway as part of its Ilford to Woodford via Hainault route. Central Line trains reached here on 14 December 1947 via the tunnel section through Redbridge from Leytonstone, then operated north of here from 31 May 1948 (although empty stock movements between Newbury Park and Hainault Depot had run prior to this). The former GER line to and from Ilford was closed and lifted, although traces can still be seen at the Newbury Park end of the station between where the Central Line tracks part to go into tube tunnel. Several trains from central London terminate here using the centre reversing siding on the Hainault side of the station. This siding is double ended and is also used in the autumn to reverse the Rail Adhesion Train after it arrives here from the Hainault direction. Newbury Park station still retains many GER features; also of note is the grade II listed bus station alongside the station entrance which features a copper clad barrel vaulted roof.

Under the copper clad barrel vaulted roof of the adjacent bus station, the entrance to Newbury Park Underground station can be seen on the right of the picture. This picture was taken during 2016, despite the profusion of vintage buses. RTL554, RTL139 and RM1962 were on a photographic tour of London during the small hours of 7 February 2016.

North Acton ⬤ Central (zones 2 and 3)
Opened 5 November 1923.
This station was upgraded in the 1990s, when the eastbound platform was converted into an island platform so that a third could be added. Today, platform 1 is normally used by westbound trains and platform 3 by eastbound trains. Platform 2 is mostly used by trains that reverse here. To the west of the station is North Acton Junction where the West Ruislip lines and the Ealing Broadway lines split.

North Ealing ⬤ Piccadilly (zone 3)
Opened 23 June 1903.
Opened by the Metropolitan District Railway on in 1903, North Ealing still retains a fine example of a District Railway station building.

Northfields ● Piccadilly (zone 3)

Original station opened as Northfield (Ealing) 16 April 1908.
Renamed Northfields & Little Ealing 11 December 1911 and closed 18 May 1932.
Current station opened as Northfields 19 May 1932.

The original station, opened by the District Railway in 1908, was slightly further west than the current one. It was closed in 1932 and replaced by the current station just prior to the introduction of Piccadilly Line services. Today, Northfields is a four track station with a fine example of a Charles Holden designed station building. At one time there was a separate entrance from Weymouth Avenue to the east and the remains of a concrete walkway can still be seen. At the west end of the station is Northfields Depot, one of two main depots on the Piccadilly Line. Beyond Northfields, the Piccadilly reduces down to two tracks towards Heathrow.

North Greenwich ● Jubilee (zones 2 and 3)

Opened 14 May 1999.

A three platform station on the JLE, the centre platform is used mainly to reverse trains from the central London direction, several of which are booked to do so. All platforms have platform edge doors fitted. This is the station to use for the O2 Arena and the Emirates Air Line, which is a cable car which crosses over the River Thames. There is also a large bus interchange here.

North Harrow ● Metropolitan (zone 5)

Opened 22 March 1915.

Although opened in 1915, the current station buildings date from 1930 and were designed by Charles Clark. This station only has platforms on the local lines, with the northbound and southbound main lines passing alongside.

Northolt ● Central (zone 5)

Opened 21 November 1948.

Located on the West Ruislip branch of the Central Line, this station has a centre reversing siding which is used by several trains which are timetabled to turn back here. The Network Rail line between Old Oak Common West Junction and Northolt Junction runs parallel to the Central Line here.

North Wembley ● Bakerloo (zone 4)

Opened 15 June 1912. First served by the Underground 16 April 1917 until 24 September 1982.
Re-served from 4 June 1984 onwards.

Situated on the Watford DC line and first opened by the London & North Western Railway, North Wembley is served by both Bakerloo Line and London Overground trains. The station still retains its LNWR station building and platform buildings.

Northwick Park ● Metropolitan (zone 4)

Opened as Northwick Park & Kenton 28 June 1923.
Renamed Northwick Park 15 March 1937.

Northwick Park station consists of an island platform which is reached via a subway. The platform serves only the northbound and southbound local lines, with the fast lines passing by outside them. The two tracks of Network Rail's Chiltern line also run parallel to the northbound fast. The station is located very close to where the West Coast Main Line, Watford DC line and Bakerloo Line pass beneath the Metropolitan and Chiltern lines. It is a very pleasant 10 minute walk across the park between Northwick Park and South Kenton stations if you wish to change lines on a nice day.

Northwood ● Metropolitan (zone 6)
Opened 1 September 1887.
Northwood station only has platforms on the local lines, with the northbound and southbound main lines passing by on the west side. Northwood has a reversing siding which can be used to turn back trains from the north. There is also a short stub siding which has been used in the past to remove redundant rolling stock for scrap.

Northwood Hills ● Metropolitan (zone 6)
Opened 13 November 1933.
Like Northwood, this station only has platforms on the local lines, but was a later addition, not opening until 1933.

Notting Hill Gate ● District ● Circle ● Central (zone 1)
Opened 1 October 1868 (Circle and District lines) and 30 July 1900 (Central Line).
The sub-surface station served by the District and Circle lines is one of the finest on the Underground. It has been sympathetically restored with replica old style lighting suspended from the roof. Interchange is available here between the sub-surface station and the deep level Central Line. Although the sub-surface station was opened by the Metropolitan Railway in 1868 and the deep level Central Line was opened by the Central London Railway in 1900, it was not until 1 March 1959 that the two were linked, both having separate entrances until then.

Oakwood ● Piccadilly (zone 5)
Opened as Enfield West 13 March 1933.
Renamed Enfield West (Oakwood) 3 May 1934 and Oakwood 1 September 1946.
One stop west of the Piccadilly's Cockfosters terminus, several trains start and finish their journeys here as it is located at the western exit of Cockfosters depot. Look very closely where the tracks enter the depot and you will find a World War II pill box guarding the depot entrance.

Old Street ● Northern (zone 1)
Opened 17 November 1901.
There is interchange between the Northern Line (Bank branch) and the former Great Northern & City Railway. To the north of the station, the Northern Line turns to the west and passes through the abandoned City Road station which closed 8 August 1922.

Osterley ● Piccadilly (zone 4)
Original station opened as Osterley & Spring Grove 1 May 1883 and closed 24 March 1934.
Current station opened as Osterley 25 March 1934.
Osterley was opened in March 1934 to replace the former Osterley & Spring Grove station, the abandoned platforms of which can still be seen at the east end of the station. The station building was designed by Stanley Heaps.

Oval ● Northern (zone 2)
Opened as The Oval 18 December 1890.
Renamed Oval circa 1894.
The station building here dates from the 1920s, but a recent refurbishment has seen it given a rather modern appearance. The station takes its name from the nearby Oval cricket ground. This is one of only two stations with only four letters in its name, the other being Bank.

Oxford Circus ● Central ● Victoria ● Bakerloo (zone 1)
Central – Opened 30 July 1900.
Bakerloo – Opened 10 March 1906.
Victoria – Opened 7 March 1969.

This station serves the busy west end shopping district and the main subway entrances are conveniently located on the corner of Oxford Street and Regent Street. The original Central London Railway and Baker Street & Waterloo Railway station buildings still exist on either side of Argyll Street and are used mainly as retail outlets, although there are exits from the station in each building.

Paddington ● District ● Circle ● Hammersmith & City ● Bakerloo (zone 1)
Circle and Hammersmith & City – Opened as Paddington Bishop's Road 10 January 1863.
Renamed Paddington 10 September 1933.
Circle and District – Opened as Paddington (Praed Street) 1 October 1868.
Renamed Paddington 11 July 1948.
Bakerloo – Opened 1 December 1913.

The sub-surface lines have two separate stations at Paddington, with Hammersmith & City and Circle line trains on the Hammersmith branch using platforms 15 and 16 alongside the mainline station.

The Circle Line, along with the District Line, also serves the station in Praed Street which is situated on the west side of the 'inner circle' and still retains its overall roof. At deep level is the Bakerloo Line. The station here is on a sharp curve and the platform walls are decorated with a design celebrating the Greathead shield and the tunnel boring machine. Recent construction work on the Bakerloo Line station is preparing new connecting passageways for the coming of the Elizabeth Line (Crossrail) which is due to open in 2018.

A train of S Stock led by 21527 arrives at Paddington platform 15 with a Hammersmith & City Line service for Hammersmith. 14 January 2017.

Park Royal ● Piccadilly (zone 3)
Original station opened as Park Royal & Twyford Abbey 23 June 1903 and closed 5 July 1931.
Current station opened as Park Royal 6 July 1931.
Renamed Park Royal (Hanger Hill) 1 March 1936 and Park Royal in 1947.

The current station was opened on 6 July 1931 ready for the Piccadilly taking over the line from the District. It replaced the former District station at Park Royal & Twyford Abbey, which closed the previous day. The station building was designed by Welch & Lander, heavily influenced by the work of Charles Holden. To the north of the station, the Piccadilly crosses over the top of the Central Line close to Hanger Lane station.

Parsons Green ● District (zone 2)
Opened 1 March 1880.

Parsons Green was opened in 1880 as part of the MDR's extension from West Brompton to Putney Bridge & Fulham. On either side of the station are sidings where seven trains stable outside traffic hours.

Perivale ● Central (zone 4)

Opened 30 June 1947.

Perivale has a delightful curved station building designed by Charles Holden which is grade II listed. It is at street level, with stairs leading up to an island platform. To the east of the station is the impressive art deco Hoover building, part of which is now a supermarket, while other areas of the building are about to be converted into luxury flats. Regardless of what is inside, the building is still very impressive to look at and is very visible from passing trains.

Piccadilly Circus ● Piccadilly ● Bakerloo (zone 1)

Opened 10 March 1906 (Bakerloo Line) and 15 December 1906 (Piccadilly Line).

The station ticket hall is well worth exploring with its circular concourse which retains many 1920's features including art deco style pillars and a linear world clock.

A 2016 addition to this area is a memorial to Frank Pick (pictured), the former Managing Director of the Underground Electric Railways Company of London and Chief Executive Officer of the London Passenger Transport Board. He was largely responsible for ensuring that the expansion of the transport systems in London was done in a considered way from a design point of view. As it says on the plaque alongside this memorial, Frank Pick had a conviction that good design contributes decisively to the quality of city life.

Down at platform level, the station is decorated in cream, green and red tiles, offset with brown tiles on the Bakerloo and blue tiles on the Piccadilly. The station layout on the Bakerloo is quite unusual, as there is a section at the north end of the platforms where the northbound and southbound tracks share the same tunnel to accommodate a trailing crossover. At one time this open section had a scissors crossover. There are very sharp curves at the ends of the Bakerloo platforms – passengers are urged to Mind the Gap!

Pimlico ● Victoria (zone 1)

Opened 14 September 1972.

The Victoria Line extension to Brixton opened on 23 July 1971, but Pimlico station did not open until 14 September 1972. It serves the Tate Britain and is the only station on the Victoria Line that does not interchange with any other Underground or Network Rail line.

Pinner ● Metropolitan (zone 5)

Opened 25 May 1885.

Opened by the Metropolitan Railway in 1885, Pinner served as the MR's northern terminus until the next section to Rickmansworth opened on 1 September 1887. The two platforms serve only the local lines, with the northbound and southbound main lines running parallel alongside the station.

Plaistow ● District ● Hammersmith & City (zone 3)
Opened by the London, Tilbury & Southend Railway in 1858.
First served by the Underground 2 June 1902.

The station buildings here date from 1905 and there are several platform canopy brackets with the letters LTSR cast into them. A bay platform at the west end of the station allows trains from the west to be turned back, but this is only used by a few trains. The Network Rail lines in and out of Fenchurch Street run parallel on the south side of the station. There are still platforms against these tracks, but they are disused and no longer cared for.

Preston Road ● Metropolitan (zone 4)
Original station opened 21 May 1908 and closed southbound 21 November 1931 and closed northbound 2 January 1932.
Current station opened southbound 22 November 1931 and opened northbound 3 January 1932.

This station has an island platform with platform faces only against the local lines. The northbound and southbound fast lines are located on the outside of the local lines while the two tracks of the Chiltern line of Network Rail run parallel alongside the northbound tracks. The station building is located on Preston Road which crosses over the railway at this point. Opened on 21 May 1908 to serve the clay pigeon shooting venue of the 1908 Olympic Games, the current station, however, dates from 1931 and is on the opposite side of Preston Road to the original.

Putney Bridge ● District (zone 2)
Opened as Putney Bridge & Fulham 1 March 1880.
Renamed Putney Bridge & Hurlingham 1 September 1902 and Putney Bridge in 1932.

Opened as the Putney Bridge & Fulham terminus of the MDR on 1 March 1880, it became a through station after Fulham Rail Bridge opened in 1889. The name Putney Bridge is a little misleading as Putney is on the opposite side of the River Thames; the station is in fact named after the nearby Putney Bridge which carries the A219 road over the River Thames. At the north end of Fulham Rail Bridge adjacent to the station is a World War II pill box which was built to guard the railway bridge.

The revised layout at Putney Bridge with two trains of S Stock passing. The track in platform 3 can just be made out above the WWII pill box, but this is redundant, having been disconnected at both ends.

Since the last book, there have been a number of alterations at Putney Bridge with the track in platform 2 and the large hydraulic buffer stop against which it ended, both removed. This platform was only long enough to reverse trains of C Stock and could not accommodate the longer D Stock and S Stock trains. With the C Stock now withdrawn, there was little need for this track. A remodelling of the layout during May 2016 saw the westbound track diverted through platform 2, the crossover removed and platform 3 taken out of use.

Queensbury ● Jubilee (zone 4)
Opened 16 December 1934.

What do you do if you build a railway station in the middle of nowhere and that place does not have a name? Make a name up of course! This is how Queensbury got its name. The Metropolitan opened the station here in 1934 in what were open fields at the time in the hope that it would attract residential development. As the next station down the line was Kingsbury, the name of Queensbury was decided on. Of interest here is the roundabout opposite the station on which a large roundel is mounted.

Queen's Park ● Bakerloo (zone 2)
Opened by the London & North Western Railway 2 June 1879.
First served by the Underground 11 February 1915.

The first station here was opened by the LNWR in 1879 on their London to Birmingham route. The railway was expanded here in 1912 with the building of the Watford DC line (often referred to as the 'new line') between London Euston and Watford Junction. It was built to increase suburban capacity, while keeping the slower trains out of the way of the expresses on the adjacent main line. The Bakerloo Line was extended from Kilburn Park to Queen's Park on 11 February 1915; they share tracks with the Watford DC trains (now operated by London Overground) north of here.

Queen's Park is where the Bakerloo Line rises out of tube tunnel from central London (or descends into it depending on your direction of travel). Alongside is Queen's Park South Carriage Shed where four trains stable outside traffic hours. The southbound and northbound Watford DC tracks to and from Euston are located on either side of the track formation here. Bakerloo Line trains can head towards Euston on these tracks, but only as far as Kilburn High Road, empty, to reverse. This is a rare move to witness.

The station has six platforms, two of which are located on the adjacent West Coast Main Line and are seldom used. Watford DC Line trains (now operated by London Overground class 378s) use platform 1 southbound and platform 4 northbound. Bakerloo Line trains use the two middle platforms (2 southbound and 3 northbound). To the north of the station platforms is Queen's Park North Carriage Shed. The Watford DC Lines pass at either side while the Bakerloo tracks merge with them on the north side of the carriage shed, which has four roads numbered 21 to 24. Roads 22 and 23 are used to reverse trains that terminate at Queen's Park, while road 21 is used by northbound Bakerloo trains and road 24 is used by southbound Bakerloo trains. This means that passengers actually pass through the shed. Outside traffic hours, all four roads can be used to stable trains.

Queensway ● Central (zone 1)
Opened as Queen's Road 30 July 1900.
Renamed Queensway 1 September 1946.

There used to be a reversing siding to the east of the station, but it has been removed and replaced (unusually) with a facing crossover. The position of vertical supports and tunnel walls did not allow enough room for a trailing crossover. It is only used to turn back trains at times of disruption and can be used in both directions. The station still retains its original Central London Railway station building designed by Harry Bell Measures.

Ravenscourt Park ● District (zone 2)

Opened by the London & South Western Railway as Shaftesbury Road 1 January 1869.
First served by the Underground 1 June 1877.
Renamed Ravenscourt Park 1 March 1888.

Although this is listed as a District station and only District Line trains call here, Piccadilly Line trains also pass through non-stop. To the east of the station can be seen the remains of the old Studland Road Junction where the line to Hammersmith Grove Road and Addison Road used to branch away.

Rayners Lane ● Metropolitan ● Piccadilly (zone 5)

Opened 26 May 1906.

At the London end of the station is Rayners Lane Junction where the Piccadilly and the Metropolitan join together before they share tracks all the way to Uxbridge. Some Piccadilly Line trains terminate here and reverse using the central reversing siding at the west end of the station. The station was opened in 1906 and takes its name from a local farmer of the time. The station buildings date from a rebuild in the 1930s and were designed by Charles Holden and Reginald Uren.

Left: Rayners Lane station building, designed by Charles Holden and Reginald Uren. Right: A Piccadilly Line train of 1973 Tube Stock in the reversing siding at Rayners Lane. Note the central position of the points, set like this as a safety measure to prevent a train from running away onto the main lines.

Redbridge ● Central (zone 4)

Opened December 1947.

Situated on the Leytonstone to Newbury Park section, Redbridge is a mere 17 feet below the ground and was built using the cut and cover method with the tracks descending into tube tunnel at either end.

Regent's Park ● Bakerloo (zone 1)

Opened 10 March 1906.

This is one of the quietest stations in central London with only around three million passengers starting or finishing their journeys here. There are no station buildings and access is via a subway entrance on Marylebone Road. Although not listed as a connection on the Underground map, it is very easy to change from here to the Metropolitan, Hammersmith & City and Circle lines at Great Portland Street, as it is only a very short walk between the two stations. Very handy if you want to avoid the hustle and bustle of Baker Street.

Richmond ● District (zone 4)

Opened by the London & South Western Railway 1 January 1869.
First served by the Underground 1 June 1877.

Richmond station is served by the District Line, London Overground and Network Rail. Platforms 4 to 7 are all suitable for use by Underground trains and all are terminal platforms.

Rickmansworth ● Metropolitan (zone 7)

Opened 1 September 1887.

A fan of five sidings to the south of the station, two to the north and number 23 siding alongside the northbound line to the south of the station (which can hold two trains) are used for stabling nine trains outside traffic hours. The station is on a curve with a water tower still at the north end that dates back to the days of steam. At the south end is a bay platform, but the track here has been disconnected.

Roding Valley ● Central (zone 4)

Opened by the London & North Eastern Railway 3 February 1936.
First served by the Underground 21 November 1948.

This is officially the least used station on the Underground with an average of less than 600 passengers per day. It is on the Hainault loop, but it is very close to Woodford Junction where the Hainault loop splits from the Epping line.

Royal Oak ● Hammersmith & City ● Circle (zone 2)

Opened 30 October 1871.

Located alongside the throat of Paddington mainline terminus, the station is formed of an island platform serving only the Underground lines, but at one time it also had platforms on the main line too.

Ruislip ● Metropolitan ● Piccadilly (zone 6)

Opened 4 July 1904.

When the Metropolitan Railway opened its line from Harrow-on-the-Hill to Uxbridge in 1904, Ruislip was the only intermediate station. The station buildings date from that time. There is also a Metropolitan Railway signal box at the London end of the station, but it hasn't signalled a train since the mid 1970s, although it has recently been restored (it is a listed building).

Ruislip station and footbridge.

Ruislip Gardens ● Central (zone 5)
Opened 21 November 1948.

Located alongside RAF Northolt, this is the last station before the Central Line terminus at West Ruislip. Some trains start and finish their journeys here as just to the west of the platform ends here is the entrance to Ruislip Depot.

Ruislip Manor ● Metropolitan ● Piccadilly (zone 6)
Opened 5 August 1912.

The station sits on an embankment and is reached by stairs from street level. It was not opened until 1912, although the railway through here opened in 1904.

The west end of the station, including the station entrances, was rebuilt in 1939, while the east ends of the platforms were rebuilt in 2005.

Russell Square ● Piccadilly (zone 1)
Opened 15 December 1906.

At street level, this station still retains its Leslie Green designed red tiled building and its unique design of green and cream tiling at platform level. Leslie Green stations in the central area all had their own individual tiling designs to help the illiterate to identify them. Illiteracy was more common when the line opened in 1906.

St James's Park ● District ● Circle (zone 1)
Opened 24 December 1868.

This station's entrance is incorporated into 55 Broadway, a grade II listed Portland Stone clad building designed by Charles Holden. Currently the headquarters of London Underground, LU is expected to vacate the premises soon, after which the building is likely to be converted for residential use. At platform level there is some confusion. Is the station called St James's Park or St James' Park? One roundel, at the east end of the eastbound platform, says St James' Park while all the others say St James's Park.

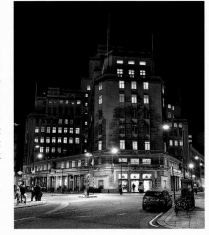

55 Broadway at night.

St John's Wood ● Jubilee (zone 2)
Opened 20 November 1939.

Opened as part of the new tube line between Baker Street and Finchley Road as part of the '1935-1940 New Works Programme', this station still retains a great deal of 1930's character including roundels and the station name cast into the ceramic tiles along the length of each platform. At street level, the station building designed by Stanley Heaps is still in place, although a block of flats has been built above it.

St Paul's ● Central (zone 4)
Opened as Post Office 30 July 1900. Renamed St Paul's 1 February 1937.

This station was opened as Post Office, a name believed to have been chosen to differentiate it from the nearby South Eastern Railway station called St Paul's. The SER station was renamed Blackfriars in 1937 and the Underground station took the name St Paul's. As the name suggests, it is conveniently located for St Paul's Cathedral. The westbound tunnel is situated directly over the eastbound tunnel here.

Seven Sisters ● Victoria (zone 3)

Opened 1 September 1968.

This is where the track to and from the Victoria Line's depot at Northumberland Park joins the main Victoria Line. The station has three platforms: number 3 is for northbound trains, 5 for southbound and platform 4 is for terminating trains from the south, and for staff special shuttles from Northumberland Park Depot. Trains can also reverse just beyond the station using the tracks leading to and from the depot, while selected trains from the south terminate here and continue to depot empty, mostly at the end of service. The tiles in the seat recesses here depict seven trees which were known as the Seven Sisters and gave the area its name (see picture, right).

Seven Sisters is the most convenient London Underground station for Tottenham Hotspur's White Hart Lane football ground and can become extremely busy on match days.

Shepherd's Bush ● Central (zone 2)

Opened 30 July 1900.

The original terminus of the Central London Railway, this has been a through station since the opening of Wood Lane on 14 May 1908. Trains heading west from here go round the Caxton curve, which is the tightest on the Underground.

Shepherd's Bush Market ● Hammersmith & City ● Circle (zone 2)

Opened as Shepherd's Bush 1 April 1914.
Renamed Shepherd's Bush Market 12 October 2008.

This station opened at the same time as Goldhawk Road and replaced the former Shepherd's Bush station which was located roughly halfway between here and Goldhawk Road and which closed on 31 March 1914. Until 2008, this station was just called Shepherd's Bush, but it was renamed to avoid confusion with the station of the same name on the Central Line.

Sloane Square ● District ● Circle (zone 1)

Opened 24 December 1868.

This station had an overall glass and steel roof which was destroyed in the war when it took a direct hit from a German bomb. Thirty-seven people were killed and the blast also destroyed the recently rebuilt station building and the newly installed escalators. The retaining walls and brackets which supported the roof can still be seen. Passing over the top of the station is what appears to be a large green pipe. This carries the River Westbourne, a small tributary of the River Thames that starts in Hampstead and flows through Kilburn and Knightsbridge and into the River Thames near to Chelsea.

Snaresbrook ● Central (zone 4)

Opened by the Eastern Counties Railway as Snaresbrook & Wanstead 22 August 1856.
Renamed Snaresbrook and first served by the Underground 14 December 1947.

Snaresbrook still retains many 19th century features including station building and ornate canopy brackets. There used to be a bay platform here on the eastbound side of the station which was used for terminating trains from the Stratford direction. This bay platform was not used by Underground trains though, first being used in 1893 and taken out of use in 1947. The area previously occupied by the bay is now part of the station car park.

South Ealing ● Piccadilly (zone 3)
Opened 1 May 1883.
South Ealing is one of two stations whose name contains all of the vowels (the other is Mansion House). It is on a four track formation which runs from Acton Town to Northfields (where it reduces to two). The two centre tracks are the fast lines, while the outer tracks are the local lines. The eastbound local also doubles up as a test track; between South Ealing and Acton Town a section is fitted with water sprays to simulate wet weather conditions.

Southfields ● District (zone 3)
Opened 3 June 1889.
The closest station to the Wimbledon Tennis Club becomes very busy during the Wimbledon Tennis Championships. The island platform is usually decorated as a tennis court during this period (as pictured below).

Southgate ● Piccadilly (zone 4)
Opened 13 March 1933.
The east end of the Piccadilly Line is above ground except for this station which is in a short section of tube tunnel beneath a hill. Looking west, it is possible to see a glimmer of daylight, but the tunnel mouth can actually be seen to the east. The station building is a circular art deco design by Charles Holden with an illuminated 'Tesla Coil' fixed to the centre of the roof..

South Harrow ● Piccadilly (zone 5)
Original station opened 28 June 1903 and closed 4 July 1935.
Re-sited station opened 5 July 1933.
In 1935, South Harrow station was re-sited a short distance further west and the entrance moved from South Hill Road to the main Northolt Road, on which a new station building designed by Charles Holden was built. Part of the original platforms and one of the original District Railway station buildings, now

used as staff accommodation, can still be found at the east end of the station. At its east end are six sidings where four Piccadilly Line trains stable outside traffic hours. Travelling by train towards Rayners Lane, look out on the right hand side for the remains of the junction into the former South Harrow Gas Works, which used to be served by regular freight trains. That site is now occupied by residential properties.

The remains of the spur into the South Harrow Gas Works as seen from a passing train. This siding saw use between 1910 and 1954.

South Kensington ● Piccadilly ● District ○ Circle (zone 1)
Opened 24 December 1868.
Opened in 1868 by the Metropolitan Railway and the Metropolitan District Railway, the station is served today by the Circle and District lines at sub-surface level and by the Piccadilly Line at deep tube level. The sub-surface station consists of one island platform, but it used to be much larger with seven platforms (inner rail Circle, outer rail Circle, a double sided Circle bay, eastbound District, westbound District and westbound District bay). There are still signs of the former layout with the retaining wall that used to support an overall roof and a formation that is much wider than the current layout requires. The Piccadilly Line runs directly beneath the District and Circle lines and interchange between the lines is available.

South Kenton ● Bakerloo (zone 4)
Opened 3 July 1933.
Served by the Underground until 24 September 1982.
Re-served from 4 June 1984 onwards.
Consisting of a single island platform, South Kenton is served only by the Bakerloo and London Overground, although it is located alongside the busy West Coast Main Line. The station was opened in 1933 and platform buildings are to a concrete and glass art deco design. Access is via a subway tunnel which also links the residential areas on either side of the railway. Due to a lack of space, there are no ticket barriers at this station.

South Ruislip ● Central (zone 5)
Opened 21 November 1948.
Situated on the West Ruislip branch of the Central, South Ruislip also has platforms on the adjacent Network Rail Chiltern main line and interchange is available.

Southwark ● Jubilee (zone 1)
Opened 20 November 1999.
Southwark is on the Jubilee Line Extension and has platform edge doors fitted. Interchange is available with Network Rail's London Waterloo East station. Its design features an upper concourse with a 16 metre high glass roof and a 40 metre long glass wall consisting of 660 pieces of specially cut blue glass. This feature was designed by Alexander Beleschenko. Escalator shafts at ninety degrees to the upper concourse lead down to a lower concourse which is panelled in stainless steel and has a large illuminated feature at each end.

Southwark – the lower concourse (left), and the upper concourse (right).

South Wimbledon Northern (zones 3 and 4)

Opened as South Wimbledon 13 September 1926.
Renamed South Wimbledon (Merton) circa 1928.
Suffix was gradually dropped in the 1940's.

Despite the name, this station is actually in Merton. It has a very attractive curved Portland Stone building designed by Charles Holden.

South Woodford ⬤ Central (zone 4)

Opened as South Woodford (George Lane) 22 August 1856.
First served by the Underground 14 December 1947.
Renamed South Woodford in 1950.

Opened by the Eastern Counties Railway in 1856, the Central Line took over the railway through here on 14 December 1947. Despite the suffix (George Lane) being dropped in 1950, some platform roundels still show it. There used to be a level crossing at the Woodford end of the station, but it was removed when the line was electrified, severing George Lane. An entrance at each side of the line is linked by a footbridge outside the ticket gates. A public subway beneath the railway links the two halves of George Lane.

Stamford Brook ⬤ District (zone 3)

Opened 1 February 1912.

This station lies on the section between Hammersmith and Acton Town where Piccadilly Line trains run non-stop and only District Line services call here. The eastbound fast (normally used by Piccadilly Line trains) does not have a platform face against it, but the westbound fast and westbound local run either side of an island platform.

Stanmore Jubilee (zone 5)

Opened 10 December 1932.

The northern terminus of the Jubilee Line, Stanmore was opened by the Metropolitan Railway on 10 December 1932. The original station building still exists at street level, however the ticket office has been moved down to platform level near a newer entrance from the car park. The addition of a third platform in 2011 has caused a slight anomaly, as the existing platforms were not renumbered to suit; as you enter the station, from left to right, the platforms are 2, 1 and 3. On the east side of the station is a fan of sidings where trains stable outside traffic hours.

Stepney Green ● District ● Hammersmith & City (zone 2)

Opened 23 June 1902.

This is a sub-surface station served by the District and Hammersmith & City lines, with a few gems to look out for. The westbound platform is fitted with a modern dot matrix indicator to tell passengers the destination of the next trains, but those on the eastbound platform receive this information via an old style light box. Also look out for the 'To the Trains' sign at the top of the stairs leading down to the platforms from the ticket hall.

Stockwell ● Northern ● Victoria (zone 2)

Opened 18 December 1900 (Northern Line) and 23 July 1971 (Victoria Line).

This was the original terminus of the City & South London Railway until that line was extended in 1900 to Clapham Common. The site of the original terminus station was slightly to the north of the current Northern Line platforms and is now the location of a trailing crossover. A tunnel branches off which used to serve Stockwell Works and Depot; trains used to reach the depot by being hauled up a steep incline by cable, which was later replaced by a hydraulic lift before being taken out of use in 1924. With the opening of the Victoria Line through here in 1971, the station buildings were replaced with modern structures and cross platform interchanges were provided between the two lines.

Stonebridge Park ● Bakerloo (zone 3)

Opened by the London & North Western Railway 15 June 1912.
First served by the Underground 1 August 1917.

At platform level, Stonebridge Park is quite modern in appearance but the original station building still survives down at street level. At the north end of the platforms, two tracks branch to the right into the Bakerloo's Stonebridge Park Depot. Some trains terminate here and reverse in the entrance to the depot. Alongside the station at a higher level is Stonebridge Park carriage sidings where the Anglo-Scottish sleeper stock is maintained.

Stratford ● Central ● Jubilee (zones 2 and 3)

Opened by the Eastern Counties Railway 20 June 1839.
First served by the Underground 4 December 1946 (Central Line).
The Jubilee Line opened 14 May 1999.

The first station on this site was opened by the Eastern Counties Railway as far back as 1839. The first Underground line to reach here was the Central Line when the first section of the eastern extension opened as far as Stratford from Liverpool Street in December 1946. A second Underground line reached here in 1999 with the opening of the Jubilee Line Extension.

The Central Line is in tube tunnel at both ends of Stratford station, but climbs up to serve platforms 3 and 3a (westbound) and platform 6 (eastbound). Westbound trains open their doors on both sides here. Stratford is the eastern terminus of the Jubilee Line, which has three platforms located alongside the DLR's Stratford International branch, at a lower level to the part of the station served by Network Rail and the Central Line. There is full interchange between the Jubilee Line, Central Line, Docklands Light Railway, Network Rail, London Overground and local buses. The station also serves the Westfield shopping centre and Olympic Park. Stratford is one of only two places on the Underground where passengers entering the station travel up an escalator to reach their train (the other being at Greenford). The escalators at Stratford lead from the lower concourse to the westbound Central Line platform and are the shortest on the Underground with a rise of just a little over 4 metres.

Sudbury Hill ● Piccadilly (zone 4)
Opened 28 June 1903.

Opened in 1903 by the Metropolitan District Railway, the station was rebuilt in 1931 to a design by Charles Holden ready for the line's transfer to the Piccadilly.

Sudbury Town ● Piccadilly (zone 4)
Opened 28 June 1903.

One of the finest examples of a Charles Holden designed station is at Sudbury Town, which has a typical Holden brick box with concrete lid. The interior and platform areas have also been restored to as near to original condition as is possible and still retain many original features such as concrete canopies, lamp standards and footbridge, original glazing, old signage, a wall mounted barometer and an old news stand.

Swiss Cottage ● Jubilee (zone 2)
Opened 20 November 1939.

Opened as part of the new Bakerloo Line branch from Baker Street to Finchley Road in 1939, Swiss Cottage retains many 1930's features such as 'Art Deco' uplighters on the escalators and roundels cast into the ceramic tiles on the platform walls. The opening of this station and of St John's Wood, resulted in the closure of Lords, Marlborough Road and Swiss Cottage on the neighbouring Metropolitan Line.

Temple ● District ● Circle (zone 1)
Opened as The Temple 30 May 1870.
Renamed Temple shortly afterwards.

The station is located on Victoria Embankment, with the railway running very close to the River Thames here. The station was rebuilt for the District Railway in 1915 by Harry W Ford in a style to match the nearby Somerset House. On top of the station building is a large public area with seats where time can be passed watching the boats pass by. At platform level, the cast iron support columns are the originals dating back to 1870.

Theydon Bois ● Central (zone 6)
Opened by the Great Eastern Railway as Theydon 24 April 1865.
Renamed Theydon Bois December 1865.
First served by the Underground 25 September 1949.

Opened by the Great Eastern Railway in 1865, the station became a part of the Central Line from 25 September 1949, when the Loughton to Epping and Ongar section was transferred over to London Transport.

Tooting Bec ● Northern (zone 3)
Opened as Trinity Road (Tooting Bec) 13 September 1926.
Renamed Tooting Bec 1 October 1950.

This station boasts entrances on both sides of a busy crossroads, which were designed by Charles Holden and clad in Portland Stone. The smaller of the two - a subway entrance on the south side of the road - is a three sided building with a glazed roundel on each side.

Tooting Broadway ● Northern (zone 3)
Opened 13 September 1926.

This station has its very own safe door - few stations can make such a claim! The site on which it was built was once a bank; the safe door was too heavy to remove and so was left in position. It is in the escalator machinery room and not visible to the public. There is a centre reversing siding to the south of the station, used only at times of disruption these days. Like all the stations on the Morden extension, Tooting Broadway has a Charles Holden designed station building clad in Portland Stone (pictured below). In front stands a statue of King Edward VII, who, as Prince of Wales, opened the first section of the City & South London Railway.

Tottenham Court Road ● Northern ● Central (zone 1)

Central – Opened as Tottenham Court Road 30 July 1900.
Northern – Opened as Oxford Street 22 June 1907.
Renamed Tottenham Court Road 9 March 1908.

This is a very busy station with interchange between the Northern and Central Lines. It is coming to the end of a major rebuild to increase capacity and accommodate the Elizabeth Line (Crossrail) which is currently under construction. A set of mosaics by Eduardo Paolozzi have been a feature of the Central Line and Northern Line platforms since the 1980s. Some of these have been restored at platform level on the Central Line platforms, along with several in a cylindrical circulating area known affectionately as 'the echo chamber' (pictured right). Some other parts of the mosaic have been removed to be displayed at the University of Edinburgh, in the artist's home city.

Tottenham Hale ● Victoria (zone 3)
Opened 1 September 1968.

The tiled seat recesses here show a ferry (or 'hale') crossing the River Lea nearby. Interchange is available with Network Rail.

Totteridge & Whetstone ● Northern (zone 4)
Opened by the Great Northern Railway as Totteridge 1 April 1872.
Renamed Totteridge & Whetstone 1 April 1874.
First served by the Underground 14 April 1940.

Opened by the Great Northern Railway in 1872, this station is part of the Northern Line's High Barnet branch today, but still retains its GNR buildings.

Tower Hill ● District ● Circle (zone 1)
Opened as Tower of London 25 September 1882 and closed 12 October 1884.
Re-sited station (slightly further west) opened as Mark Lane 6 October 1884.
Renamed Tower Hill 1 September 1946 and closed 4 February 1967.
Re-sited station opened as Tower Hill (on the site of the original Tower of London station) 5 February 1967.

The current station here has three platforms; the centre one is used to reverse trains from the west, several of which are timetabled to terminate here, usually District Line trains to and from Wimbledon. The station serves the nearby tourist hot spot of the Tower of London and is also handy for Fenchurch Street main line terminus and the Tower Gateway station of the Docklands Light Railway. The current station opened in 1967 on the site of the original Metropolitan Railway Tower of London station, replacing a station slightly further west that had opened as Mark Lane. There are still some remains of the old Mark Lane station in situ (pictured below).

Tufnell Park ● Northern (zone 2)
Opened 22 June 1907.
This station boasts a very fine three sided Leslie Green designed station building which occupies a street corner.

Turnham Green ● District ● Piccadilly (zones 2 and 3)
Opened by the London & South Western Railway 1 January 1869.
First served by the Underground 1 June 1877.
Just west of the station is Turnham Green Junction where the Richmond branch drops down towards Gunnersbury Junction. The eastbound District from Richmond passes underneath the District and Piccadilly lines to and from Acton Town to avoid conflicting movements. During the day the station is served by District Line trains, with Piccadilly Line trains passing straight through. Piccadilly Line trains do call here, but only from the start of traffic until 0650 Mondays to Saturdays, until 0745 on Sundays and from 2230 every evening. The station is also served by the Piccadilly Line Night Tube service at weekends.

Turnpike Lane ● Piccadilly (zone 3)
Opened 19 September 1932.
This station features a very large Charles Holden designed brick box and concrete lid station building with two large ventilation towers.

Upminster ● District (zone 6)
Opened by the London, Tilbury & Southend Railway 1 May 1885.
First served by District trains 2 June 1902 until 30 September 1905.
Then served again from 12 September 1932 onwards.
Upminster is the eastern terminus of the District Line and the furthest east that passengers can travel on the Underground. It is not the furthest east that the Underground reaches though, as trains can continue beyond the east end of the station to reach Upminster Depot. The District shares the station with Network Rail's Fenchurch Street to Southend / Shoeburyness line and London Overground's Romford to Upminster branch.

Upminster Bridge ● District (zone 6)
Opened 17 December 1934.
The railway here is on an embankment and is the only station between Barking and Upminster that is reached by a subway. Inside the station building is a reversed swastika pattern in the floor tiles, a common decorative pattern when the station was opened in 1934.

Upney ● District (zone 4)
Opened 12 September 1932.
Consisting of an island platform serving only the tracks of the District, this station was opened by the LMS in 1932 and has only ever had platforms against the District tracks. The name Upney is derived from Old English and means upper-stream.

Upton Park ● District ● Hammersmith & City (zone 3)
Opened by the London, Tilbury & Southend Railway in 1877.
First served by the Underground 2 June 1902.
The station building which fronts on to Green Street dates from 1904. At platform level,

the canopies still have LT&SR cast canopy brackets. The disused platforms are still in place against the Network Rail tracks.

Uxbridge ● Metropolitan ● Piccadilly (zone 6)
Original station opened 4 July 1904 and closed 3 December 1938.
Current station opened 4 December 1938.

The Metropolitan Railway opened to Uxbridge on 4 July 1904. The original station was in Belmont Road, roughly where a Sainsbury's supermarket now stands. This station closed on 3 December 1938 with the new one opening on High Street the following day. The current stations has three tracks, but with platform faces on both sides of the centre track, there are four platforms. The design of the station is very similar to the one at Cockfosters at the opposite end of the Piccadilly, both of which were designed by Charles Holden. There are several things to note here, including the stained glass windows by Ervin Bossanyi above the main circulating area which represent heraldic associations of the area, the large clock and the 'next train' indicators by the entrance to the platform. There is a fan of sidings just outside the station where Metropolitan Line trains park outside traffic hours. One Piccadilly Line train also stables at Uxbridge, but this stables in the station.

Vauxhall ● Victoria (zones 1 and 2)
Opened 23 July 1971.

Interchange is available here with local bus routes and the Network Rail station which is located on the main lines in and out of London Waterloo.

Victoria ● Victoria ● District ● Circle (zone 1)
Opened 24 December 1868 (District and Circle lines) and 7 March 1969 (Victoria Line).

Until 7 March 1969, the Circle and District were the only Underground lines serving this busy location which has a mainline railway terminus, a large bus station and coach station. From that date, the Victoria Line also served Victoria, initially as its southern terminus and as a through station after the Brixton extension opened in 1971. It is currently being refurbished, both at sub-surface and deep tube level. Intended to increase capacity and passenger flow, this includes new entrances, enlargement of the south ticket hall, new cross passages, new escalators and improved step free access.

Walthamstow Central ● Victoria (zone 3)
Opened 1 September 1968.

The northern terminus of the Victoria Line has two platforms, with each line continuing for a short distance beyond the platforms where there is room to stable two trains outside traffic hours. Interchange is available with London Overground's Chingford line and also with several local bus routes. The tiles in the seat recesses here show an adaptation of a pattern by local textile designer William Morris.

Wanstead ● Central (zone 4)
Opened 14 December 1947.

Wanstead is the first station after Leytonstone on the line to Newbury Park. At the start of the war, this tunnel was built but not fitted out and it saw use as a bomb proof aircraft components factory operated by the Plessey Company. The first tracks in here were 18 inch tram lines used for transporting materials and products between the different sections of the factory. After the war, the tunnels were emptied and the railway completed, eventually opening to traffic on 14 December 1947.

Warren Street ● Victoria ● Northern (zone 1)

Northern – Opened as Euston Road 22 June 1907.
Renamed Warren Street 7 June 1908.
Victoria – Opened 1 December 1968.

Opened in 1907 by the Charing Cross, Euston & Hampstead Railway as Euston Road, the station was renamed Warren Street in 1908. The original name can still be seen in some restored tiles on the southbound Northern Line platform. The Victoria Line opened to here on 1 December 1968, providing interchange between the Victoria and the Northern. The station is located at the top of Tottenham Court Road where it meets Warren Street and Euston Road. Although not shown on the Underground map, it is quick and easy to change (at street level) to the Metropolitan, Hammersmith & City and Circle lines at Euston Square.

Warwick Avenue ● Bakerloo (zone 2)

Opened 31 January 1915.

This station serves the 'Little Venice' area where the Regent's Canal meets the Grand Union Canal. It is a simple two platform tube station with a sub-surface ticket hall and subway entrances at street level.

Waterloo ● Bakerloo ● Northern ● Waterloo & City ● Jubilee (zone 1)

Waterloo & City – Opened 8 August 1898. Became part of the Underground 5 April 1994.
Bakerloo – Opened 10 March 1906.
Northern – Opened 13 September 1926.
Jubilee – Opened 24 September 1999.

Waterloo is a large interchange that links the Underground lines of the Bakerloo, Northern (Charing Cross branch), Jubilee and Waterloo & City with the mainline terminus above. The Jubilee Line section of the complex is the most recent addition as it is part of the JLE and has platform edge doors. The Jubilee Line is linked to the Northern and Bakerloo lines via a long moving walkway.

Watford ● Metropolitan (zone 7)

Opened 2 November 1925.

The Metropolitan Line terminus at Watford is on borrowed time as a new spur is being built to divert Metropolitan trains into Watford Junction station instead. This is not likely to open until about 2020 but when it does, the current terminus is likely to close to passengers and become just a stabling point. The station opened in 1925 and features a building designed by Charles Clark which stands at the end of an island platform serving two tracks with additional tracks for stabling trains either side.

Wembley Central ● Bakerloo (zone 4)

Opened as Sudbury in 1842 by the London & Birmingham Railway.
Renamed Sudbury & Wembley in 1882 and Wembley for Sudbury in November 1910.
Renamed Wembley Central 5 July 1948.
First served by the Underground 16 April 1917 until 24 September 1982.
Re-served from 4 June 1984 onwards.

The London & Birmingham Railway first opened a line through here in 1837. The first station opened here in 1842 with the name Sudbury. The LNWR 'New Line' (or Watford DC Line) opened through here on 15 June 1912. Bakerloo trains didn't reach here until 16 April 1917 when the station was called Wembley for Sudbury. It was later renamed Wembley Central in July 1948 and is today a modern looking station, located beneath office buildings, retail outlets and a hotel. There are also platforms here on the adjacent West Coast Main Line which are served by a number of London Midland and Southern services. It is possible to interchange between these and the Bakerloo and also the London Overground service which shares tracks with the Bakerloo.

Wembley Park ● Metropolitan ● Jubilee (zone 4)
Opened 12 May 1894.

Of the six platforms here, four are used by the Metropolitan and two by the Jubilee. The latter serves platforms 3 and 4 through the centre of the station, with the northbound Metropolitan through platforms 1 and 2 and southbound Metropolitan through platforms 5 and 6. The Jubilee has a central reversing siding to the north where trains are timetabled to reverse. Alongside the southbound Metropolitan tracks are Wembley Park sidings where several S7 trains from the Hammersmith & City and Circle lines are booked to stable outside traffic hours. The long closed Wembley Park signal box also stands at the north end of platforms 2 and 3. At the south end is a complex of lines where the Metropolitan reduces from four tracks to two and there is access to and from Neasden Depot, including a dive-under which emerges between the northbound Metropolitan and northbound Jubilee. The station serves the nearby Wembley Stadium and Wembley Arena and can become incredibly busy when an event takes place. It is now served by the Jubilee Line's Night Tube service at weekends, during which nocturnal period of operation, the Metropolitan Line platforms are cordoned off as there is no Night Tube service on this line.

West Acton ● Central (zone 3)
Opened 5 November 1923.

The station building here is a brick box with glass and concrete frontage designed by Brian Lewis and completed in 1940 to replace an earlier station building as part of the '1935-1940 New Works Programme'.

Westbourne Park ● Hammersmith & City ● Circle (zone 2)
Original station opened 1 February 1866 and closed 31 October 1871.
Re-sited station opened 1 November 1871.

The current station here is slightly further to the east than the original which closed in 1871. The line curves through the station here to bring it alongside the Great Western Main Line. Until 1992, there were platforms on the GWML but these have been demolished. Heading towards London, the Underground lines descend into Subway Tunnel which passes beneath the GWML to emerge close to Royal Oak station.

West Brompton ● District (zone 2)
Opened 12 April 1869.

The West London Line has a station alongside the District here and interchange is possible between the two lines. On days when the District is not operating to Kensington (Olympia), passengers can change from the District onto a main line train here as an alternative method of reaching Olympia. Look out for the signs here that break away from the standard London Transport font and have the tops of the W on West Brompton crossing over.

West Finchley ● Northern (zone 4)
Opened by the London & North Eastern Railway 1 March 1933.
First served by the Underground 14 April 1940.

Although the High Barnet branch was opened by the Great Northern Railway on 1 April 1872, the London & North Eastern Railway (successor to the GNR) didn't open West Finchley station until 1 March 1933. It became a part of the Northern Line when the High Barnet branch was transferred to the Underground on 14 April 1940.

West Ham ⚫ District ⚫ Hammersmith & City ⚫ Jubilee (zones 2 and 3)

Opened by the London, Tilbury & Southend Railway 1 May 1901.
First served by the Underground 2 June 1902.
Renamed West Ham (Manor Road) 11 February 1924 and West Ham 1 January 1969.
Jubilee Line opened 14 May 1999.

This station has a high level and a low level which cross each other at right angles. The low level runs north to south and consists of the Jubilee Line and the Docklands Light Railway's Stratford International branch. On the high level, on an east / west axis, are the Hammersmith & City and District lines, with Network Rail's main line in and out of Fenchurch Street running parallel. Interchange is possible between all lines. At the east end of the high level station is a central reversing siding which can be accessed from both ends.

West Hampstead ⚫ Jubilee (zone 2)

Opened 30 June 1879.

First opened in 1879 and served by the Metropolitan Railway, the station was served by the Bakerloo Line's Stanmore service from 20 November 1939 and then by the Jubilee Line when it took over the Stanmore service on 1 May 1979. Metropolitan trains ceased to call here after 7 December 1940 and today there are no platforms against the Metropolitan tracks. The station has an island platform serving the northbound and southbound tracks of the Jubilee Line only, with the northbound and southbound Metropolitan lines on either side. At the north end of the station is a central reversing siding, which can be used to reverse northbound trains (southbound trains can also go back into the siding).

West Harrow ⚫ Metropolitan (zone 5)

Opened 17 November 1913.

This is the only intermediate station on the Metropolitan Line's Uxbridge branch to be served only by the Metropolitan. The next station - Rayners Lane - and all stations between there and Uxbridge are also served by the Piccadilly. The line through here opened on 4 July 1904, but West Harrow station was a later addition, not opening until 1913.

West Kensington ⚫ District (zone 2)

Opened as North End (Fulham) 9 September 1874.
Renamed West Kensington 1 March 1877.

This is a two platform station adjacent to West Cromwell Road and close to Lillie Bridge Depot. At the east end is a junction where a single line accesses the depot, which several trains are booked to use at the start and end of service. Behind the westbound platform there used to be a goods yard that was reached from the cutting at the west end of the station.

Westminster ⚫ District ⚫ Circle ⚫ Jubilee (zone 1)

District and Circle - Opened as Westminster Bridge 24 December 1868.
Renamed Westminster in 1907.
Jubilee – Opened 22 December 1999.

The original terminus of the Metropolitan District Railway when it opened as Westminster Bridge on Christmas Eve in 1868, it became a through station when the MDR extended to Blackfriars on 30 May 1870. The station was heavily modernised to accommodate the Jubilee Line extension which opened through here in 1999. There is interchange between the sub-surface District and Circle lines and the Jubilee Line. Some of the modern architecture here is very impressive.

A train of S Stock led by 21490 passes slowly through West Kensington out of service on 29 October 2016. This is the 0045 Hammersmith to Lillie Bridge Depot, which is about to take the short branch to Lillie Bridge.

West Ruislip ● Central (zone 6)

Opened as West Ruislip (for Ickenham) 21 November 1948.
Suffix gradually dropped.

The western terminus of the Central Line consists of a single island platform serving two tracks. Parallel to these are the Network Rail platforms served by Chiltern Railway's trains and there is interchange between the mainline and the Central Line. There is also a link between Network Rail and London Underground's Ruislip Depot which passes alongside the Central Line platforms, which is used to deliver engineering materials and also the new S Stock trains when they are delivered from Bombardier. The large Ruislip Depot can be seen from the east end of the platforms; it is responsible for maintaining the Central Line fleet (along with Hainault) and is also home to the London Underground engineering fleet. The station was originally called West Ruislip (for Ickenham) and it will be noted that the line map on the westbound platform at Holland Park still displays this name in full (see picture on page 133).

Whitechapel ● District ● Hammersmith & City (zone 2)

Opened as Whitechapel (Mile End) 6 October 1884. Renamed Whitechapel 13 November 1901.
East London Line platforms opened 31 March 1913 and last served by the Underground 22 December 2007 (to become part of the London Overground network).

Whitechapel is currently a construction site as work associated with Crossrail is taking place. Once complete, the Underground station is expected to emerge with modern features and bear little resemblance to how it looked before the work began. The former East London Line, now part of London Overground, passes beneath the Underground station here and interchange is available. Between Whitechapel and Aldgate East are traces of the former St Mary's Junction where there was a connection between the District / Hammersmith & City and the East London Line used to branch off. At one time this was used by passenger trains, but latterly only by empty stock trains; since the ELL has been transferred to London Overground, the connection has been removed.

White City ● Central (zone 2)

Opened 23 November 1947.

Westbound trains emerge into daylight here for the first time since Stratford. Right hand running occurs here (for reasons stated in the 'History' section of the Central Line). The station was opened in 1947, replacing the one at Wood Lane which was built to serve the Franco British Exhibition in 1908. It was this event that gave the station its name, as most of the buildings making up the exhibition were white in colour, earning it the nickname the 'White City'. There are three tracks through here, the centre track mainly being used by trains from the east that reverse here. There is also a reversing siding at the country end of the station. The tracks revert to left hand running via a flyover at Wood Lane Junction. At the London end of the station, inside what used to be the Wood Lane loop, were 16 sidings (which have now been built over); these have been replaced with new sidings on a new alignment, where 12 trains are scheduled to stable outside traffic hours.

Willesden Green ● Jubilee (zones 2 and 3)

Opened as Willesden Green 24 November 1879.
Renamed Willesden Green & Cricklewood 1 June 1894 and Willesden Green in 1938.

Opened by the Metropolitan Railway in 1879, Willesden Green's station building is a later addition from 1925, but still proudly displays the words 'Metropolitan Railway' in large letters just below the roof. It was served by Bakerloo Line trains on the Stanmore service from 20 November 1939 and then by Jubilee Line trains when it took over the Stanmore service on 1 May 1979. The Metropolitan last served the station regularly on 7 December 1940. Today it is only served by Jubilee Line trains, but there are still platforms on the Metropolitan tracks which can be used for Metropolitan Line trains at times of disruption. To the north of the station is a reversing siding for turning back northbound trains (southbound trains can also go back into the siding).

Willesden Junction ● Bakerloo (zones 2 and 3)

Opened by the London & Birmingham Railway 1 September 1866.
First served by the Underground 10 May 1915.

The first station at Willesden Junction was opened by the London & Birmingham Railway on their main line between the two cities (now the West Coast Main Line). The LNWR's 'New Line' (or Watford DC Line) opened through here on 15 June 1912, with Bakerloo services operating over it from 10 May 1915. The platforms on the adjacent WCML eventually closed in 1962. The station today has a high level and a low level: the high level is served by London Overground services on the North London Line while the low level is served by Watford DC Line London Overground trains and the Bakerloo Line. The low level station consists of a large island platform with a central bay (which is only used by Overground trains). The station is in the centre of a complex of lines, with the West Coast Main Line running parallel to the low level station, the North London Line passing overhead and connections between the high level and low level and with the Wembley freight yards. To the south of the station is Willesden Depot which is mainly used by London Overground, but also by the locos which operate the Anglo-Scottish sleeper trains.

Wimbledon ● District (zone 3)

Original station opened by the London & South Western Railway 21 May 1838.
First served by the Underground 3 June 1889.

The original station opened by the L&SWR in 1838 was slightly further south than the current one. It was rebuilt on its current site to coincide with the opening of the L&SWR's line from Putney Bridge & Fulham (following the opening of Fulham Railway Bridge) over which the District had running powers. Wimbledon today has eleven platforms, which include two for Tramlink (10 and 10b), five for Network Rail (5, 6, 7, 8 and 9) and four for London Underground (1, 2, 3 and 4). All four used by the District Line are terminal platforms. There is a link between Network Rail and the District at Wimbledon North Junction just outside the station; Network Rail trains can run along the District tracks from here as far as East Putney Junction and several empty stock workings are scheduled to do so.

Wimbledon Park ● District (zone 3)

Opened 3 June 1889.

Between Wimbledon and Wimbledon Park, the District runs along the west side of Wimbledon Depot, which is used to service the South West Trains fleet. Network Rail trains (South West Trains) can share the tracks with the District between Wimbledon North Junction, Wimbledon Park and East Putney Junction, where they can use a spur to travel to or from the Barnes to Clapham Junction line. These trains run empty along this stretch of line. The main line trains along here reflect the fact that the L&SWR built the line, which did not pass into London Underground ownership until 1994. Wimbledon Park station consists of an island platform serving two tracks with a station building at street level above.

Woodford ● Central (zone 4)

Opened by the Eastern Counties Railway 22 August 1856.
First served by the Underground 14 December 1947.

Woodford station has three platforms, with number 1 being a bay. Alongside platform 1 are five sidings which are used to stable trains outside traffic hours. To the south is a reversing siding which is mainly used by trains which have arrived via the Hainault loop, terminated at Woodford and are reversing to form a train back round the Hainault loop. Trains can also be reversed in the platform via a crossover at the Epping end of the station.

Wood Green ● Piccadilly (zone 3)
Opened 19 September 1932.

This station has a reversing siding in tunnel for turning back trains from Central London. It is only used at times of service disruption these days. The station building was designed by Charles Holden.

Wood Lane ● Hammersmith & City ● Circle (zone 2)
Opened 12 October 2008.

Built in 2008, this station is located on the Hammersmith branch on an embankment where the railway crosses over Wood Lane opposite the former BBC Television Studios. It is a very short walk along Wood Lane to the Central Line's White City station, which is shown on the Underground map as an interchange. Wood Lane was built without a ticket office, which was unusual at the time, but seems irrelevant now that they have been phased out across the Underground. There was a station at Wood Lane which opened as Wood Lane (Exhibition) on 1 May 1908 to serve the Franco British Exhibition. It closed on 31 October 1914, but re-opened on an ad hoc basis. It was renamed Wood Lane (White City) on 5 May 1920, to just Wood Lane at some point in the 1930s and White City in November 1947. Last used on 21 October 1959, it burnt down on 25 October 1959. The old Wood Lane station was slightly closer to Hammersmith than the current one. The new station has an old roundel from Wood Lane on display beneath one of the arches of the brick viaduct on which it sits, but this is from the original Central London Railway station of the same name.

An old roundel on display at the bottom of the stairs to the westbound platform at Wood Lane. This is from the former Central London Railway station of the same name.

Woodside Park ● Northern (zone 4)
Opened by the Great Northern Railway as Torrington Park 1 April 1872.
Renamed Woodside Park 1 May 1882.
First served by the Underground 14 April 1940.

Opened by the Great Northern Railway at the same time as the branch to High Barnet (1 April 1872), this station was originally called Torrington Park and was renamed to Woodside Park in 1882. Today it is part of the Northern Line's High Barnet branch and still retains many Great Northern Railway features, including the station building, platform canopies and footbridge. Perhaps the most remarkable survivor is the old signal box on the north end of the northbound platform. It is no longer used to signal trains, but is kept in very good condition. Opposite the signal box is a large car park, on the site of what used to be the goods yard. Even after the Underground took over from the LNER, goods trains operated by the LNER and later BR, still served the goods yards at Woodside Park, High Barnet, Finchley Central, East Finchley and Totteridge & Whetstone until 1962.

USEFUL REFERENCES

The London Underground – A Diagrammatic History by Douglas Rose

A diagram of the Underground with details of opening dates, closing dates and station re-namings. Known for its accuracy, this has been used to check a lot of information within this book. Published by Capital Transport. **ISBN 978-1-85414-404-1**

London Underground Railway Society (LURS)

Membership of this society comes highly recommended by the author. All members receive the excellent monthly magazine called Underground News which contains fantastic articles, colour and black and white photographs, up to date news from around the system, details of society events, features about modelling the Underground and regular fleet updates (which will help keep your London Underground Guide Book up to date). The magazine is worth the membership fee alone, but the society also organises occasional visits to Underground related locations and there are monthly society meetings held near Great Portland Street station. These usually take the form of a talk by former and current Underground staff and management, photographers and historians. More details can be found at:

http://www.lurs.org.uk/

Transport for London Working Timetables

Working timetables for all London Underground lines can be found online and can prove to be very handy.

https://tfl.gov.uk/corporate/publications-and-reports/working-timetables

First and Last Tubes

This gives details of the first and last trains on each line, a very handy quick reference, especially when you don't want to miss the last train.

https://tfl.gov.uk/modes/tube/first-and-last-tube

London Transport Museum

This site can be used to plan your visit to the London Transport Museum. Details of forthcoming events such as open days at Acton Museum Store, visits to abandoned stations and heritage train operations can also be found here.

http://www.ltmuseum.co.uk/

Epping & Ongar Railway

A private railway operating heritage trains over a former part of the Central Line, the Epping & Ongar Railway is well worth a visit. More details at:

http://eorailway.co.uk/